THE GROWTH
of
MUSWELL HILL

By

Jack Whitehead

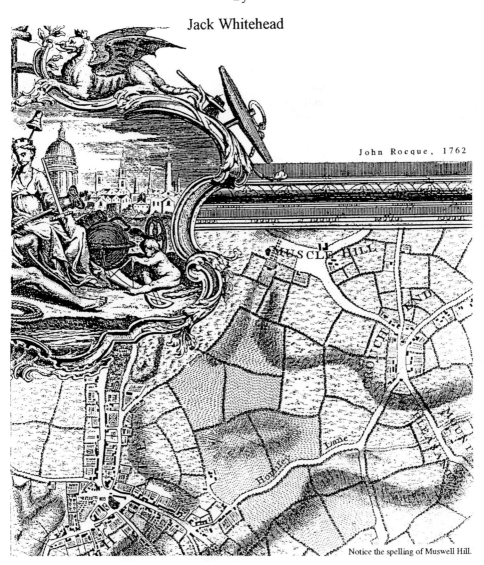

John Rocque, 1762

Notice the spelling of Muswell Hill.

I

ISBN 0 9509362 3 5
1995

Published by Jack Whitehead
55 Parliament Hill, London NW3 2TB

Printed by Biddles Ltd
Guildford Surrey GU1 1DA

Also by Jack Whitehead

The Growth of Stoke Newington: a model for other
local studies
The Growth of Marylebone and Paddington
The Glacial Drifts of Muswell Hill and Finchley
Graphic Communication Made Simple

From local bookshops or by phone or post from
55 Parliament Hill London NW3 2TB
0171 435 3302

To Jack and Pat

and their Collins house

Contents

Acknowledgements

First I should like to thank my wife for her meticulous editing and fruitful suggestions. Without these the book would never have been completed.

I should like to thank Mrs Read at Haringey History Archive at Bruce Castle Museum, Mr Steve Gould of Haringey Planning Department and officers in Haringey Building Control Department, who were all so helpful with drawings; Isobel Stokes of Haringey Reference Library and members of Hornsey Historical Society; the librarians and archivists at the British Library, The Clothworkers Guild, the Royal Institute of British Architects, Barnet Local History Library, the Church of England Record Office, Essex Records Office, the Guildhall Library, the British Library, the Greater London History Library, Islington Library and Islington Architects Department, the Greater London Record Office, the City of Southampton Society, Mr Cobb and Mrs M. Watkins of the Hampstead Garden Suburb Archives Trust and Mill Hill School.

Many local people have helped me with advice, comment and documents. I should particularly like to thank David Adler, Anna Alston, Robert Andrewes, and Peter Curtis who suggested the format for this book, Paul Dickinson & Associates and Taylor Walker for the Firkins pub drawings, Ken Gay, Andrew Golland, whom I have tried in vain to contact, Joanna Haydon Knowell, Mrs S. Heathcote for the Odeon Cinema material, Tom Helcke, Mrs Elsie Higgins, John Kilburn Topping, Mr and Mrs Kraushar, David Jones for details of Highgate Woods and the Billy Collins interview, Jennifer Jones for her drawings of the Scissors Flats, Marianne McKnight for the Road Widening file and other information, Mary Marden for alerting me to the Queen's Wood campaigns, Mrs Niblett for some excellent stories, Vic McRae for lending me a very rare book, Ruth Phillips, Eric Robinson, Wolf Suschitzky, Mrs Tomkins for showing me a book even the British Library no longer holds, Bill Tyler, Peter Walker, Dick Whetstone for his many old photographs and Tom Whitehead for his professional photography.

The book draws on my memories and later research, but also on an enormous amount of research done by others. In this, of course, the main sources have been the back files of the Hornsey Historical Society which have proved invaluable. I hope that all of these published sources have been acknowledged, but if any have been omitted I apologise and will correct the oversight in any future edition.

Finally, I should like to thank Henry Hagger for the fine front and back paintings which he made especially for the book and which so enhance it. After seeing them, everyone will want to come to live in Muswell Hill.

Introduction

This book is about Muswell Hill where I was brought up and went to school. It was my childhood experiences, growing up surrounded by houses which were perpetually encroaching on the open fields, that led me to my lifelong interest in history and architecture. Thus the book begins with a small amount of autobiography, recalling the exhilaration of growing up in Muswell Hill in a world almost unrecognisable today. It traces the growth of estates and the people who built them. It describes campaigns to protect buildings and other ones to protect open spaces. Some of these campaigns are unfinished. I hope readers will enjoy the story so far and add their own later chapters.

The Arrival

Moving from our old house to Muswell Hill held no attractions for me. Why leave familiar rooms and streets for the unknown? I was happy at home and happy at school, but my mother was most anxious to go.

"All I want is my own front door and a garden", and then would follow the familiar story of the man downstairs who had refused to give her some soil for a pot of bulbs. He had dug a fish pond in his garden large enough to swim in so that the evacuated soil, rich and black, was piled in a slope all round the garden walls, yet he had refused her a pailful. Anyone else would have been glad to dispose of the surplus soil, but he had refused. Clearly there had been other differences over the years which had culminated in this ridiculous quarrel about a bucket of soil. My mother took earth resentfully from the front garden, which was no-man's-land, but the privet hedge had been exhausting the soil for fifty years so that it was now dry, grey and dusty. She dug out some with the coal shovel and planted her few bulbs, yet when they bloomed they were not a triumph, but a further excuse for returning to her anger.

To my father the new house was far less important: he was willing enough to move if it made my mother happy, yet his London was always to be the streets of the West End and the City, while Muswell Hill remained a dormitory. The other children in the family were too young to have any opinion on moving, leaving me alone in my love of the old house and the railway line behind, where I used to spend so much of my time. I climbed out of the window above the back-addition, under my mother's careful eye, crawled down the slate roof to the garden wall, again neutral territory where the man downstairs had no power, and walked along the wall to the railway embankment. High above ran the branch line from Finsbury Park to Muswell Hill. This was my playground, a tiny copse of elderberry trees and cow parsley; an isolated world shared only with the boy next door, where nobody else came and as familiar to me as the living room carpet. Nobody else in the family knew how warmly I felt about this small patch of scrub.

There was also the mulberry tree in the garden on the other side, beyond the fish pond. Each year we could see the red and purple berries, tantalizingly delicious. Two old ladies lived in the house next door, but they did not pick the mulberries, which lay unheeded on the grass. When I was eight, the year before we moved, my mother came back from the shops with a message inviting me to pick the mulberries. The ladies would be happy for me to pick them, but I was not to go through their house to reach the garden. Nobody said why I should not go through the front door in the normal way. It was a decision made for me.

Instead, my mother and I, leaning out of the first floor back window, planned a route

Black Mulberry

1

to the tree avoiding the garden below. I climbed out of the window and down the sloping slate roof as usual, lowered myself to the garden wall and walked along to the railway embankment. From there I walked along to the next garden wall and climbed from the wall into the mulberry tree. I had no basket or bag to collect the fruit. It had never occurred to me to pick the fruit to give to the ladies or my mother. Perhaps that part of the message had not penetrated. I simply ate the fruit and when I was satiated, came away. Weeks later I wondered if I should have harvested the fruit, instead of just eating it and resolved to do this the following year, but before the fruit ripened again, we had moved. The mulberry tree was another reason why I did not want to move to Muswell Hill, but I was overruled.

For days my mother had been packing, clearing cupboards and wrapping crockery. We had hardly enough plates to eat off and nothing could be found until one morning we left it all and went by bus to the edge of Muswell Hill, where my life was to change completely.

By the time the pantechnicon carrying our furniture arrived the whole family was standing at the door of the new house. Within two hours it was all roughly in place and the removal men had gone, to move yet another customer.

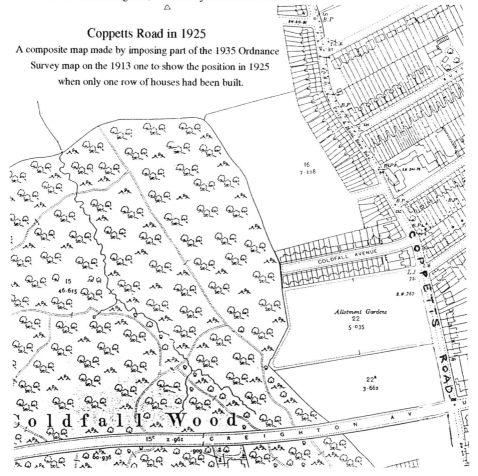

Coppetts Road in 1925

A composite map made by imposing part of the 1935 Ordnance Survey map on the 1913 one to show the position in 1925 when only one row of houses had been built.

"Never ending," they said. "Carrying things into the van, driving a few miles and carrying them out again." Families with pianos, families without pianos; easing furniture down narrow staircases, or up basement steps; tea at both ends till it came out of your ears. People from all over Hornsey were arriving at the new houses as if they were coming to a fair.

Beds were put up and a fire was soon alight in the cold house. At first the smoke billowed out into the room but, as the chimney warmed, the fire began to draw better. We older children kept dashing to the sink in the kitchen to see if the water from the back-boiler behind the fire had started to run hot. This patented boiler had been well advertised in the council's description of the houses and was a wonder. The living-room fire would heat that room as an ordinary open fire, heat the oven behind, and heat the hot water for the sink and bath. Economical, efficient, and 'modern'. We had come from the upper half of a house in Florence Road, Stroud Green. The kitchen of the house was in the lower flat, so all our cooking arrangements had been improvised. We had had a

The 1935 Ordnance Survey map showing the complete estate,
newly built Coldfall School and the earlier houses
in that part of Creighton Avenue.

3

good living room fire and small bedroom ones, a gas stove and sink in the back-addition kitchen but no hot water apart from a kettle on the gas. Here, for the first time in my life, we had a purpose-made kitchen.

It was 1925. Hornsey Borough Council had put up a long row of council houses on the remote edge of Muswell Hill, backing on to fields and woods. A single row of houses, in blocks of six or eight, stood new and untouched along Coppetts Road, in a sea of emptiness. Front gardens were marked out by short concrete posts with spiked iron chains looped between them, and a narrow path of black clinker from the municipal gas works led to each front door. Apart from this nothing had been done. The ground was as the builders had left it; yellow clay with brick ends and bits of cement, but the houses were symbols of momentous change.

Behind the houses were long back gardens bordered by concrete posts holding round

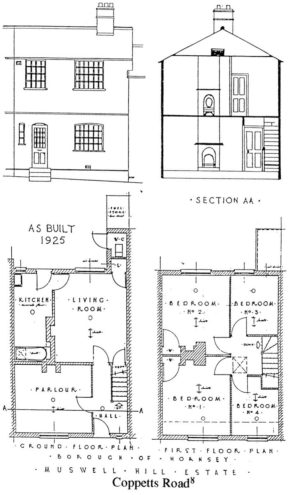

· SECTION AA ·

AS BUILT
1925

· GROUND · FLOOR · PLAN ·   · FIRST · FLOOR · PLAN ·
· BOROUGH · OF · HORNSEY ·
· MUSWELL · HILL · ESTATE ·
Coppetts Road[8]

The drawings show a typical parlour-type house, with the bath in the kitchen, an outside WC and fuel-store and a cold-water tank in an unboarded loft. This design and a non-parlour one were the standard designs of the estate.

4

iron bars at waist height. All over the estate, generation after generation of children were to turn over on those unending bars. Between each block of houses was a path to the remains of a narrow field and the forest trees beyond.

Coppetts Road itself was still a gravelled lane with houses on one side, while behind the houses was the edge of Coldfall Woods, a remnant of the ancient Middlesex Forest. From about 1900, speculators had ventured into building rows of houses between Colney Hatch Lane and Coppetts Road. Villas had been built up as far as Coppetts Road and now the Council was at work on the other side of the road. The first new people were moving in and we children from older London streets were suddenly to become country dwellers.

Huge oaks, the Quercus Robur which had built the wooden ships of England a dozen wars before, stood thick at the end of the garden. Further into the wood were clearances of hazel and hornbeam, the typical woodland of Middlesex. To us as children this was a magic land. Our old upper-floor rooms in Finsbury Park had been without a garden, so our stamping ground had been the streets and shops. In a single day we had been transported to the edge of a thousand year old forest, immense and exotic. We did not know then that much of the timber would be felled. We would watch it go with excitement and regret, but for the first few years we were forest children, free to roam and climb at will.

During the first week we began to settle in as the bedrooms became our own. The front parlour was tightly packed, for the new room was smaller than the old Florence Road one. An upright piano, a black-japanned chiffonier, a glass cabinet with a glass door which survived unbroken by some miracle for the whole time we lived in the house, a large sofa and an arm chair, crowded the room but, once seated, it was a warm place to read in.

The houses were built to a design which was appearing all over the country at that time. Two-storey houses in red or yellow brick, with red-tiled roofs, pebble dash on the first floor, and small glass window panes in steel Crittal window frames. A small entrance hall with a staircase; a tiny front parlour and a larger living room behind, with a pantry in one corner and a kitchen with a concrete floor to the side. Upstairs were four bedrooms, two very small, with a loft above all. There was no bathroom and the W.C. was outside in an attached outhouse, next to a coal bunker.

These council houses did not have bathrooms, or inside W.C.s. Middle class houses had had them for fifty years, but not most council houses. An outside W.C. with a cistern which froze every winter was the norm. With it came the ubiquitous chamber pot. There was still something blind and punitive about the thought behind the design of these houses - together with a need to cut cost. The houses were solidly built of good materials, to last the full sixty years it would take for the rents to pay for them. Instead of a bathroom there was a fixed cast-iron bath at the end of the kitchen and the bath was therefore never easily private. One had to negotiate with the rest of the family; lock the kitchen and garden doors so that nobody could come bursting in; not stay in the bath too long in case someone else wanted a drink from the kitchen sink. Above all one had to avoid the lid, for the bath was covered by a heavy wooden lid which hinged up and was held by a metal catch.

In theory things could be placed on the bath-top but, as it had to be cleared each time the bath was used, this was of little use. Instead, the lid was a source of terror. In my early dreams the lid crashed down and I woke in a sweat. Eventually I tamed the thing, removing it completely to make a woodwork bench in the garden, useful and safe at last.

Seven years after the Armistice the returning soldiers were being settled. Next door was Mr Lawrence, a giant of a man, who had arrested Roger Casement and taken him to the Tower. Mr Rogers had been in the Infantry, as had Mr Dalgleish and others along the road. Albert Whitehead, my father, was one of five brothers, all in the infantry. One was killed and one lost a leg. Similar family histories were common.

Over the mantlepiece in the sitting-room was the picture of Uncle Cyril, the youngest brother of the family, in a small round photo-frame, with last year's Armistice Day poppies arranged above it. The face, rather stiff and uneasy in some photographer's grotto, was undeveloped. Taken during his last leave, he was still a lad, smartly turned out, potentially handsome, but raw. Like so many others his life was before him until, in 1918, in the eleventh month, he was killed. This was the last picture of him, all in fact that remained, and each year the poppies were replaced by new. Many houses had similar photographs which continued to exert their influence throughout the Twenties and Thirties on all political parties, right up to Munich. In 1925 the soldiers who had survived were home and this estate would begin to house them. Others were waiting impatiently for more houses to be built on the land behind. It was like a Roman legion, disbanded after a war, being settled as a new small town in some foreign valley.

Some extracts from the Medical Officer of Health's Reports which led to the houses being built can be found in Appendix 1. [6]

6

The Gardens

While the front gardens of the houses were mere squares, the back ones were very long, for the planners had seen gardens as part of the family economy. Tenants would grow their own vegetables and live a healthy life. It was part of the 'garden city' concept which had built Letchworth and Welwyn Garden City at the turn of the century. This was a garden estate.

That first season the gardens presented a serious challenge to town people unused even to a window box. Acres of brown clay were divided by concrete posts and round iron bars painted red. At the back door was a concreted area leading to the W.C. and coal shed with, at the far end of the garden, a gap in the railing but no gate. All between was open and bare.

The local ironmonger must have sold a lot of spades and forks that season as each household began digging over the soil inexpertly. On the day we bought a spade my father marked out a path from the house to the gap, disliked the spade and, so far as I can remember, never picked one up again. There was little we children could do to help except to collect the brick ends and stones to throw on the pathway. There, with the ashes from the fire, a sort of path emerged but it was a long process. My mother paid a neighbour ten shillings to turn over the soil and a few weeks later she raked a patch smooth before sowing a lawn. Slowly things began to grow.

It was in the gardens that the differences in family age and income between one household and the next first showed. One man, manager of the butchery department of a large local chain-store, had grown-up children and only one still at school. The butcher came home to lunch each day carrying a small piece of meat - nothing excessive - but it would have cost other people money. Three children were already working, but still living at home. Four wages were coming into the house with only one rent and reduced food bills. The result showed in the garden. Instead of pecking weakly at the clay like most other people, the family had the manpower to double dig the garden all over, turning it up as if it were wartime trenches. Then, leaving it ridged and ready for the winter frosts to break it up, large wooden posts and trellis work were delivered, to the amazement of the neighbours. For a month the smell of creosote and the sound of sawing filled the air. The family completely fenced their back garden to a height of eight feet, cutting themselves off from the sight of everyone else. Compared with what other people could achieve it was as if Louis XIV had come to live in a council house.

Most people were far more modest. A small lawn in most front gardens, to be cut by shears and behind, a grass patch for the children to play on. Beyond that it depended on the energy and dedication of the family. Everyone grew runner beans, some cabbages and potatoes. Some gardens grew them well and some less well, but within a twelvemonth most people had something in the garden. We had a rose pergola made of hornbeam poles, hard and durable, but difficult for beginners to use. "One nail for deal and three nails for hornbeam because you bend the first two," but once built, a mass of single yellow roses flowed over the pergola and arch, protecting the house from view and making it beautiful.

7

Obdurate plants lasted best; Michaelmas daisy, marguerites, roses which liked the boulder clay, and in May, still in full leaf and ready to provide yet another cutting of green leaves, the curly kale. In summer most of the gardens were a fine sight in a workmanlike, allotment sort of way. Very few were designed as pleasure gardens and none looked like the modern patios, full of expensive plants from garden centres. Most were far more untidy, with children's soap-box carts under construction and plants which had survived rather than been imported full of flower.

There were exceptions. Mr Dalgleish was a real gardener. He had had a wife who died soon after they came to the house, but apparently no other family. How he and his wife had obtained the house was never explained. All other families had several children, some young and some already grown up, but here was a solitary couple and the wife ill. Perhaps there had been a family and some tragedy had overcome them. Perhaps the wife's illness had caused them to scatter instead of drawing the family together. Adults in the road may have known but it was never discussed in front of the children and any such questions were firmly discouraged.

"We live in everyone else's pockets here. There is no need to notice what's in them".

Not having a family must have been a sadness, for Mr Dalgleish loved children. A very handy man, with a neat way with tools and a love of 'finish', he made us our first mouse cage. It was a splendid wooden box made of clean Quebec Pine, etched all over with a pattern of minute gum sacs and without a knot in it. He must have made it from an old drawing board, for there could have been no other source for that particular wood. Perhaps he worked in some drawing office and had access to such exotic material. Really, we children knew nothing about Mr Dalgleish.

The cage had a glass front sliding in neat grooves. Inside was a flat floor with a slope leading to a sleeping balcony above, where the bedrooms had round entrance holes, cut with an exciting centre-bit drill. A pitched roof hinged up for cleaning purposes and across the front Mr Dalgleish lettered 'Mouse Villas' in beautiful copperplate writing. This first experience of seeing a man shape wood, and such clean, yielding wood as good pine, opened up wide vistas of creation. Anything could be made. Everything was possible. He had provided two white mice which quickly produced naked young.

However, it was mainly in the garden that he showed his quality. The front garden had slightly raised beds with never a weed to be seen and the edges trowelled smooth at a slope, as if they were worked cement. He used a plasterer's float, working the black earth in flat slopes on either side of the path, from the gate to the front door. Then, with his beds laid out, he planted his flowers in studied array, as if in a Victorian park. Ice plants along the sloped edges, with their silver grey leaves and pink flowers nodding,

individual spot plants set at measured distances, varigated foliage plants and a never ending succession of annuals in season. No flower was allowed to fade and everyone of them stood up straight. In another world, Mr Dalgleish would have been a happy gardener in a noble house, smartly turned out in polished leather leggings and trying not to smile when praised, standing to attention by his beds as the owner made his daily inspection.

His house was a plant factory. Each window-sill held pots and dishes, some covered with slips of glass, some with ingenious wicks leading from bowls of water to below the flower pots, so that the plants did not dry out. As the seedlings grew they were potted on in ever larger pots until it was their season for planting out. Thus Mr Dalgleish's garden was unlike that of anyone else. It was a nursery and flower shop which happened not to sell flowers but to show them to all those who chose to look.

But it was Mr Lawrence who first amazed us. In the first week he took some twigs of privet from the Isolation Hospital hedge and made them grow. We watched as he took out a shallow trench along the front edge of his garden. Then he walked across the pavement to the edge of the road and swept the sand and gravel which had washed into the gutter into a heap. He carried this ponderously to the trench and mixed in a little soil. With a large clasp knife he trimmed his privet stems and carefully pressed in a double row across the garden. We had done this many times, making gardens of stones and twigs. Clearly Mr Lawrence was playing, although he seemed a little old for it. In a few days' time the twigs would die, but instead, Mr Lawrence's cuttings thrived. He watered them regularly: in a year there was a dense little hedge which grew and flourished till well after he himself was dead.

Watching this transformation of mere cuttings into sturdy plants was a formative experience, especially for Phyllis who became a very keen gardener. In later years she took cuttings of all kinds. It was a game to produce a bed created entirely from cuttings taken from other people's front hedges: a source of pleasure and fun. One of the oddest sights years later was to see a party of middle-aged women from the Co-op Guild on a visit to a stately home. Enthusiastic gardeners, they came with a battle plan. These upright people, who would have walked half-way across the parish to return a penny undercharged, were marauders who gloried in their wickedness. They had strict rules. Only one cutting from any plant. Never touch a plant which was too small to suffer it. Only one cutting for each person per visit. They concealed small paper bags in their pockets and, on seeing a likely quarry, descended in a chattering flock. Then, with them all crowding round so that nobody else could see, the robber secured the cutting and dropped it in her bag. The group dispersed, leaving the guilty one ostentatiously writing down the Latin name in a notebook, as any other plant lover would do. The cuttings, mature and carefully tended, became a source of never ending conversation and memories of their riotous middle-age. Today, when far greater numbers visit stately homes, this would be frowned upon but then there was less pressure on the plants and the sin was venial.

The effect of gardens in the new Coppetts Road Estate was revealed over twenty years later, after the Second World War. Coldfall School had been built to serve the estate, backed by the woods, and with its own playing field, now sadly sold off and lost for ever. Each year the children from all over the borough came together for the Inter-School Sports. The fastest and most vigorous children from every school appeared in shorts and vest as if on some medical parade and teachers could pick out the 'Coldfall Type'. Children bigger, rangier and more active than the rest, who had been fed on good food for the whole of the War. One cannot dig for victory in a five-storey block of flats, but in the War years, the estate gardens became one enormous allotment. Every inch was cultivated and the children thrived. The Inter-School Sports Days displayed the result.

The Woods

Oak trees started quite close to the back of the gardens, rising steadily for about one hundred and fifty yards to a gentle ridge. The edge of the wood was surrounded by a thick fence, but there were soon gaps in it. As children we walked through the edge of the wood to reach the stream and the meadow beyond, but we never went far into the wood, for it was private, owned by the Ecclesiastical Commissioners. People living in houses which backed on to the wood could pay a fee to walk in it, and many of the houses in Tetherdown, Durham Road and Fortis Green had back garden gates which led directly into the trees. For them the woods were their back garden, stretching from Fortis Green to Coppetts Road.

Most of the wood was large oak, but there was a coppice of hazel and hornbeam, for this had been a 'managed' wood for centuries. Trees had been felled carefully and individually as one culls a herd of deer, killing a few each season, but leaving the herd intact. Hazel and hornbeams had been cut to the ground time and again, so that the old, gnarled roots spread out like the arms of ungainly starfish, throwing up crop after crop of slender poles. The first must have been cut centuries earlier to be used as fencing, or to hold up runner beans, or even to make wattle and daub cottages. Each time new poles had sprung up, to be lopped in their turn a few years later. The local ironmonger sold bundles of pea-sticks made from the tips and bundles of bean poles, all cut from similar coppiced trees.

The forest clearing was a favourite spot, with a brighter, more dappled light than under the oaks. Nowhere in the wood was there the heavy, dense shadow such as one finds in beech woods, but always the open, airy feeling of oak, with great branches high above naturally bent, to sharp angles, those L shaped timbers which would perhaps some day join the sides to the decks of wooden ships, heavy and strong. But the open hazel coppice had a charm of its own, clear, fresh and light. Bright sun glinted through the leaves as if on rippling water and at dusk the light became a mysterious blue grey, full of glancing shadows. This was the time for 'sugaring' moths. Our Aunt Winnie had

to make up the mixture of treacle and sugar in an old saucepan and pour it in a golden column from a spoon held high above to test its consistency.

We brushed the sweet sticky mixture of treacle and sugar on the trees in the early twilight and returned with nets half an hour later to collect the moths. In they came, gently fluttering, settling to drink at the trees with wings folded, camouflaged dull against the bark. Tiger and poplar moths, hawks, yellow under-wings, and small strange semi-moths with five-leaved wings, which were clearly not normal moths and could not be found in our insect books.

Over the years, long after this first coppice had been cleared, we collected and bred butterflies and moths, beautiful, exotic, ephemeral beauties in a myriad of forms. It is hard to realise today that in the twenties the fields were full of butterflies, some common and some rare. Their shapes and colours were so familiar to us that we could tell them apart at fifty yards, floating and staggering in their erratic flight. Later we bought insect eggs from L.Hugh Newman, at the Butterfly Farm in Bexley, Kent. He was a real enthusiast who had transformed his house into a breeding centre for butterflies and moths, to start a cottage industry and become known world wide for his insect eggs and nature photographs. On several occasions we bought eggs of the Comma butterfly as these seemed to be rare in Muswell Hill. Once I did see a Comma which may have been from our breeding, but no doubt most did not survive. Reintroducing a lost species often defeats experts and is well beyond any child.

In season we collected the more common caterpillars from bushes and trees and placed them in white muslin sleeves tied round their favourite food plants. Then, when the caterillars had pupated, they were placed in some sheltered corner to overwinter. I watched one goat moth caterpillar until it pupated and then kept it in a Palm Toffee tin in my bedroom for nearly another year, despite the pungent smell, before the moth emerged with one unfortunate wing damaged.

At this period, before the introduction of chemical sprays which have obliterated butterflies, the hedges and streets were full of caterpillars, so that sometimes one could not walk on the pavements without treading on looping caterpillars. In the first year of the Second World War there was a bounty on Cabbage White butterflies. A hundred for fourpence. When the children were evacuated to the country I, as a young teacher, had to count tins full of mangled bodies, beaten down by children waving jackets in the surrounding cabbage fields to save the crops. I was sad in some ways to pay out that bounty.

In 1942, sitting on the wing of a Wellington bomber in North Africa, replacing an emergency life-raft, I saw a swallowtail butterfly walk out of the torn canvas and fly off in the direction of the Suez Canal. To the amazement of everyone else, I slid down to the back edge of the mainplane, dropped off, and raced across the desert, following this wisp of England. The day before I had been on duty and had accepted the planes, newly arrived from England. Ten bombers, now being prepared to attack Tobruk, which had been only a few days earlier in Norfolk.

Inside the wing, warmed by the Egyptian sun, the butterfly had emerged from its pupa and now its great wings were fluttering across the foreign sand in an arid desert, with the mirage forming across the Canal as it does each day at noon, so different from the lush wide reeds of Norfolk. The Suez Canal was hidden beyond a row of sand-hills, but in the mirage it appeared to float and shimmer on the horizon, offering water to a thirsty traveller. At twelve noon each day, the mirage of the Cairo to Suez train seemed to

11

travel across the mirage of the Canal, a mirage riding on a mirage. Can a butterfly recognise a mirage? Was it really trying to reach the fancied water? Certainly this butterfly appeared to be flying towards the water, looking in vain for the misty reed beds and wide open skies of its native Norfolk. As the butterfly began its erratic flight, and the two mirages met, a sand-devil skittered across the desert floor. Noonday heat always produced these whirling spirals of air, blinding columns of furnace-hot dust which moved erratically across the desert. Four completely unreal elements performed a ballet on a piece of barren desert: the mirages floated unsteadily above, while the sand-devil and the butterfly danced their erratic steps until, after perhaps five minutes, each one disappeared in turn and life became normal again.

To most people it had been a butterfly, or moth, or piece of litter. To me it was a message from home and a memory of childhood. I had signed for ten bombers, new to this theatre of war and said to be worth £50,000 each. If this figure was correct, the planes were worth half a million pounds in old money. At this time a new bungalow on an arterial road leading from London could be bought for £495. A good house in Muswell Hill cost perhaps £900 or £1000, so a £50,000 bomber was worth a row of houses and ten Wellingtons were worth a housing estate. Here, two days later, was a present, a tip, a sort of pour boîre - a swallowtail.

As children we had never seen swallowtail butterflies in the wild, but had admired them longingly in the Butterfly House in the Zoo. They were the largest British butterfly, brilliantly veined in yellow and black, with the long tails which made them stranger and more elegant than any others: the birds of paradise of their world. On one visit the keeper had kindly given us three dead swallowtails. Lately dead, because the wing muscles were still flexible enough to be spread out without breaking. We had pinned the bodies in the groove of our largest setting board and gently spread out the wings on either side. There they dried and later were displayed in a shallow glass case, the pride of the collection. Now, in a foreign country, I had found the butterfly I had never seen in the wild before. A rare, unearthly moment.

This love of butterflies was strange. Most children were not so butterfly struck, having their own obsessions, but the cult went on in the family for years. It was perhaps the extraordinary transformations which insects achieve which had us in their thrall. The

hawk moth caterpillar, richly coloured, with its spiked tail, the looping Magpies and the fierce, hairy ones we called pussy-cats. The variety was immense and they were everywhere. Cabbages had holes through them, garden peas were full of maggots, apples had small cavities with, at the bottom, fat caterpillars gorged with eating. It is difficult to look back from today, when supermarkets select for cosmetic reasons, not taste, to realise that many apples and other foods have always been shared with caterpillars. No wonder we were so interested in Nature.

The notebooks of Farbre, Bates in the Amazon, Darwin, Wallace, were all in the house and were read, off and on, by everyone in the family. At eleven, my paternal grandfather, William Whitehead, gave me a well-worn copy of The Voyage of the Beagle. A 77th edition, in green cloth binding, worth perhaps a shilling, but given at exactly the correct time. The small print and crude woodcuts would make it look dull compared with bright modern editions, but how well that book was read. It was picked up and studied at random for years.

It is doubtful if William Whitehead ever realised the effect of that book. He was a man of no formal education, but a persistent, omnivorous reader, who had left school at the minimum age and had worked for years as a packer in the tea department of the Cooperative Wholesale Society. Each Christmas the family received a tin of tea so that, over the years, the tins accumulated and everything was stored in fancy tea tins.

Grandfather William had a combatative mind, hard and rather dour. He read philosophical books in the Thinkers Library and thought that Balzac was the greatest writer who had ever lived. He got no sympathy in this from his wife, who read nothing but The Universe, the Roman Catholic newspaper.

She was a tiny, vital woman, who was said to have had Italian blood. This must have been at least one generation remove, if true at all. Certainly she was dark haired, with a slightly sallow complexion, but she knew no Italian and had little particular sympathy with anyone from abroad. She was a Roman Catholic and had brought up the children in that faith, to her husband's resigned dislike. Five boys and one girl, all with voices, all singing in choirs at one time but Albert, my father, outstanding. A boy soprano, his first choir payment was a half-guinea in gold, shining, brilliant and his own. He ran home exultantly to give it to his mother, the first money ever earned by his generation, tossed it up and saw it slip down a drain, never to be recovered. People gathered round. A policeman was called, but the coin stayed in the drain to be found by someone unknown.

At the age of fourteen his voice broke, as happens to all boys, and he was doubtful if it would ever return to allow him to sing professionally again. For two years he took a nondescript clerical job, but at sixteen his voice came back better than ever. A rare alto voice, warm and full, able to float and soar. He joined the choir of Westminster Cathedral and sang there for many years, making the transition each day from marble and plainsong in the West End cathedral, to a cottage on the edge of Muswell Hill, another butterfly transformation.

The Stream

Coppetts Road had only recently been covered in macadam but further down, beyond the Isolation Hospital, it was still gravel. A country lane between rather bleak fields, leading down at the far end to the smell of the Sewage Farm. At the bottom the road curved round beside a stream called, of all things the Strawberry Brook, before joining Colney Hatch Lane and the old road to the north. One of the tributaries of the Strawberry Brook rose as two springs in the woods behind our house, hidden one on each side of Creighton Avenue. Beside the thick forest fence and the hazel copse was an open field, expanding across a gentle valley to the edges of Finchley.

To the north, the woods behind the house continued solid and unbroken to Fortis Green, at the top of the hill. Essentially it was still the old Middlesex Forest, cut round the edges generations before to make a fringe of fields and houses. The field soil was deep black earth, product of long ploughing and cattle grazing, very different from the shallow forest floor. Today the stream is still there, but as a travesty of its rural self. At that time it was a country brook running through a shallow valley, washing the roots of great willow trees. When in full spate, after a period of heavy rain, it was still only a foot or so wide and half that deep, but it had some power. Our dams were always brushed aside by the time we returned next day. Sometimes we planned to make a great assault on the stream; to get more stones and timber to make a real dam; to build a mill pond which would drive machinery, harnessing all that wasted power but, when we returned with what stones could be found in the clay soil, our first attempt had gone. We used to talk of living in a countryside where the building stones were to hand, where we could build great structures of natural blocks, moved into place with levers and backed with clay, but here the attempts to make dams failed each time.

We held boat races with lengths of stick, started off formally with the waving of a handkerchief, with 'boats' jostling each other for the lead in the moving water. They would be snagged in turn on some tree root and the race abandoned, but there was always the dream of a clear run, the full length of the field and away to join the Strawberry Brook as it flowed along the valley bottom from Finchley to Bounds Green.

For a few weeks after we arrived there were cows in the field beyond the stream, but they soon disappeared. Either the land had already been sold, or the farmer was not prepared any longer to risk his cattle near hordes of town children and their dogs.

Not that the dogs were fierce. There were no large dogs. No alsatians or rottweilers. Who could have afforded to feed dogs of that size when people had trouble finding enough to feed themselves? There was no money to keep large dogs and there was little to protect anyway. The houses were bare of valuables. Who ever heard of stealing a cat's-whisker wireless set, yet these were the height of technology at that period. There were none of the electronic gadgets so easily stolen and sold off in pubs today. People had the bare necessities of living and a few trinkets of sentimental value, hardly worth stealing. Lastly, the area was open to view. Every inch of ground was covered by a dozen windows. Thus there was no need for large dogs. We had one of the largest dogs. A cross between a chow and a collie, golden haired, with the cocky, curled tail of a chow and the gentle, loveable nature of a collie. We had commandeered him by accident. My father had offered to act as a messenger, taking the dog from one friend to another. He collected the dog one day and brought it home. The next day he would take it to the new owner, but for that one night, the dog would be at our home.

People object to crossing breeds, but that particular cross is handsome and without the viciousness of some chows. Above all, it can be trained. When everyone sat down to eat, the dog went quietly to lie down in the corner. There was not a sound. It did not look appealingly from one to the other for food. No wimpering. No movement. We were able to eat our meal in comfort and calm. His behaviour was a revelation. After the meal we all fed the dog, finding tit-bits, stroking, patting and encouraging, yet during the meal there was peace.

The next day we refused to allow the dog to go. My father had to meet his friend and tell him that the dog was in custody and could not be released. What arrangements were made I never knew. Certainly the man never got his dog. Jock stayed with the family until he died of old age, by which time we were almost grown up.

Our cats were another story and came later. One day my father arrived with two cats in baskets. One, Tigger, was a handsome ginger and the other, Soo, a smooth-haired, black female. They had come from Peter Warlock the composer. To us Peter Warlock, with his pointed beard and buccaneering look, was a cult figure, always in the Radio Times. He was the musician Philip Heseltine who suddenly changed his personality, grew a beard and wrote different music. His house was always full of cats and my father had apparently offered to look after two of them. It was only later that I learnt that Peter Warlock had died and much later that it was probably by suicide. In Philip Gray's biography he talks of Peter Warlock putting a saucer of milk out for his kitten the night before he died. Soo may have been that kitten for she was tiny when she came. Strange to remember this in Peter Warlock's centenary year.

Peter Warlock

The cats could not have been more different in nature: Tigger out marauding while Soo was almost always at home, not unlike Peter Warlock's two different personalities. Sometime after she arrived Soo produced a nest of kittens which she kept moving until we learnt not to worry her. This was the first of many litters so presumably there are by now many descendants of Peter Warlock's cats in Muswell Hill.

When we first explored the field beyond the stream, years before Soo and Tigger, it was a hay meadow thick with buttercups. The grass in June came up to our waists full

15

of summer sap, making a sweet-smelling forest through which we tramped out hot paths. I cannot remember that anyone objected. No angry farmer appeared to chase us away. Presumably the Borough Council had already bought the land so that year it became a glorious playfield. We could crawl through high grass with no thought that we were damaging a valuable crop. So far as I know nobody cut the hay: no cattle browsed there: nobody cut it to make a playing field. For one glorious year it returned to nature and to us, before law and order took over again. That summer we owned all the grasses of a mixed pasture, with their varied seed heads and long, succulent stems. There were pimpernel, poppies and vetch, but the main impression was of buttercups and more buttercups, rich on those wet slopes.

In the midst of this idyll reality struck. Mr Speller was a bus conductor wearing a heavy blue serge uniform in winter. On May the First he put a white cotton cover on his cap and wore a light summer jacket so that London buses all became brighter and more cheerful that day, but one May there was a quiet disaster. Nobody spoke of it. Nobody took sides or ventured an opinion to another, though Mr Speller spoke of it to everyone he met.

" I never did it," he said. "They claimed I sold a dead ticket. They said I took a fare and gave the man a ticket which had already been punched. Sacked out of hand! Two men on the bus, in ordinary clothes, not in uniform as they should have been, said the ticket was not a good one. I had taken a penny, they said, and then sold the ticket again to another man. I told them I had not. Said it came off the pad of tickets in the proper order. Every day for a week I went down to the terminus to try to see the passenger. Try to pick him out. Make him come forward to say I had given him a good ticket, but I was confused. I couldn't remember his face. You don't look at their faces. You sell tickets to hands. One hand after another, time and again in the rush. You don't see their faces."

"There was a long enquiry. I had to go down to the Head Office. I sat there all day. Didn't even have a drink. I was so nervous I didn't even think of it. I didn't have a drink all day. The Union did what it could. Went through my good record. Nothing like this ever in fifteen years and a safe, good job gone for nothing. I never sold a bad ticket. I never did." He was almost crying.

This story was rehearsed with everyone he met, young and old. Poor Mr Speller told everyone. I was sure he had not done it. Busmen were known for earning wages well above the London average, and here was a man going to lose all his security.

"What reference will they give him?" asked my mother. "It will be a terrible blow."

"But to sack him for a penny!"

"It's not the penny. It's all the other pennies. If he did it, he's lost his job. If he didn't, he's lost it for nothing, but which it is nobody knows, and talking won't change that. It's his wife I'm sorry for. She hasn't spoken to anyone for weeks poor soul. Not like him - he's justifying himself to everyone he meets, but what can she say? She doesn't know the truth any more than we do, but she's the one who has to put the food on the table."

A few months later I became aware that the family was no longer there. I had not noticed their moving and I was vaguely sad when new people moved in.

The Shops

In the 1920s, Olney's, the butcher's, was at the corner of Wilton Rd and Colney Hatch Lane. It had an open front, closed at night with shutters, and inside large hanging rails for sides of meat. In Wilton Rd was a side entrance to the back of the shop, which was furnished like a stable. Just before Christmas each year a young heifer and a few sheep were herded to the shop from some farm and stabled there. The animals were penned as if in a zoo, bedded in thick straw and fed from large troughs. The Roman Catholic church was showing its model of Christ in the manger and here was a real example. We thought, as children, that the live animals seemed better versions of the models. We visited the stable several times and fed the animals with grass, but when we returned one day the animals were gone.

Mother had great difficulty in explaining that the animals had been killed for Christmas. Their bodies now hung in the shop as sides of beef and mutton for people to eat. It was a traumatic shock. Until then meat and animals had been completely different things, as they are to children buying meat in supermarkets today. Now reality had entered and I was never to see a painting of the Nativity after this without wondering what had happened to the animals when the artist had finished painting.

On the opposite corner of Wilton Road was an off-license and next door a newsagent. Further along came an ironmonger's, with garden tools, brooms and all the other clutter spread over the pavement, selling a multitude of things, mostly loose. Nails and screws were weighed or counted, but many other things which we now buy packaged, or do not buy at all, were sold loose. Loose washing soda; balls of whiting used to whiten the front steps; creosote bought by the pint - bring your own tin; putty from a barrel; spirits of salts for cleaning the lavatory; and a hundred other things.

When I was twelve I first saw the effect of dipping copper or brass into acid. Dull metal quickly gleamed bright, transformed in a moment. From this I read about etching and engraving and decided that, while I could not yet engrave metal, I could etch. Engraving involved careful cutting of metal with a sharp burin. Clearly this was a skilled job, while etching was mere scratching through a protective surface so that the acid could cut into the metal. I could certainly etch.

I filed a rectangle of copper to the size of a visiting card and polished it highly. I covered the copper with beeswax, the nearest I could think of to an etcher's protective ground, and scratched my name neatly through it with a large needle. When the metal was put in a bath of acid, the beeswax would protect the copper from the acid. The acid would cut away only at the lines of the name. This would give a set of grooves like engraved lines and the card could be printed. Nothing could be simpler.

I washed a small stoneware oven dish to make my etching bath and went off to the ironmonger to buy some spirits of salts. The ironmonger had no bottles, so he sold me, a twelve year old boy, two pennyworth of hydrochloric acid - spirits of salts - in an open baked bean tin, the only container he could find. This I carried the full length of Wilton Road and the copper was etched with my name and a small leaf pattern. With no etching press I had to print the cards by squeezing them in a vice, an awkward, cack-

17

handed process. The card was just about acceptable. The etching had disappointing blotches, the lettering was shaky and imperfect. It was interesting to have done, but I abandoned etching for many years.

Nobody else knew how the acid had been carried home in an open tin. No unfortunate child bumped into it in all the length of that careful walk home. It was not until nearly sixty years later, when trying to buy some acid, that it suddenly appeared such a bizarre event. Today, when car batteries are sealed, and lavatory basins are cleaned with proprietary cleaners, raw acid is simply not available over the counter to the general public, let alone to a child of twelve.

The main shops were at Muswell Hill Broadway. Harvey Hicks, the butcher, had a shop at the top of Colney Hatch Lane where private houses had been converted. These were the 'tower houses' included in the 1880 sale of The Elms. Single-storey shops had been built over the front gardens, but from the corner of Queen's Avenue one can still see the two square towers which used to stand beside a gravelled Colney Hatch Lane. Harvey Hicks was a typical butcher's shop of the period, with sawdust on the floor, wooden chopping blocks, and men with blue-red hands. They delivered to the Estate, arriving in a small covered van with cut meat ready for sale. Shoulders of Australian mutton cost two shillings and ninepence, which appears to be 14p, but represented one and a half hour's work for a skilled bricklayer. Translate that to modern wages and the price was clearly very much higher.

Sainsbury's stood at the top of the hill, on the site of The Elms', between Duke's Avenue and Muswell Hill itself, in the centre of all the winds. When one saw mythical pictures of gods blowing the winds and scattering ships in all directions, one thought of Sainsbury's. It was a traditional Sainsbury building, with tiled walls, wide counters with huge blocks of butter and enormous cheeses, sides of bacon and large blocks of processed meat, ready to be cut by an army of assistants in white aprons. A dozen grades of bacon lay in piles on the marble counter. Along the front were square tins of biscuits, while tinned foods stood in decorative piles at intervals, separating the different counters. Outside, surrounded by cases of eggs, was a young lad exposed to every wind. One could tell the temperature by the colour of the egg boy. As the weather became colder, he became more and more blue until, by January, he looked like the North Sea. People used to say that he was allowed into the refrigerator every two hours to warm up.

18   The Exchange, Muswell Hill, 1903 [92]

Muswell Hill Broadway in Winter   *Denis Higgins '53*

Muswell Hill Broadway under Snow
by Denis Higgins [93]

The old Sainsbury shop can be seen in the picture above, on the right of the bus shelter. It was the white frontage which is catching the full sunlight and the reflection of the snow. Baine's Baptist Church is seen in the centre.

Denis Higgins was a gifted etcher and engraver who probably illustrated Muswell Hill and local people more completely than anyone of his generation. Originally he was a Muswell Hill postman and lived for years in Grand Avenue, so he had seen the district in every mood, while his figures have all the charm of Ardizonne.

He studied etching at Hornsey College of Art evening classes and later exhibited at the Royal Academy, the Royal Society of Painter-Etchers and Engravers, and at International Exhibitions in Berlin, Brussels, Lisbon, Madrid (Bronze Medal) Naples and Paris (Silver Medal).

Denis Higgins taught etching at the Working Men's College, where he won the Lowes-Dickenison Memorial Art Scholarship. His work can be seen in Hornsey and Islington Library Collections and the Post Office Chairman's Official Suite. Perhaps someone should arrange a retrospective exhibition of his work in Muswell Hill.

19

St James's School

St James's Elementary School stood on Fortis Green, next to the fire station, about half a mile away from the new estate. It was a single storey building with a high slate roof and no ceilings, so that the steep wooden rafters were an unfailing source of pleasure. One could sit in a lesson with the mind wandering and imagine the carpenters up there sawing their joints and putting together this immense structure. If someone had asked, "What are you dreaming about?" the reply would have been, "Watching the carpenters make the roof. There is one of them who could do with a hand if only I could get up there." A far more pleasant way of spending the afternoon than fussing about arithmetic or geography.

I had been surprised when I first saw St James's School because it was so different from my earlier one. Stroud Green School, in Finsbury Park, had been enormous, in red brick with white dressings, full of architectural exuberance. That building had been typical of the London School Board design brought in after the 1870 Compulsory Education Act, with huge windows and classrooms built without corridors, round a sunny hall. St James's School was completely different, much older, and showing by its shape how it had been enlarged over the years. A small front building linked by cloakrooms to a larger one behind and, off to one side, yet another addition. One could trace in imagination how the school had grown over the years, adding and accreting like a snail's shell. By 1925 the school was surrounded by flats and a large fire station. The Headmaster, Mr Plant, later wrote a short history of his school, full of telling detail. [21]

Fortis Green c.1910[92]

Fortis Green showing Tetherdown on the left, Queen's Avenue ahead, and Fortis Green Road to the right, taken from the top of Leaside Avenue. The front gable of St James's School can be seen on the extreme left.

Mr Plant wore his whiskers sharp-pointed, waxed and military. His hair, which had been auburn, was now pale straw. His hands were clean, with well kept nails. No speck of dust would have had the impudence to fall on his clothes. He gave the impression of the very best type of non-commissioned officer, efficient, vital and capable of getting on with the job. Everything he did was vigorous, but dignified. As he walked up Tetherdown each morning, he would help push the milkman's float up the slope. His bowler hat stayed on straight and nobody would have thought of smiling at his behaviour. This is what decent people did. Teach by example.

His two great loves were arithmetic and music. He taught simple mathematics and algebra so well that my sister Phyllis, for one, came across nothing new to her in mathematics in her grammar school until the third year. Some days Mr Plant would walk into a maths lesson and take over, allowing the teacher to go off to do some other work. We children never knew when this would happen: perhaps the teacher did not know either.

Instantly there was a change of speed. Arithmetic became more urgent, more insistent. There would be quick questions and answers, rapid ways of doing things, short cuts for this and tricks for that. It suited some pupils and bewildered others. Mr Plant did a lot of good to some, making them quick and facile. Able to answer simple questions too easily. He got a lot of them through the Scholarship Examination at eleven, but he was caviar to the general. He did not teach them why they were doing anything, or what they were doing, just tricks for doing puzzles quickly. He was a conjuror, bewildering his audience. Kind, willing, hard-working man that he was, he spent his life teaching people to do the three-card trick and failed. While some gained from his teaching, he convinced three quarters of the class that they could not do mathematics and that idea stayed with them for the rest of their lives.

His other great love was singing. There was a special anticipation in his back as he rolled down the tonic sol fah chart and took up his pointer.

Mr Plant would walk between the rows of children, listening and conducting. He taught folksongs and sometimes sent messages home asking if my father knew of part arrangements of particular songs. Sometimes I would bring to school a piece of music specially obtained from Boosie and Hawkes and once or twice, almost under protest, my father set and wrote out the parts for a particular song. I took them in the next morning feeling that my father had been imposed upon. I was quite glad to leave that school before someone was rude.

The History of St James's School

Before 1850, when the school was built, the nearest schools to Muswell Hill had been the National Schools in Hornsey, in Priory Rd, near what is now Warner Rd, and at St Mary's Church further along. These were too far for children under eight to attend, so an appeal to local residents raised money and an Infants School was built. It must have been part crêche, for children from eighteen months were admitted[84] and at eight years old children left to walk to the National Schools in Hornsey. At St James's School, parents paid twopence a week for the first child and one penny for each subsequent child. There were regular public appeals for voluntary contributions and, since many of the people in Muswell Hill were prosperous, the school was able to expand. The only other source of income was a government grant for average attendance and for each child who passed a fresh stage in an examination. This was the 'payments by results system', with all its implications of rote learning.

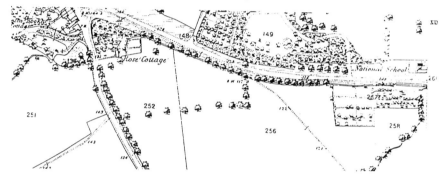

The 1865 Ordnance Survey map showing the National School in
Priory Road, at the bottom of Muswell Hill.

The first school had been built in 1850, to a design by Salvin, the famous local architect, at a total cost of £790 which included the classroom, school-house, complete furnishings of both buildings, and the salary of the schoolmistress for the first year 'of £40 and coals'. The site, on a country lane and backed by dense woods, was so remote that 'the comparative isolation is somewhat obnoxious to the residence of a single woman.' [21] Her first classroom later became the Infants Department.

Soon a second, larger building was added parallel to the first and the older girls, and then the older boys, who had been walking the long distance to Hornsey, were also accommodated on the site. An evening school on three nights a week was started soon after the building was opened. In 1856 there is a bill for 5 shillings and 9 pence for 'candles and ink for the Night Class.' Gas was installed in 1864. There were extensions in 1861, 1887, 1912 and 1931.

In 1887 about £1500 was spent on building a long room capable of being divided into classrooms while still suitable for evening use for choirs and entertainments.

In 1912 an additional classroom was attached to the Long Room, divided from it by a glass and wooden screen.

Thus when I first saw the school, it was a group of inter-connected bungalow buildings

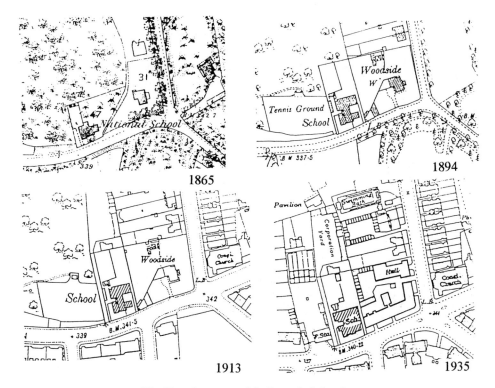

1865

1894

1913

1935

The Development of St James's School
Built 1850, demolished 1970.

with high slate roofs. The Infants were in the original building, near the road, with the
school-keepers' house next to it. A much larger room ran parallel, divided in half by a
wooden partition and the two halves were each divided into two by curtains, so that
lessons on either side had to be kept quiet. In addition there was the fifth classroom
which had been added in 1912. I never saw the 1931 additions which were made after I
left.

In 1925 I had no conception of why the roof rose so high. That penny did not drop for
thirty years and is discussed more fully in Appendix 2. When I first sat in the room my
pleasure was in the huge vault; in working out how the joints fitted together; how the iron
tie bars prevented them from spreading and the whole ridge from collapsing. Pleasure in
the way the iron had been hammered to form long, smooth welds and that magnificent
central eye. It was like sitting under a great cathedral roof and feeling the joy of the
structure.

An imaginative young teacher had started these dreams. One afternoon he sprang to
life, acting out being a building. He stood against the wall and became that wall. The
class had felt the weight of the bricks pressing down on the top of his head, so heavy that
he almost buckled at the knees. Then, when the walls had been built to door height, he
acted the bricks above the doorway, unsupported and loose, raining down on his head.
This made us laugh, but he found a solution: a lintel. A beam of wood or concrete over
the head of the door would bridge the gap and support the bricks above.

However, the roof was the best part. Two children were made to stand facing each other in front of the class to act as two opposite walls. The teacher stood on a chair between them and put his hands on their heads. His arms sloped down like the rafters of a roof and, as he pressed down, the force along his arms pushed the 'walls' outwards. The children were gently pressed backwards on their heels as the 'roof' pushed downwards and outwards.

Suddenly the weight of the roof became clear. Huge baulks of timber suspended over our heads, trying every minute of the day to fall. Blown by gales, soaked by rain, why did the roof stay up and why, above all, did it not push out the tops of the walls? The teacher tied a length of string between his two wrists so that his straight arms and the string made a triangle. Try as he might, his arms could not stretch further apart than the length of the taut string. Now when he stood on the chair and pressed down, his weight rested on the top of the children's heads: they were not pushed outwards. The children were walls. They would have been toppled sideways if the 'rafters' had spread out, but were able to hold great weights which merely pressed straight downwards.

Thereafter the roof was a living thing, with its great rafters pressing down and trying to move outwards, but the tie bars holding them firmly together in a grip literally of iron.

It was only years later, teaching in modern classrooms with their low ceilings, that the reason for the high open roof, without a ceiling, became clear. I had first seen the high roof in 1925, when I was nine. A number of years earlier Aunt Jessie had developed tuberculosis and had had to go to the clean air of Mansfield to recover. This she did over a long period of years, but never returned to live in the smoggy air of London for fear that the infection would recur.

Tuberculosis was rife. Almost every family knew of someone who suffered from the disease, or had died of it. The only known cure was fresh air. Sixty children in one classroom could rapidly infect each other, so each child needed plenty of fresh air which was changed regularly. Therefore schools were built with very high ceilings and windows on each side to give ventilation. Medical Officers of Health were perpetually writing about the 'Cross-draught Theory'.

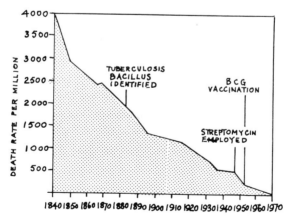

The Graph of Deaths from Tuberculosis

In 1840 there were 4000 deaths per million from tuberculosis. Slowly better living conditions, better food, and the cult of open-air exercise, reduced this but, by the time

24

the tuberculosis bacteria was identified in the 1880s, there were still 2000 deaths per million. There was then no prospect of an early cure and though the death rate had been halved, this was only part of the story. TB made it difficult for the patient to earn a living: there were long periods of sickness at home, or in hospital. Patients had to be supported by their relations since there was no free health system and no unemployment pay, so one tuberculosis patient could bring distress to a whole family.

This was years before the modern drugs which are available today had been invented. The list of medicines for Paddington Childen's Hospital in 1914 consisted of:- Bromide of Potassium, Carbonate of Bismuth, Cod liver oil, Glycerine, and Quinine. No others are mentioned in the King's Fund list. [25] These, with crude disinfectants, were the pharmacoepia with which the army fought the First World War. No wonder the deaths from wounds were so high: no wonder children needed to be tough to survive in peacetime. This is why fresh air and exercise played such a large part in the conscious planning of child health.

The London County Council developed open-air school sites on the outskirts of London, for example in Muswell Hill. Classes from the centre of London visited them for one day a week, to work in open-air classrooms, botanise, and play games away from the befouled town. In town, schools had lessons and exercise on the roof. This emphasis on physical exercise which would ensure deep breathing, was the other side of the coin. Exercise yards can still be seen on the tops of some London Schools.

This is discussed more fully in the Appendix

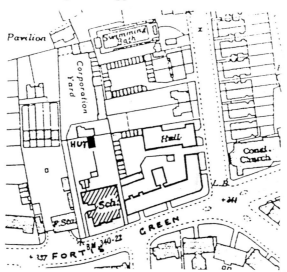

The 1935 Ordnance Survey map showing the hut in the playground,
marked in black.

As St James's had a large playground, there was no need for roof-top marching, but there was the same stress on fresh air. An open wooden classroom stood between the two playgrounds, beyond the two huge oak trees. The shed had a pitched roof and wooden walls reaching to above eye level, with open sides above. Light came in through these gaps and the open doorway. So did snow. The oldest class had the majority of their lessons in this open hut and others used it at least once a week. TB killed people year after year and the only hope at that time was to make people tough enough to resist. Doctors drummed into everyone that the only way to survive was to become resistant to disease. It was to be many years before the arrival of our modern drugs.

Under the two large oak trees in the playground were wooden desks. In anything but steady rain, the trees gave protection, so lessons were held outside whenever possible. Though the desks were dirty, covered in dust and soot so that one tried to carry a rag to rub them down, the grime was accepted. What was a little dirt when one could be in the open air? It is surprising how deeply this idea of healthy open-air life penetrated. For years we children slept with our windows wide open and the curtains flapping in the wind. Only when rain was coming in were the windows closed.

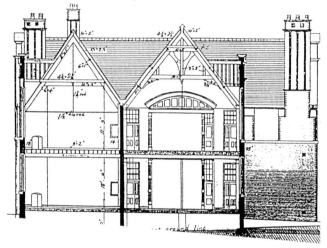

The original pitched roof at Queen's Head Street School, Islington.[34]

Queen's Head Street School is discussed in the Appendix on page 224. St James's School was a bungalow but had a similar shaped roof, with a steel tie-bar in place of the heavy beams and king post shown in the Queen's Head Street drawing.

Coppett's Farm

At the corner of Wilton Road and Coppetts Road was the Farmhouse where we brought small groceries, but the building was always a mystery. Why was a farmhouse surrounded by houses? It was old: the roof tiles were a deep, rich red completely different from the grey slates of Wilton Road or the hard red tiles on our house; its walls were built in irregular bricks with weather-worn corners, set in soft white mortar and covered with ivy; roof and walls were solid enough but they sagged and slumped. It was a farmhouse, yet how could there be a farm without fields or animals? The photograph shows the ivy-covered Coppetts farmhouse when it was still a working farm, surrounded by fields, with the footpath running beside Coppetts Road in the foreground. By 1925, the fence in the picture had disappeared, swept away twenty years before when Wilton Road was built. The farm outbuildings had been demolished and built over, but the farmhouse still existed, with a shop on the ground floor selling groceries, and the old farm-entrance yard converted into a garden.

It was the last relic of the economic life of Muswell Hill in the eighteenth and early nineteenth centuries. Then, before the coming of the railways, London lay in the centre

Coppetts Farm [2,92]

27

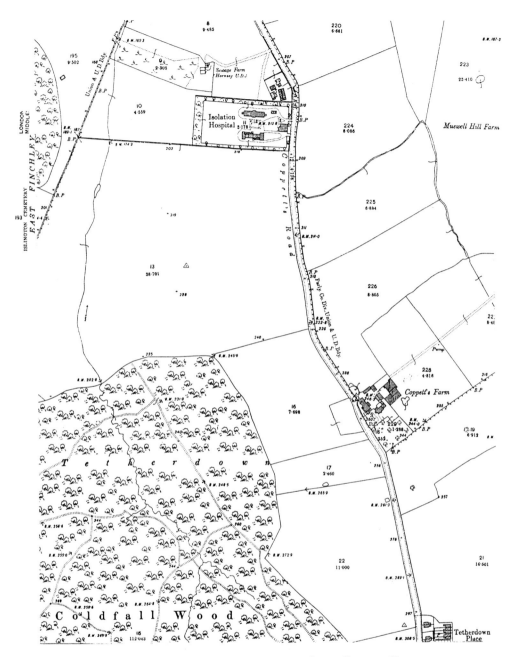

The 1893-4 Ordnance Survey map shows Coppetts Farm
and the Isolation Hospital before any
housing development had started

of a ring of farms which supplied its daily milk and meat and hay. Wilton Road was built on old farmland and symbolized the change from milk to houses.

Coppetts Farm had been cleared from the woodland in the 16th century, and until the mid-nineteenth century, was the only building in Friern Barnet south of the Bounds Brook. The borough boundary ran through what are now the back gardens of Greenham Road. The 1815 Map of Hornsey, from the Victorian County History, not reproduced here, shows that Coppetts Wood extended up to the corner of Fortis Green and Tetherdown, with only a narrow strip of common trailing down beside Tetherdown and Coppetts Road, but Coppetts Farm is not shown in the map because it was in Barnet.

The Victoria County History map of mid-19th and early 20th century development, below, shows how Coldfall Woods were reduced and a Sports Field was developed in the 1930s. This part of the map, at least, is 20th century. It was certainly not a sports field in 1925, but was the lush, sloping meadow described earlier.

The early records of Coppetts Farm are lost. Dairy farms have been linked and split up again over the years and Friern Manor Dairy Farm (Park Farm) was one of those which changed hands from time to time. In 1987 the Company put together a centenary

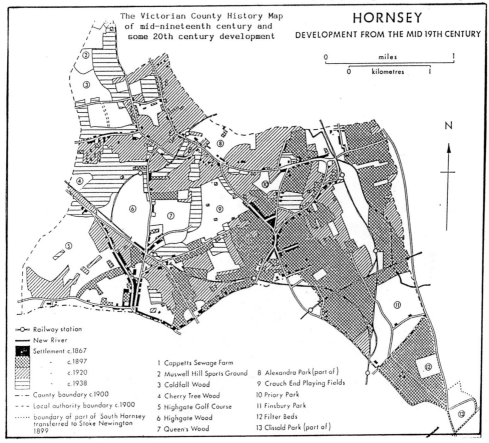

The Victorian County History Map of mid-nineteenth century and some 20th century development

HORNSEY
DEVELOPMENT FROM THE MID 19TH CENTURY

N

Railway station
New River
Settlement c.1867
          c.1897
          c.1920
          c.1938
County boundary c.1900
Local authority boundary c.1900
boundary of part of South Hornsey transferred to Stoke Newington 1899

1 Coppetts Sewage Farm
2 Muswell Hill Sports Ground
3 Coldfall Wood
4 Cherry Tree Wood
5 Highgate Golf Course
6 Highgate Wood
7 Queen's Wood
8 Alexandra Park (part of)
9 Crouch End Playing Fields
10 Priory Park
11 Finsbury Park
12 Filter Beds
13 Clissold Park (part of)

pamphlet[2] which mentions an article in the London Illustrated News of 11 June 1853, with an illustration of the Great Meadow of Friern Manor Dairy Farm, but says that this was situated in Peckham. The Company had been founded in 1836, so the consolidation of many different farms into one was very early. Presumably Friern Manor Farm had been the aggressor and taken over others, including one in Peckham. The detail is lost but the pattern of take-overs sounds very familiar.

The 1893-4 Ordnance Survey map on page 28 shows Coppetts Farm in Coppetts Rd. The farm must have extended right down the the hill, because Coppetts Wood at the bottom of Coppetts Rd was beyond the Sewage Farm.

By 1889 there were eight dairies in the company. One of them, at the corner of Hanley Rd and Crouch Hill, is still famous for its terra-cotta murals showing the methods of dairying and milk distribution years ago. Every child in the neighbourhood is still taken to see the cattle and the pretty milkmaids in their bonnets.

The dairies were well known to everyone but the profit was abysmal. They amalgamated with others until, by 1904, the number of dairies had increased to eighteen but, faced with competition from further afield, the overall profit had sunk even lower.

Even before this however, the Company had began to realise that its extensive land holdings were more valuable as building lots than as farmland. About the turn of the century, Coppetts Farm began to sell off its fields. By 1901, Greenham Rd, Wilton Rd, and Sutton Rd were planned and Greenham Rd was partly developed. One side of Greenham Rd has parts of the back gardens in Muswell Hill, but all the houses are in Friern Barnet, so clearly the Farm was developing from the District Boundary and working down the hill.

The Great Meadow of Friern Manor Dairy Farm, Peckham.

Manor Farm Dairy at the corner of Queen's Parade and Queen's Avenue about 1905.
Milk was served from the churns into the customer's own jug.

Wilton Rd had not been started in 1901, but by 1903/4 was partly developed. In 1905 the Hornsey Journal was advertising seven roomed houses for £425 or £40 a year rent. Sutton Rd was not in the 1903/4 Directory, but had been fully developed by 1911.

It seems probable that the company had hoped to sell land as building lots right to the bottom of the hill, because in 1925, the fields opposite the Isolation Hospital and down to the stream at the bottom, were called 'The Waste Lots'. Presumably these were building lots which did not sell. Perhaps one day someone will find an estate development map in some lost archive.

Friern Manor Dairy Farm Limited was a very large concern with twenty-six shops all over London and a Chief Office in Hatton Garden, E.C. In 1929, the firm had become the United Dairies (London) Ltd (Park Farm).

Some districts have preserved maps giving the old field names from centuries ago. Romantic names - Primrose Meadow, Milking Field, Lark Field, Cowslip Meadow, are all to be found, for example, on the Stoke Newington Estate Map[43], which I published in The Growth of Stoke Newington, but we have no such details about Coppetts Farm. About 1900 a developer bought a single field on the other side of Coppetts Road, almost opposite the farmhouse. It is shown on the 1893-4 map leading straight to the edge of Coldfall Woods, just wide enough to take a central road and two rows of houses. This became Coldfall Avenue, where the houses were to stand by themselves, with fields on either side and the woods at the end, for over twenty years. According to the Street Directory the road was fully developed by 1903/4, with houses bearing romantic names such as Darien, Haycote, The Ferns, Wisteria and Lucerne. Halliwick

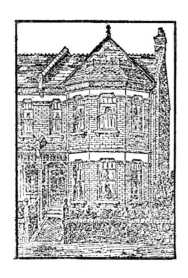

WILTON ROAD,
COLNEY HATCH LANE,
MUSWELL HILL.

———

Superior and Substantially Well-Built

7 ROOMED

HOUSES.

Side entrances, long gardens.

Price £425.　　　Ground Rent £7 7s.
Rent £40.

For full particulars, Apply to Foreman
on the Works, or to

W. GRAHAM,
69, HAMPDEN ROAD, HORNSEY, N.

The Hornsey Journal, 1905

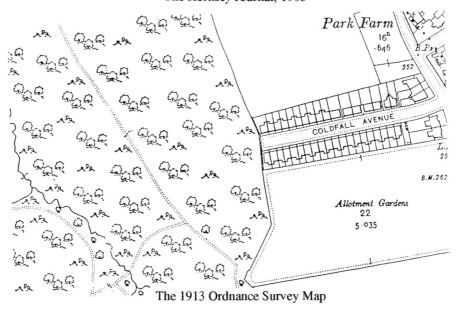

The 1913 Ordnance Survey Map

Road, on the other side of Coppetts Road, was marked out by 1907/8, but it developed only slowly as the market appears to have been pretering out by this time. Even housing would not solve all the Company's problems.

During the 1914-18 War the Dairy had difficulty in obtaining labour, so in 1916 the North London milk rounds were amalgamated with Emerton & Sons Ltd, who served the same area. In 1920, about twenty shops were sold to the United Dairies Ltd, in return for shares, but Friern Manor Dairies still retained ten shops in the City of London. They tried to diversify into ice-cream, supplying the cinemas of South

London and converted some shops into milk bars, which were a such a feature of the City in the 1930s.   Gradually the Company continued the process begun in Greenham Rd, gave up the milk side, while retaining its shares in the United Dairies, and became a small property company.   The whole story shows a company changing direction, slowly and perhaps reluctantly, from farming to property development as economic pressures drove it.

Coppetts Farmhouse continued to trade as a small shop for some years.   It appeared in the 1934 street directory but this was to be the end. The oldest house in the area was demolished and the Wilton Court flats were built on the site.   In the Wilton Road hedge-line was a noble old tree, so the architect built around it, preserving the tree and with it the old farmyard. As a result Coppetts farmyard is still open to the air and I like to think that, on a quiet night, one may still hear cattle walking up the lane to be milked.

The area south of the Coppetts Road Estate had always been a borderland between Hornsey, Finchley, and Friern Barnet, remote from the three centres.   Therefore they had built their Isolation Hospital in this spot, in the open air.   There also, as in later days countries would build their nuclear power stations on coastlines or borders, far from cities and the mass of people who might protest, so the councils built their sewage works in the valley between the three boroughs.   In a bad wind, the stench was everywhere, effectively halting all house building for years.   It was only in the 1960s that the nuisance was moved elsewhere and housing began to venture into the valley.

33

The Felling

The houses woke to the sound of axes. Shirt-sleeved men swinging silvery axes were chopping a wedge out of the bottom of a huge tree. By the time we had dressed and rushed out, there was a wound nearly a foot deep on one side of the trunk and a man with spiked boots was walking up the tree leaning backwards against a belt. Well above the first branch he fastened a wire cable round the tree and slid down. Children crowded near but the men waved us back to a safe distance, where we stood silent and astonished.

The end of the wire was taken far away from the tree to a large metal machine which had a lever like a signal-box points lever. This machine was anchored to the base of another tree and the cable levered taut so that when the tree fell, it would fall in a safe direction, as the men required. Now two men took a long, double-handed saw with enormous teeth and sawed from the other side of the trunk towards the wedge. The sharp smell of fresh-cut oak, a smell that would evoke oak all our lives, filled the air. That sharp tang of pyrogallic acid is like no other smell on earth, clearing the brain like wine. Other woods have their own smells but oak has a special sharpness.

As the saw bit deeper and deeper into the trunk, the hawser was drawn tighter and, at last, there was a slight movement. The men released the saw and ran to drag on the steel lever. Slowly the tree moved towards them and a space opened up in the sky as the huge canopy of branches fell to the ground, dragging in a gush of light. Great branches cracked like sticks under the impact. Twigs littered the ground and, finally detached, broken from its branch but still closely woven and complete, was a bird's deserted nest which I kept for years.

By the time we came back from school, almost a dozen fine trees had been felled. The lumberjacks had sawn or chopped off the side branches so that the trunks were stripped ready for the carters to take them to the timber yard. Larger branches were stacked,

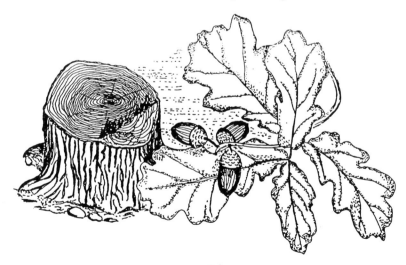

34

ready to be carried away, but the smaller pieces still littered the ground. Instead of a dense wood there was an open prairie with flat-topped tree trunks spaced at intervals and light reached the ground as it had not done for a thousand years.

That evening the wood was alive. Children played on the flat tree stumps, jumping on and off in an enormous natural gymnasium. Some young ones sat solemnly round a tea table laid with a toy china tea set and extra acorn cups picked up from the ground. The householders and the older children were gathering winter fuel. Branches were carried off and secreted in gardens all along the road, though how they would cut them nobody knew. Many pieces were far too thick for the tiny saws most people owned. Children rested them between stones and jumped on them but only ricked their ankles. Some branches hung about for years, too long to fit into any fireplace, and were finally burnt in some Guy Fawkes blaze years later. Small twigs were gathered in baskets and sheets, to be stacked near the coal cellars to dry. By the next day most of the area had been cleared.

After a few days, when plenty of trunks were ready for moving, the timber wains arrived. Not lorries as I remember it, but horse-drawn wains with two pairs of wooden wheels joined by enormous curved axles, which swept up between them. When the wains were drawn forward over the trunks, the curves of the axles stood higher than the trunks. The trunks were winched up below the axle curves to be held suspended a few inches above the ground and the wain was ready to move. Then a team of two, or four, huge shire horses drew the wain away slowly to the local timber yard. At this period London still had its small timber yards, with their power saws and stacks of timber being seasoned slowly in open-sided sheds.

When the great hurricane struck London in 1987, a wealth of timber was felled, but by then there was no local equipment to deal with it. In the end large amounts of good timber were turned into mere fibreboard, soulless and dull because there were no saws to cut it up.

In 1925 England was still in an early manufacturing age, doing many things as they had been done a century earlier. Building and construction were still largely hand-worked, with processes carried out by traditional handicraft methods, using long-remembered skills. These trees would be cut in local yards to make oak fencing for perhaps quite local use.

Ever since they had begun cultivating their gardens, the householders had made secret attacks on the wood for leaf-mould. This litter layer, far thinner then they had expected, had been taken in small amounts. A pail here and a pail there to help a particular plant, or lighten the soil along a row of beans. Now, with the area cleared and building about to start, this was their last chance. People went out with pails in both hands and returned to build small heaps of rich black leaf mould to enliven their heavy clay.

We children were fascinated by the flat tops of the tree stumps. We tried to count the annual rings to find the age of one large tree. We knew that a tree adds one ring each year and these ones were clear to see. Start at the middle and count outwards. That gave the age of the tree, but we continually lost count. In the end I went back to the house and collected the nails left over from making the rose pergola and the full collection of tools the house could provide - a coal hammer and a gimlet. A ludicrous kit. There had been a proper hammer, used to build the pergola, but I could not find it. Presumably it had been left in the garden and would turn up later. The coal hammer, which weighed about a pound and a half, was very far from a carpenter's tool. A rough forged head, straight from the steam hammer, with a straight pane like a blunted axe blade at one end and a four-sided point at the other. It would break coal well enough, but hitting a nail was another matter, while the gimlet was a tool of the devil. It was like a corkscrew, with a wooden handle across the top. In theory one pushed the point into the wood and slowly twisted so that it screwed into the wood, cutting a neat hole. In fact the point was blunt and the tool would skid rather than penetrate. We were not well equipped, but fortunately we did not realise this.

Back at the tree trunk we carefully counted ten rings from the centre and hammered in a nail. It was very difficult. The hammer point was too small and rounded and the straight pane too narrow for us to be able to hit a nail cleanly. In the end, after several missed strokes and barked fingers, we took to hitting with the flat side of the hammer and made some progress. Slowly the nails moved across the trunk at ten year intervals until there were twenty-three nails and three more rings outside. After a lot of discussion we agreed that this made 233 rings and that was the age of the tree.

It meant that this huge oak had first sprouted from its acorn in AD 1717, more than two centuries earlier. We looked it up in a history book and found that King George I had been on the throne. When we told Mother she said in an off-handed way,

"Yes. He was the first German. Never spoke a word of English you know."

This was one of those shocks that one remembers all one's life. A king of England who did not speak English and, more than that, a German! It was 1926 by now and we children had all those blind prejudices that young people absorb through their pores. Three years earlier, at my previous school, I had moved from the Infants to the Junior School. To celebrate, my Mother had bought me a satchel unlike any worn by any other child in the class. It was brown canvas, with short crossed straps so that it sat high up on the shoulder blades, instead of hanging by the hip like any respectable satchel.

I was horrified. "I can't wear that. It's German."

Mother did not try to persuade me, but went back to the shop and changed it. This was when Germany was trying to rescue her economy from its pit of despair by expanding exports. The Dawes Plan to rescue German children from starvation had only just been agreed, and here was one export being rejected by a boy who had to be like his friends. The Germans were still the enemy and suddenly I had discovered that a British king was German.

Felling continued until there were no trees left behind the houses and there was clear land as far as the field edge. All was stumps and devastation. The woods to the right were still there, but our original row of houses would never again look out on a green forest: some of the romance was gone. Only the people of Barrenger Road, in the far corner of the Estate, were to have trees up to their back gardens for ever.

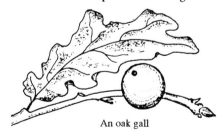

An oak gall

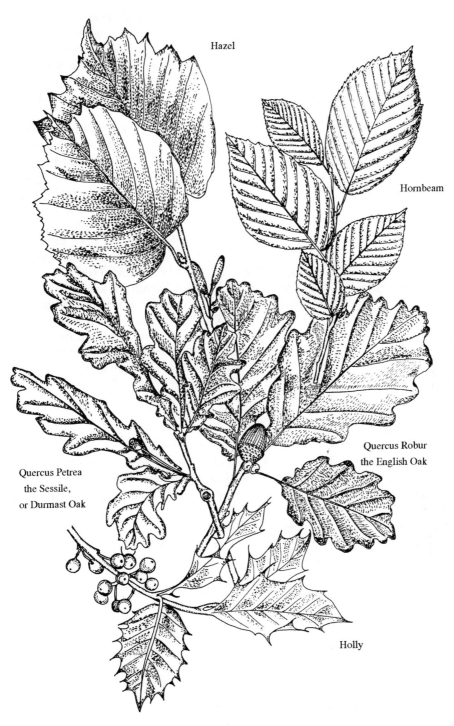

Hazel

Hornbeam

Quercus Robur
the English Oak

Quercus Petrea
the Sessile,
or Durmast Oak

Holly

The Major Trees in Coldfall Woods

The Clearing and Building

When the timber had been removed, the slope became a pattern of tree stumps, dotted like mushrooms. Then men with pickaxes and narrow digging spades cut round each stump, chopping off the roots, exposing the sides, undercutting where possible. A chain was passed round the exposed stump and a huge shire horse, its flanks shining and glistening with sweat, pulled and heaved until the stump began to move. At that moment Phyllis, after the first occcasion, turned away and winced, for no sooner did the stump move than the carter cut the horse violently with his whip. Each time this produced a frenzied whinny and a scrabbling with the hooves as the horse dragged harder and the stump broke clear. Soon Phyllis could bear it no longer and ran home crying, with me following, trying to comfort her.

By the time we ventured back next day the stumps had been piled in long heaps and burning had started. Not with great blazes, but slow combustion, tardy and fitful because the wood was wet and full of sap. The men kept returning to their fires, pushing them together as the centres burnt to ash, shaping the mounds and coaxing the stumps to burn.

A few days later there were piles of wood ash all over the site and unlevelled pits left from the tree stumps. The burnt-out watch fires of a vanished army near their abandoned fox holes. When I pointed this out to my father he said, "Too much like Flanders," and refused to say any more.

The more knowledgeable gardeners collected some of the wood ash to put on their flowers, but most of it washed away. By the autumn weeds and grass had sprung up, colonising a landscape which had, for centuries, been too shady for them to grow.

Within a month there were men marking out the site with pegs and strings in a way that we children could not understand. Trenches were dug for no apparent reason. Great heaps of gravel and sand arrived in two wheeled carts, drawn by the inevitable shire horses, with their huge hooves and hair-fringed anklets. These carts were always exciting because the carter backed them into position, pulling on the cheek harness where it met the horse's bit until the cart was in the correct place. Then he knocked out a holding wedge and the cart body tipped up, suddenly and violently, depositing its load in exactly the right position.

These mountains of sand and gravel were to be features of the landscape for some years to come. Each time the same process was repeated. Two or three men began wheeling so many barrowloads of sand, so many barrows of gravel, so many sacks of cement, into a huge pile which they turned until it was all the same grey-yellow colour. Then they made a hole in the centre, filled it with water and carefully turned the dry mixture into the centre. Steady turning, controlling the water so that it could not escape from the centre, watchful mixing, to produce a great lake of concrete, ready to be poured into the narrow trenches to form foundations for the houses.

This mixing process would be repeated along road after road as the houses were built, year after year, until the estate was complete. The first mix was for foundations. They would use different proportions and different materials for the bricklaying mortar, but the process of batch mixing would be used on all occasions. There were no concrete mixers. No ready-mix concrete was delivered to the site in revolving conical vases, carried on huge lorries. These machines were still light years away. Bricks were delivered by lorry, or cart, and unloaded one by one. The impression the whole time the estate was being built was of armies of men, with their different skills, working by hand, following each other in turn from house to house, without any of the modern machinery we expect today.

When the concrete had been mixed, men shovelled it into wheelbarrows which were then wheeled off along lines of planks to the foundation trenches. Two lines of planks, with full barrows moving along one and empty ones returning along the other. Wide wooden barrows, white from the layers of dried on mortar, handles polished by perpetual use, wooden wheels hooped with iron. The builders' labourers with their sleeves rolled up, trousers tied with string below the knee, wearing waistcoats, knotted scarves, and flat tweed caps, followed each other up and down the planks.

At the trenches other men, more skilled, tamped down the concrete with baulks of wood to pack it tightly into the trenches, forcing the trapped air to the surface so that the concrete would be solid and then placed a long spirit level on top. Only when the bubble in the level lay exactly in the centre was the top of the concrete level and they could move to the next section. These were the bricklayers, kings of the building trade. They never mixed concrete, or wheeled a barrow, or carried a brick. Those were the labourers' jobs. Bricklayers were craftsmen who had served apprenticeships. They got threepence or fourpence an hour more than the labourers and expected everyone to recognise it.

Three days after the first foundations were poured came the lorries with thousands of bricks. They had been piled into the lorries by hand and were taken out in the same way. A man inside the lorry threw them over the side to another man on the ground, who caught them and threw them to a third. The third man stacked them in a neat pile. Flying bricks, caught time after time, without a miss. The men's hands were so hard and calloused that even the sharp brick edges did not cut them. By the pile was a foreman with a clipboard who counted and checked to make sure that the full number of bricks of each sort was delivered. There were Flettons, in one pile, pink and smooth, and in the others, deep red facing bricks and white/yellow Gaults.

When the lorries were emptied the men sat down for a break. They brewed tea in a can over a wood fire, dropping the tea leaves into the water as it boiled, and took out thick sandwiches, or a loaf of bread and a piece of cheese.

Then began the bricklaying. Labourers mixed batches of mortar on a platform made of wooden boards, using sand, lime and cement to make a stiff porridge. When the mortar was ready, they brought forward a tall frame which leant at an angle against two wooden stays. Over the frame was a thick felt blanket made of animal hair, like a huge horse-cloth. They beat the cloth with sticks so that the hairs fell into the mortar. They mixed the hairs into the mortar, beat again and mixed again, until the mortar was threaded with hairs. These would hold the mortar together and, years later, I could still recognise them in the tiny gap between the wooden front door frame and the bricks. Hair mortar was the traditional bricklaying material, now long forgotten.

Then the labourers each stacked a dozen bricks in a carrying hod and carried them on their shoulders to the foundations. They built piles of bricks at intervals along the wall and set out mortar on small mixing boards. All was ready for the brickies. Swiftly a bricklayer spread a layer of mortar on the foundations, picked up a red facing brick, examined it to find the best corner and laid it down on the mortar. He tested it with a spirit level in both directions, tapped the high corner with the handle of the trowel and tested again. It appeared so easy. Quick, assured movements, perpetual checking, a well trained eye. We children were fascinated to watch for long periods as the men spread the mortar, buttered the brick and tapped it true.

Slowly the walls rose to waist height round the first block of houses. One could see the shape arising, but the rooms seemed so small, rooms for dwarfs. Later, when the men had gone, we paced out the rooms and were surprised to find that they were the same size as our own papered rooms.

Now came the scaffolders, quick, lithe men who threw piles of tall larch poles on the ground. These rang out with high, bright notes as they landed on the pile, which became an enormous xylophone. Grown in a forest, close packed like grass, they had shot up straight and tall, with their side shoots weak from lack of light. Now, stripped of bark, with any side shoots cut off and bleached by the sun, they were to be erected as another forest round the new house walls like a giant Meccanno; to be put up and taken down time and again as the building of the estate progressed, in a never ending dance.

Nearby were a huge pile of scaffolding boards, with metal cleated ends, and another pile of puttocks,short baulks of timber about four feet long, adzed to about four inches square. These were the cross- members which would carry the scaffold boards, for at this period there was no metal scaffolding. All scaffolding was still of wood as it had always been. The larch poles were tied together in a square lattice with standard lengths of sisal rope. These ropes, with their neatly whipped ends to prevent fraying, were bound tightly round each joint of the framework in a traditional joint. Scaffolders carried special hand axes with a blade at one end and a sharp point at the other. We children were fascinated at the way these axes were used for a dozen jobs. The scaffolders dug the point into a piece of wood to pull it towards them; they wrapped the end of the rope round the axe and levered it tight to bring their poles together; they wound the rope end round the scaffolding pole and the axe tip, removed the axe, slid the rope end through the gap left and pulled it tight. With the axe they bound the scaffolding tight and safe without using one single knot. Without the axe this would have been impossible to achieve.

RATES OF WAGES IN THE BUILDING TRADE.

The following are the rates of wages in the building trade in England and Wales. Every endeavour is made to ensure accuracy, but we cannot be responsible for errors that may occur:—

The Builder, 1923

	Masons.	Bricklayers.	Carpenters, Joiners.	Plasterers	Slaters.	Plumbers	Painters.	Masons' Labourers	Bricklayers' Labourers	Plasterers' Labourers
Grimsby	1/8	1/8	1/8	1/8	1/8	1/8	1/8		1/3	
Great Yarmouth	1/4	1/4	1/4	1/4	1/4	1/4	1/4		1/0	
Guildford	1/4½	1/4½	1/4½	1/4½	1/4½	1/4½	1/4½		1/0½	
Halifax	1/8	1/8	1/8	1/8	1/8	1/8	1/8		1/3	
Harrogate	1/8	1/8	1/8	1/8	1/8	1/8	1/8		1/3	
Hartlepools	1/8	1/8	1/8	1/8	1/8	1/8	1/8		1/3	
Hastings	1/4	1/4	1/4	1/4	1/4	1/4	1/4		1/0	
Hereford	1/5	1/5	1/5	1/5	1/5	1/5	1/4		1/0¾	
Huddersfield	1/8	1/8	1/8	1/8	1/8	1/8	1/8		1/3	
Hull	1/8	1/8	1/8	1/8	1/8	1/8	1/8		1/3	
Ipswich	1/4½	1/4½	1/4½	1/4½	1/4½	1/4½	1/4½		1/0½	
Lancaster	1/8	1/8	1/8	1/8	1/8	1/8	1/8		1/3	
Leamington Spa	1/6½	1/6½	1/6½	1/6½	1/6½	1/6½	1/6½		1/2	
Leeds	1/8	1/8	1/8	1/8	1/8	1/8	1/8		1/3	
Leicester	1/8	1/8	1/8	1/8	1/8	1/8	1/8		1/3	
Lichfield	1/6½	1/6½	1/6½	1/6½	1/6½	1/6½	1/6½		1/2	
Lincoln	1/8	1/8	1/8	1/8	1/8	1/8	1/8		1/3	
Liverpool	1/9	1/9	1/9	1/9	1/9	1/10	1/9		1/4½	
Llanelly	1/8	1/8	1/8	1/8	1/8	1/8	1/8		1/3	
London	1/8	1/8	1/8	1/8	1/8	1/8½	1/7		1/3	
Loughborough	1/8	1/8	1/8	1/8	1/8	1/8	1/8		1/3	
Luton	1/4½	1/4½	1/4½	1/4½	1/4½	1/4½	1/4½		1/0½	
Maidstone	1/4	1/4	1/4	1/4	1/4	1/4	1/4		1/0	
Manchester	1/8	1/8	1/8	1/8	1/8	1/8	1/8		1/3	
Mansfield	1/8	1/8	1/8	1/8	1/8	1/8	1/8		1/3	
Merthyr Tydfil	1/8	1/8	1/8	1/8	1/8	1/8	1/8		1/3	
Middlesbrough	1/8	1/8	1/8	1/8	1/8	1/8	1/8		1/3	
Newcastle-on-Tyne	1/8	1/8	1/8	1/8	1/8	1/8	1/8		1/3	
Newport, Mon.	1/8	1/8	1/8	1/8	1/8	1/8	1/8		1/3	
Northampton	1/6½	1/6½	1/6½	1/6½	1/6½	1/6½	1/6½		1/2	
Norwich	1/4½	1/4½	1/4½	1/4½	1/4½	1/4½	1/4½		1/0½	
Nottingham	1/8	1/8	1/8	1/8	1/8	1/8	1/8		1/3	
Oakham	1/5	1/5	1/5	1/5	1/5	1/5	1/5		1/0¾	
Oldham	1/8	1/8	1/8	1/8	1/8	1/8	1/8		1/3	
Oxford	1/4½	1/4½	1/4½	1/4½	1/4½	1/4½	1/4½		1/0½	
Plymouth	1/6	1/6	1/6	1/6	1/6	1/6	1/5		1/1½	
Pontypridd	1/8	1/8	1/8	1/8	1/8	1/8	1/8		1/3	

Prices in shillings and pence when the average wage was about £3 a week.

Carpenters

Surely the most enjoyable job on the new houses was carpentry. Open-shouldered work, using big, sweet smelling materials, quickly cut with sharp saws and nailed vigorously with a fine swinging of the arm. I always enjoyed watching the carpenters fixing their heavy floor joists and then nailing the floor boards with crudely sheared cut- nails. The men never seemed to mind a couple of small children watching through a window, examining everything they did.

The carpenters arrived when the bricklayers had finished building the walls. They climbed the scaffolding and began creating the roof. Rafters were cut to standard lengths, with the end joints set at the correct angles with bevels. It was a pleasure to see them cutting so accurately to the thick pencil lines with cross-cut saws. No machinery. There was not a power machine on the site. In 1925, almost everything was done as it had been done a century before. Of course they no longer squared their roof joists with an adze, or sawed them with two-handed saws in saw pits. Those practices had gone out long before. Joists arrived at the site already sawn to width and thickness by power saw; floor boards came machine planed; skirting boards were machine moulded, but from then on everything was cut by hand. No small electric saws or planes. No electric sanders. These small tools were still far in the future.

When the ridge beam was in place, with the raking corner rafters, the rest of the rafters were cut and nailed in place. It looked easy, but cutting the correct angles every time took years to learn. Last they nailed in place the eaves boards, ready to take the gutter brackets.

Each man had his tools in a circular 'straw', a shallow bag of strong canvas, with two large handles on the rim. Presumably they used to be made of straw and the name had stuck. Tools were always laid back on the straw, so that they would not be scattereed and lost. Then, when the carpenter was ready to move, the two handles were pulled together,slipped over the shoulder and the straw was tucked under the arm and carried off. It was large enough to hold the longest saw safely and still fold over to protect the ends. At five o'clock each night we children saw dozens of men walking home and could pick out the trades by the different tools they carried.

Tools were guarded jealously. A labourer would be told sharply, "Don't touch that saw. You're not a carpenter." Carpenters were skilled men who had served their apprenticeships and did not welcome untrained men. Nor did one carpenter use another's tools. Great offence could be given that way. Each man's tools were marked, burnt in, or deeply stamped, so that there was no chance of the mark being obliterated. When tools had odd initials, there was always a story attached. "From the wife's deceased father"; -"Picked up in Caledonian Market for next to nothing"; - "Bought from a pawnshop window when I was an apprentice." Many of these stories had been polished by telling, repeated on site after site, and no doubt some acquired truth by the same process.

One day we children watched a strange ritual. A carpenter had died. Some of the men who had worked with him for years had gone to the funeral. Now there was a strange ceremony. The widow, left with her husband's tools, could not face the sight of them. There was no family; nobody who would continue to use them, yet she could not bring herself to sell them. She had asked one of his friends to dispose of them as he thought best.

That lunch time, about six men who had known him well sat round in a partly floored room, to eat their sandwiches and drink their tea. Then the straw was opened, heavy with tools. They tossed up for turns like children in the playground and then they each chose a tool in turn as a memento. A wooden smoothing plane, remouthed with boxwood, shining with wear. A cross-cut saw, a carpenter's brace together with a green baize roll of bits. Chisels chosen singly. Tobacco tins of small bits and pieces accumulated over a life-time. Each item was handled carefully and put away by the new owner in its new tool kit, where it would become the subject of a new story. Lastly the leader collected a small sum from each man to buy a present for the widow, a tea tray perhaps, or a vase, as a remembrance. The foreman's whistle went and they slowly returned to work.

After the rafters were in position, long tiling battens were nailed in place, but without any roofing felt, or other insulation below them. The tiles would be the sole protection and, from inside the lofts, one would always be able to see the sky through the draughty chinks.

When the carpenters left, the roof tilers arrived. Large boxes of red clay tiles had been delivered and now stood around the houses, scattering whisps of packing straw. Labourers stacked the tiles in their carrying hods and climbed the ladders to the top of the scaffolding, holding the ladder with one hand and gripping the hod with the other. They piled the tiles ready for use and the tilers began laying them from the eaves upwards. They hooked the tiles over the wooden battens, by their projecting nibs, nailing every fifth row. It seemed too little, but the men assured us that this was enough.

Years later I read the amusing account of Samuel Butler's house in New Zealand, where they put the roof on upside down. Samuel Butler, getting as far away as he could from his father, the Bishop, became a sheep farmer in New Zealand. There he had a house built in the traditional early colonial manner of earth blocks with a thatched roof.The thatchers were amateurs who started tying in their bundles of thatch from the ridge and worked down to the eaves instead of the other way round. As a result, the open ends of the straw thatch were pointing upwards instead of being protected by the straws above. When it rained, the water ran through the vertical thatch into the house as if the roof was made of bundles of drinking straws.

Fortunately, in the Coppetts Road estate the tilers started correctly from the bottom and worked to the ridge. Once there, they cemented in place round capping tiles along the ridge and down the corner hip rafters.

Meanwhile the carpenters were inside the houses, building the floors, fixing the floor joists and nailing down floor boards with heavy cut nails. Large open boxes of these, crudely stamped out of sheet steel, accompanied the carpenters everywhere. The hammer rhythm was absolutely regular. Tap, bang, bang, bang. A light fixing-stroke followed by three heavy blows, as regular as clockwork. One could tell from the outside of the house when a man was nailing floorboards.

43

With the floors made, everything became more finished. The sawing stools, brought inside, became seats. Stair-cases, delivered ready-made from the joiners' shop, were fixed, their treads protected by temporary pieces of plywood. Door frames and doors were fitted, skirtings and window sills were cut and fixed. There was a smell of freshly planed wood and men went home with small bundles of firewood.

Carpenters had always taken home the short off-cuts from the roofing joists, angle-shaped pieces which would light the fire, or burn as brief logs. Now there was more variety to choose from. No piece of timber longer than seven inches could leave the site. This was a rigid rule and easily enforced by a watchful foreman. One evening I watched a man take a length of floorboard and carefully saw it into seven inch lengths, tie them neatly with string, and put them aside to be taken home. A few years later I went into another carpenter's house where there was a white butler's sink with a deal draining board, neatly pieced together out of seven inch pieces, like a chess board.

When the carpenters' work was done, the plasterers moved in. In Finsbury Park, where we had come from, the house had internal walls made of lath and plaster, fine places for mice to run. We had kept down the mice by having a cat, but there was always the danger of mice returning. There were certainly mice in the coal cellar there, but in the new estate lath and plaster were banned. All inside walls were built of dark grey breeze-block, thin, hard and solid. No space for mice to run. Only the ceilings were set with lath and plaster: there was no plaster board as this had not been invented.

The plasterers brought in trestles and large mixing boards, white with dry plaster. They mixed sand, lime and cement to make a loose, sloppy mortar which they applied with wide, sweeping strokes. Then came a skimming layer of plaster, smoothed and polished by repeated strokes of the trowel. Plasterers were quick moving, wiry men, all muscle, and we were fascinated to see how rapidly the walls were covered. The dark, wet plaster seemed to set immediately and, two days later, it had dried to the palest of pinks. With the plasterers gone, the houses appeared almost finished. From buildings under construction, they were recognisable houses. Families could almost have moved in, so dramatic was the change..

Last came the glaziers, painters and decorators. Crates of cut squares of glass appeared. Glaziers with huge barrels of putty, rolled and pulled and squeezed putty into the window frames, pushed a sheet of glass into the soft putty and bevelled the edge with a quick putty knife. Here again was the speed of men doing a job they had done a thousand times, so that the familiar rhythm of work made the job easier. But their work was silent and intense. Nobody treated glass carelessly. The men never took their eyes off it and as they left, dabbed the windows with whitewash so that nobody would break them by accident.

Doors and staircases had come on site ready-primed with pink paint. Now floors were swept, damped to reduce dust, and the decorators in their white overalls painted the woodwork with undercoat and gloss paint in a pale stone colour. The older men had learnt their trade in a much more decorative period, when people had time and money to spend. They could tell tales of elaborate stencil work and multi-coloured painting, such as they had carried out in big houses in Muswell Hill before the First World War. Elaborate cornices painted in parallel bands of salmon, pale green, dark green, and salmon again; elaborate flock wallpapers, difficult to handle; deal doors painted and grained with a rabbit's tail to resemble oak, mahogany, or bird's eye maple. They some -

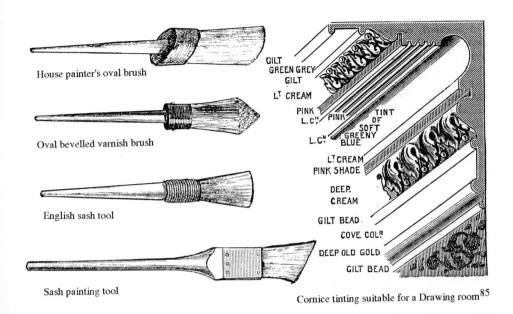

House painter's oval brush

Oval bevelled varnish brush

English sash tool

Sash painting tool

GILT
GREEN GREY
GILT
L^T CREAM
PINK
L.C^M PINK TINT
OF
SOFT
GREENY
L.C^M BLUE
L^T CREAM
PINK SHADE
DEEP.
CREAM
GILT BEAD.
COVE COL^R
DEEP OLD GOLD
GILT BEAD

Cornice tinting suitable for a Drawing room[85]

A world which had been lost by 1925

times felt that they had come down in the world to paint a complete house in one colour and then to repeat the same colour all down the road. It was against their dignity. However, the immediate job was to get people into decent, clean houses. Perhaps elaboration would come later.

In 1925 they decorated the walls with cheap, bright wallpapers, trimming the edges of the rolls with huge shears, so that we were able to collect handfulls of curly streamers and wrap them round our heads as elaborate wigs. This dressing up marked the end of building. A little carnival to celebrate the completion of the next block of houses.

These pre-war building sites would be unrecognisable today, alive with men instead of machines. Yet while there were many men, they could be hired and fired at an hour's notice. Building has always been the most chancy of trades. About 1978, the architect R.A.Bullivant, who is quoted later in the chapter on The Odeon, Muswell Hill, gave a lecture about the building of cinemas in the 1930s. He said:-

"It would not have been possible to build a 1500 seat cinema in eight or nine months if the Economy had been overheated as it was for example in the 1960s. All contractors employed a nucleus of craftsmen who had started with them as apprentices. In addition, casual labour was hired and fired as there was a large pool of unemployed craftsmen and labourers. At an inspection of one half-completed cinema I condemned a large area of brickwork on the advice of the Clerk of Works. Before I left the site that evening all the condemned work had been demolished and twenty additional bricklayers had suddenly materialized and were rebuilding the walls."

45

Books

The fact that there were several children in the family and several aunts, meant that books sometimes arrived at Christmas in sets. Thus we had 'Wayside and Woodland Flowers', 'Wayside and Woodland Trees', 'Wayside and Woodland something else'. Each had been given one, but in fact they were common property. There were always plenty of these basic reference books in the house. With them came story books and annuals, all the sorts of books for Christmas and birthdays, but most of the books in the house had been bought by my father. There were classics, of course. Complete runs of Dickens, Kipling, and Wells, with some Hardy, but very little Scott, apart from Ivanhoe. He was slightly passé by that time. My father could never resist collected essays, mostly modern, like Chesterton, Robert Lynd, E.V. Lucas; what he called 'The On books', after that never ending series by Belloc. Published at three shillings and sixpence, they could be picked up in any second-hand shop for a shilling. They were small, hardbacked and comfortable to the hand; easily slipped in the pocket and ideal for reading on buses. There was always a large selection to choose from on the shelves.

The nearest public library was in Shepherd's Hill, Highgate. It was on the 43 bus route, but normally I walked there and back. Many of the books had been rebound in strong, 'library' covers, with the name of the library heavily embossed on the front cover, for books were designed to last in those days, not discarded when the covers became creased. There were no paperbacks,

With six in the family and two books each, I chose twelve books every fortnight, rain or shine, from before I was eleven. Because I was collecting books for my parents as well as myself, the librarians gave me access to the adult section very early and I picked books for the whole family. Boys' stories, girl's stories, novels by named authors for my parents, others recommended by the librarians, it was a fortnightly treat. I can still feel the warm parquet flooring on my bare knees as I searched the bottom shelves.

As I walked through Highgate Woods there and back, they revealed themselves in all their seasons. Muswell Hill Road was still gravelled, with open-topped buses and very few cars. The fences to the woods had three open bars, without vertical palings, so that they were hedgerows rather than fences, making it a walk through the country, enjoyable in all weathers.

Not all the books were a success. My father rejected some of the Librarian's suggestions. My first example of meeting literary criticism was when I brought back a Bindle book. Bindle was a removal man who enjoyed playing practical jokes on people. Written by Herbert Jenkins, who was an astute publisher, they were very popular and I read dozens of the stories. When I offered one to my father, he looked sideways and said very gently, "But they are so cruel. He thinks it's funny to hurt people." This came as a great shock. It had never occurred to me that books could have a moral content. Later he dismissed another series of books with, "The characters never change. They never learn anything. They are the same at the end as they were at the start. They are just bits of cardboard."

But there were detective stories on the home bookshelves as well. When a superior friend, not an aunt, disapproved of the popular detective stories, Olive said, "You can't live on caviare all the time. Caviare is alright but you'd soon get sick of it every day." So the ordinary fare was the meat and vegetables of story books and thick-ear yarns, with caviare available on the menu.

At Tollington School I found the same attitude to books. There was a lending library in a tiny square room at the top of the old stairs, crammed with books and looking more like a broom cupboard than anything else. Teachers borrowed alongside the boys. Masses of detective pulp and adventure stories jostled for shelf room with good modern novels and classics, in alphabetical order. The librarian had no wish to segregate or indeed to educate' in the narrow sense. Eng. Lit. could be left to the classroom. Here you read books because you wanted to do so and because the story line was strong. When the new art deco library was opened in Muswell Hill Broadway, in 1932,[35] books became even easier to obtain and I learnt to order books from other libraries. I had heard of Pamela, by Richardson, but knew nothing about the book. It was not on the shelves, so I asked the Librarian, who said, "You could order it," showed me how to fill in an order card and charged a penny for the stamp. A week later the card came back through the post saying that the book had arrived, the first of hundreds, perhaps even thousands in a lifetime. Next day I took in the card and, to my bewilderment, was given a four-volume presentation copy of Pamela, in heavy boards, quarter bound in red leather, standing eight inches thick on the counter, and weighing fourteen pounds. It was beautifully printed in 12 point type, with enormous margins: a magnificent library edition, but not convenient for reading in bed. All for a penny. That was public library service at its best.

Unfortunately, during the last few years the appearance of the library has deteriorated badly. It is difficult today to realise what a very beautiful building the Library was when it was first opened. A revelation and a landmark. From the outside one can still appreciate the sophisticated detailing of the brickwork in its carefully contrasting colours. The pilasters and string courses light red and the rest darker, both set against Portland Stone dressings. The careful detailing and good bricklaying make it a most satisfying building.

The New Branch Library, Muswell Hill.
Mr W.H.Adams, F.R.I.B.A.   Borough Engineer and Surveyor
The Builder, 25 November 1932.25th

Fortunately it has now been listed as Grade II, so perhaps it will be treated with more respect and someone with a good eye will supervise restoration to its original graciousness and beauty.

The outside steps are carefully designed, with the splendid bronze central handrail carefully divided in two so that the main doors can slide in between, and the scrolled ends shaped to comfort the hand. Unfortunately the bronze capping has now gone from the entrance rails. When the Library is closed, with the main doors shut, one can see the elegance of the building. It is arguably the best exterior in Muswell Hill and should have been listed long ago.

The interior used to be equally distinguished, with a Reading Room on the ground floor and a small Children's Library beyond, entered from the side road. The staircase to the Library above was a delight. Sixty years of wear have not been able to damage the stair-rail, but in the 1930s it was a simple, uncluttered stairway in marble terrazzo: a suitable approach to the elegant room above.

In the Library itself there was a central reservation, with an entrance for returning books on one side and an exit for stamping them on the other. Round the walls were oak shelves, with three radiating bookcases in the centre, and every book in place. The library was lit by chaste hexagonal glass lanterns designed to give the greatest diffusion of light and so a daylight effect, making the room a delight to enter.

It was the nearest thing I knew to the secluded libraries found in novels, elegant, quiet, full of unexpected books which could take one along unknown paths to distant futures. Today the impression of the library is very different, drab and unkempt. Perhaps this is the future of libraries: jostling market places for the Information Society. If so, when do we have time to think?

Muswell Hill Library is not the only one to have been affected by underfunding, failure of civic pride and loss of direction. In half a dozen London boroughs, oak shelving has been ripped out on the excuse that it was old and splintery, when all it needed to make it

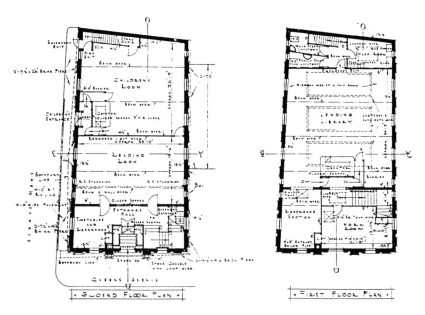

new and safe again, was two coats of good varnish. In place of oak we have been given supermarket shelving in characterless fibre-board and a sense of impermanent litter. The period of 'modernization' was quickly followed by a drastic reduction of funds and a freeze on book buying.

One can judge a civilization by its libraries and the amount of money put into them. Hornsey boasts two excellent Art Deco buildings, Hornsey Town Hall, which seems to become more elegant each time I see it, and Muswell Hill Library, for in the 1930s a rare thing happened: municipal pride and subtle designers came together to create two particularly good buildings. This lucky chance should now be celebrated by giving Muswell Hill library some loving care.

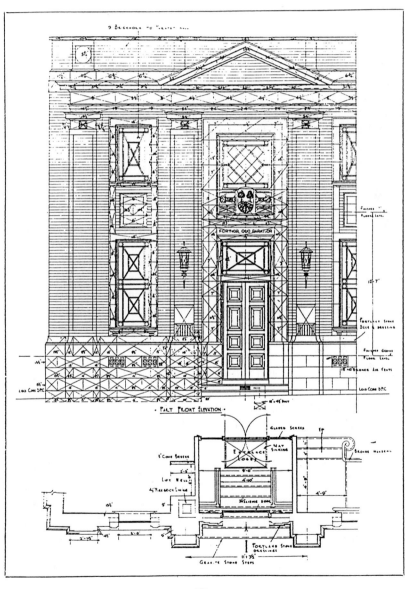

Terminal Moraine

It had snowed steadily for several days so the walk up Coppetts Rd and Tetherdown to Fortis Green was part delight and part penance. Like all the boys, I wore shorts, my bare knees were red with cold and a chilbain on one finger itched painfully. My boots were slightly wet so that my legs were ice and cold penetrated everywhere. There seemed no prospect of ever being warm again. By the time we reached school, someone had started a slide in the playground and soon everyone was skimming down the slope, making the slide longer and longer. When one of the older boys stopped the slide, we all kicked fresh snow on to the ice to make it thicker and faster. Everyone began sliding again and running back up the hill. Energetic running was the only way to keep warm. Two or three times that day the teacher made us stand in the aisles between our desks and do vigorous arm exercises. The large coal fire behind its fireguard was drawing well in the cold air, but the heat did not circulate to the back of the room and my chilblain was sore.

The young teacher began talking casually, looking out of the window, pointing out the falling snow. How cold it was. How it melted at a breath. Beautiful, light, fragile. But what would happen if it went on snowing? What would happen to the snow then? What would happen if the snow became thicker and thicker? Right across the playground, up to the window sill, up to the eaves, up to the ridge of the building? The whole school engulfed in fallen snow and above that another school and another, school piled on school and all completely buried, so thick was the snow.

A single snow flake was so light that it would be difficult to weigh. But what if the snow was half a dozen schools thick? How much would it weigh then? What would happen to the snow at the bottom? Slowly I realised that the snow would have turned into layer upon layer of ice. We would be looking out of the windows into a lump of ice taller than the school. We would live in an ice world, subjects of an Ice King, where everything would glitter like green glass. We would become used to the cold, moving slowly, pushing our way heavily through the ice so that it would take a century to move one step. To make a journey would take ten thousand years.

I was pulled back from this dreaming by the teacher holding up a photograph of a glacier flowing down a valley as a cliff of ice. That whole ice-scape had been made of separate flakes of snow, each one separate, weak and delicate, but now a powerful monster capable of destroying everything in its path.

Then he discussed sliding and why we could slide. There was no friction. Once a glacier started moving there was no way to stop it, because if there was no friction, there were no brakes and its weight was irresistible.

The teacher drew a picture of a great ice field stretching from Scandinavia, across the North Sea, to Britain. He described how this snow had fallen round rocks and completely encased them. Small pieces, pieces as big as desks, pieces as big as classrooms with ice all round them, completely wrapping them like currants in a cake. The ice was heavy - almost as heavy as water. Ice was heavy and, because it was heavy it moved down hill. Slowly the ice sheet moved, carrying its load of stones and debris, sliding slowly across the North Sea and into Britain. A great blanket of ice sliding on the frozen ground, moving stones, scoring great grooves in the rocks. Nothing could resist it.

I could imagine the school and a pile of schools above it, moving slowly but surely downhill and even uphill, forced by the weight behind, wrenching off rocks in its path and engulfing them. No way to stop itself. A cliff on castors.

A huge cliff of solid ice over a thousand feet high, moving south at less than the pace of any snail, ripping pieces of rock and stone, large and small, from the ground beneath it and carrying them away. Gathering stones and fossils from the different rock formations wherever it passed.

Now the teacher was waving a pamphlet. In 1850 a piece of Coppetts Wood had been felled to build St James's School. A little further into the wood was a Gravel Pit where people had dug gravel and sand for their paths for years. They might even have dug sand for the mortar to build this very school. In 1874 a strange discovery had been made in the Coldfall Wood Gravel Pit. A Mr Wetherell had found a deposit of fossils and rocks

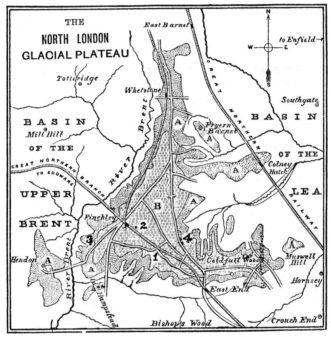

Scale, about two-thirds of an inch to a mile.   After the Geological Survey.

MAP OF THE GEOLOGY AND HYDROGRAPHY OF THE NORTH LONDON GLACIAL PLATEAU.

REFERENCES:—

Shaded parts: **A.** The Glacial Gravel. **B.** The Glacial Clay (Boulder Clay). Excavations: 1. Marylebone Cemetery. 2. Manor Brickfield, Finchley. 3. Gravel Pits. 4. St. Pancras and Islington Cemeteries. All yielding Drift Rocks and Fossils.

Unshaded parts: London Clay, with Pebble-beds at Mill Hill and Totteridge. Valley gravels (chiefly re-assorted Glacial gravel).

The original map from the 1874 pamphlet[22]

The Glacial Drifts of Muswell Hill and Finchley

51

jumbled together only a few feet below the surface. There were fossils and pieces of granite, slate and chalk, all embedded in Oxfordshire Clays. Large Chalk nodules had been found in Tetherdown, where I walked each day, yet the nearest chalk was miles away.

Mr Wetherell was a medical practitioner living at the crest of West Hill, Highgate, who examined every railway cutting or other digging in the area. He had found these strange deposits not only in Coldfall Wood, but all over the district. There were Belemnites, which were fossils of cuttlefish skeletons, and Devil's Toenails, which was the country name for fossils of the snail Gryphia. He had found stone from Scotland, Lincolnshire, and even Scandinavia, all carried here in jackets of ice and deposited as huge mounds of Boulder Clay when the ice melted.

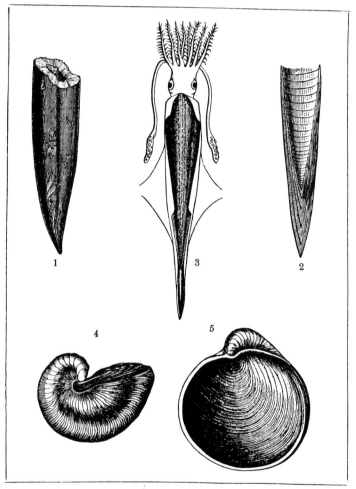

COMMON FOSSILS OF THE FINCHLEY GLACIAL CLAY.

1. A Belemnite; internal skeleton of a species of Cuttle Fish. 2 Section of a Belemnite. 3 A Belemnite restored. 4. *Gryphea incurva.* 5. *Gryphea dilatata.* (Bivalve Shells.)

Illustrations from the pamphlet [22]

St James's School had been built where this great ice sheet finally stopped. When the ice retreated, melting away in a dirty sludge, it deposited its stones to form a great ridge from Muswell Hill, along East End Road and far beyond. The teacher showed us the geological map with the Boulder Clay marked in icy blue and Fortis Green at the southern edge, at the last position of this giant bulldozer. This was why there had been a road along Fortis Green for so long. The ridge of stones and rocks rose above the surrounding countryside, dry and easy walking, with clear views to north and south. It was a secure road, not to be moved until perhaps the next ice age. A triangle of Boulder Clay stretching for four miles from Muswell Hill to Hendon, cut through by the River Brent. The Boulder Clay extended past Whetstone to Chipping Barnet, with a tongue stretching out to Colney Hatch, just beyond the Great North Road.

The foundation stone of St James's Parish Hall, in Fortis Green Road, had been laid on the 26th of September, 1925, only about six months after I came to Muswell Hill. In my last year we began to have lessons in the upstairs room now occupied by the Nursery. Mr Broad, another teacher, used to assemble us in the St James's School yard, in Fortis Green, and march us across to the new building. It was in those short walks that I first began to imagine the effect of the glacier on the surrounding area. One leg felt cold because of the immense glacier in Tetherdown towering above us, while the other leg, facing the southern sun, felt warm and comfortable. On the return journey the heat reversed itself. From then on I never walked along Fortis Green without imagining that I had one leg hot and the other cold.

The Old Gravel Pit in Coldfall Woods was best remembered later because it was just by the Tollington School cricket pitch. One day, bored with rolling the pitch, several of us dropped the roller into the pit, but this pit is recorded in the literature as follows:-

Layers of Deposits

'Boulder deposit, with fossils of various formations, lying irreguarly on the bed below,

and sometimes filling pipes that extend through the latter, 15 to 20 feet,

Laminated brick-earth 3-4 feet,

Gravel (Thickness and composition not given)

London Clay.'

Geology of London Vol 1, 1889 p.312.

Ghosts of Victorian geologists haunted that pit, for this is where the detective work on the past history of Muswell Hill had started. Over the years geologists swarmed into the area, coming out from London on Saturday afternoons to poke about in the gravel for tell-tale rocks. Learned papers were written and hours of careful drawing and analysis lavished on each specimen, yet here were idle boys dropping a cricket roller on their ghosts. Today the ghosts can rest peacefully because the Pit has been filled in and a level playing field covers the site.

The Thames Valley

Between Coppetts Road and Colney Hatch Lane was a series of roads, Greenham Road, Wilton Road, Sutton Road, straight roads of semi-detached houses in red brick, with tiled roofs. The family travelled up and down these day after day to reach the shops. Down a gentle slope from Coppetts Road to a dip and then up more steeply to the shops in Colney Hatch Lane and, beyond that, the hill went up again. When I asked my mother about the shape - the same dip in all three roads - she said,

"They must have covered up the stream when they built these houses. You can't keep jumping over a river every time you go to the shops." To my surprise she took it as a matter of course that it was the valley of a stream.

Later I saw a picture of a culvert which had held the River Westbourne, rediscovered in west London. The picture showed a man standing upright in a brick tunnel, so it was no mean stream. Perhaps one could walk underneath the road here, smuggle goods, get behind the enemy lines, and my mind wandered off.

When I was eleven, just before the scholarship examination which would take me to the grammar school, the same teacher who had explained about the ice ages and the terminal moraine, rode his hobby-horse again. For no apparent reason, sparked by a thought, or a chance remark, he began to describe the neighbourhood. How, when England was much hotter than it is today, with a vegetation like modern Malaysia, the London Basin had been under the sea. Great depths of fine silt had been laid down at the bottom of the sea to form London Clay and, millions of years later this had risen to form low, smooth hills.

A huge river system had formed at the level of the top of Muswell Hill. He asked us to imagine ourselves looking south from Muswell Hill to Blackheath and the Surrey Hills, and think of it a large plain, flat as a prairie. You could walk level across an area which later was cut out to became the valley of the River Thames. On your way you could pat

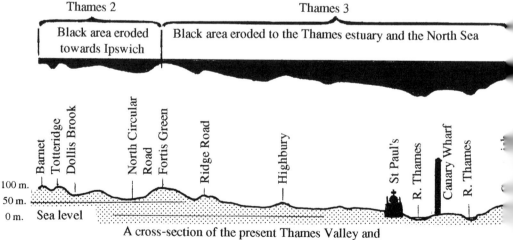

A cross-section of the present Thames Valley and
the earlier one known as the Finchley Gap

54

the cross at the top of St Paul's Cathedral, standing up like a street monument, with the rest of St Paul's, dome and church and graveyard, buried deep below the ground. On the top of this plain the rivers had laid down beds of gravel, some of which could still be found in the neighbourhood. Look for a well and you would find the gravel.

At this period the River Thames had gone straight on from Malden and flowed into the North Sea somewhere near Ipswich. This was Thames 1. Then had come an ice age and the path of the river was frozen. He showed us the map of the Thames Valley and the sharp bend southwards that the river now takes at Malden, where the river had been frozen. The Thames had had to cut a new bed. There it flowed for thousands of years, cutting the deep valley through Finchley, to the west of the Great North Road. This was Thames 2.

With the next ice age, the Thames was blocked again. Now it began to cut the Thames 3 Valley which we know today. Muswell Hill, Highgate, Hampstead, were left standing high above the river, but an immense volume of soil was carried down the river and away to the sea to form the Dogger Bank. The Thames had cut its third valley and perhaps, thousands of years from now, in another ice age, the river would cut a fourth one even further south. Geography could repeat itself.

As the teacher spoke I could see a never ending movement of soil, being built up and then moved on, sorted and resorted like sand castles built between the tides and swept away in the next flood. I watched in my mind the rain pouring on Muswell Hill and running down, cutting away the soil. The water which seeped out at Pages Hill and ran down through the allotments into the culvert under Greenham and the other roads, had cut out the valley. Coppetts Road and Colney Hatch Lane were higher up on either side, safely away from the stream. Further over, small springs started in Coldfall Woods and became the familiar stream through the meadow. These were already cutting the ground away. On the other side of the hill there must be others. A complete hill top being eroded and sliding down into the valley.

Before I went to Tollingon School, part of Coldfall Woods had long been felled to make the school sports ground. I liked to stand there looking towards Barnet and imagine myself on a narrow ridge between the two valleys. Thames 2, which once had held the mighty Thames, now carried the insignificant Dollis Brook, while the Thames had been diverted behind my back to the other side of Muswell Hill, capturing on its way the Wandle, the Falcon, The Ravensbourne, the Tyburn and the Fleet and a dozen other tributaries with romantic names from north and south. I stood in Twyford Avenue with a ghostly Thames 2 in front of me and behind me the modern Thames, waiting perhaps to become a ghost in its turn sometime in the distant future..

Tollington School

Soon after I started secondary school I found that boys from Stationers' Company School were jeering at us. They held their noses when we appeared and asked us why we could not afford soap. To eleven year olds this was an invitation to fight and there were several confrontations between young boys from the two schools. Older ones probably realised that, when you are trying to attract attention to your cause, all publicity is good publicity.

TOLLY WANTS A BATH was a clever slogan. For weeks posters in shop windows had heralded the three-day Fair to raise money for a new swimming bath to be built behind the Preparatory School in Tetherdown. Everything in Muswell Hill was to stop while we junketed to raise money. I found myself helping to wheel the Scout's track-cart from house to house, collecting articles to be sold. The White Elephant Stall had a mountain of unearthed treasures, one piece so old that I had to be told what it was. An old lady gave me a strange wooden article like a three-legged stool on the end of a broomstick. She held the stick upright with the stool downwards and turned it vigorously, showing us how to wash clothes in a tub. She so enjoyed the exercise, swirling the clothes backwards and forwards in her imaginary water with her washerwoman's dolly, that I stepped back to avoid being splashed.

Anything that might sell was welcome. We collected old pictures, pots and pans, old furniture, the contents of garden sheds and attics. Muswell Hill had a spring-clean that year and our little track cart seemed to move the lot. The Woodwork Room had been

WHEN TOLLY HAS ITS BATH

Smart Haircutting and Shampooing will be essential to those who wish to be "in the swim." No one could possibly swim the Atlantic, or the "potty" little Channel with long, untidy hair (it would look so bad in the Press "snaps") therefore, see that you frequently visit

MR. BARNES' HAIRDRESSING SALOONS

1, FIRS PARADE, — MUSWELL HILL

where Men and Boys are given special and sole attention at moderate charges, by skilled assistants who know exactly what you require. We also stock a large variety of Toilet Requisites at lowest Prices for Men and Boys.

HAIRCUTTING ONLY 9D.

SHAMPOOING, WET 1/- DRY 1/- & 9D.

OPEN 8.30 a.m. CLOSE 7.30 p.m. THURS. 1.0 p.m. SAT. 8.0 p.m.

The hairdresser's shop is still there.

turning out small, saleable items all term. Trays and small stools with woven raffia seats were popular; small book racks and a few occasional tables; all to be bought by well-wishers. The campaign to build a swimming bath had been running for some time. The sale of new school uniform had been taken over by the teachers who manned the school shop, fitting us with blazers and caps and putting the profits into the Bath account. Donations were sought everywhere and the climax was to be the Three-day Fair.

There was an elaborate bazaar programme[6] with a jazzy cover which we sold by the dozen. Someone in the school must have had some theatre connections for the three different days of the Fair were to be opened by Jack Hulbert and Cicely Courtenidge, the comedians; Angela Baddeley, then a young ingenue; and Lady Barratt who was a local notable, but not a theatrical. W.A.Darlington, the playright and theatre critic, wrote a Foreword saying that his friend Dr Draper had written saying he wanted a bath. After a few jokes about personal cleanliness, inviting Dr Draper to come round and bring his soap and other quips suitable for a school magazine, he appealed to everyone to 'fork out' to pay for the bath.

Other celebrities were assembled from the world of sport. 'Plum' Warner, the cricketer; E.H.Temme, who had swum the Channel; Dr Ronald Cove-Smith, who played rugby for the English XV; W.W.Wakefield who held a record number of rugby caps for England; and Bernard Darwin the great authority on golf, who reputedly emptied Muswell Hill Golf Course when he gave a lecture at the school. Each descended on the Bazaar in turn, attracting his particular fans.

The Fair was a great success, the money was raised and a few years later the open-air swimming bath was a reality. There was never the money to cover it, but the bath was a great attraction: the five-shilling season ticket was the best value in London.

Tollington School, Tetherdown, 1928

57

The History of Tollington School[6]

The old school building in Tetherdown, now part of a much larger complex, used to be called Tollington School, but the name did not start in Muswell Hill. In 1879 William Brown, B.A., bought a school for 50 boys in Turle Road, near Finsbury Park. At that time Stroud Green was a new suburb, still being built, with new streets being completed each month, all full of parents ambitious for their children's success, but few secondary school places available. The Compulsory Education Act of 1870 provided elementary education to the age of thirteen, but not Grammar Schools. These were still privately run and too small to cope with the demand, so the pressure for the few places was intense. Soon William Brown's School expanded, adding an extra floor and a chemistry lab in 1890. In 1897, a brand new building for 200 boys was opened in nearby Tollington Park. As each new street was built it added to the pressure for school places, so that this building too had to be expanded several times.

In 1901 Campbell Brown, son of the founder, established a school with the same name in Muswell Hill, to serve the new population flooding into this district. What Finsbury Park had needed in the 1880s, Muswell Hill required twenty years later. The same name was given to both schools and they were regarded as parallel institutions. Campbell Brown took over 'Thorntons', a big house in Tetherdown which does not appear on the 1865 map, shown on the next page, but is on the 1894 one.

At that time the Waste, or common ground, beside Tetherdown had been grazed for years, but only Muswell Lodge, Woodside, and one other house had then been built on it. Thorntons is shown on the 1894 map as a large house set well back from the road, with a

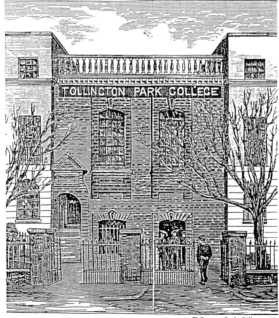

Tollington Park College, 1881

58

large garden in front and a strip cut out of the Coldfall Woods behind, to make a T-shaped site. The Old Gravel Pit, where the geological finds mentioned in the St James's School chapter had been made, was just behind the school. Tetherdown had been built up, with two rows of cottages and a few larger villas with fair-sized gardens.

The 1913 map shows that a new school building was built on the Thornton front garden. The house became The Old School House and was known by that name into the 1930s, still with its original cornices and architraves. The new school building had three floors of classrooms with high ceilings but no Hall, so presumably assemblies must have been held in the corrugated iron gymnasium erected on the edge of the wood (lined in dark on the 1913 map).

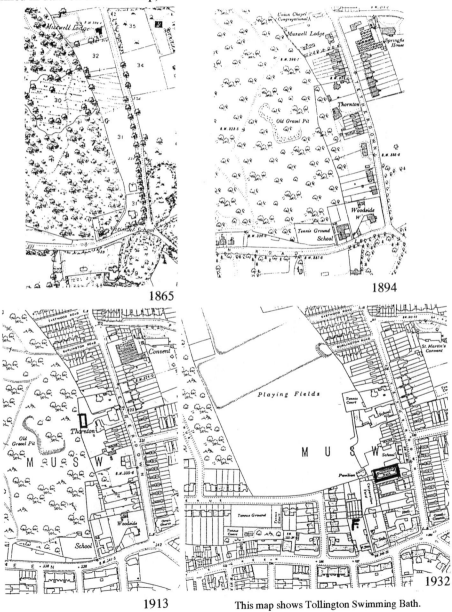

1865

1894

1913

1932

This map shows Tollington Swimming Bath.

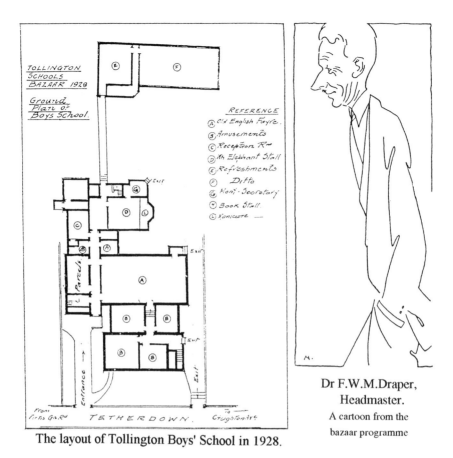

TOLLINGTON
SCHOOLS
BAZAAR 1928

Ground
Plan of
Boys School.

REFERENCE
Ⓐ Old English Fayre.
Ⓑ Amusements
Ⓒ Reception Rm
Ⓓ Ih Elephant Stall
Ⓔ Refreshments
Ⓕ Ditto
Ⓖ Honi. Secretary
Ⓗ Book Stall.
Ⓘ Manicure ⎯

TETHERDOWN.

The layout of Tollington Boys' School in 1928.

Dr F.W.M.Draper,
Headmaster.
A cartoon from the
bazaar programme

In 1910 Campbell Brown set up a parallel Girls' School at the corner of Collingwood and Grand Avenues. It began with 50 pupils and three assistant mistresses, but it soon became a most popular school and numbers grew quickly. Today the building houses Tetherdown Primary School.

Tollington Girls' School

60

At the same time, Campbell Brown had his eyes on more property in Tetherdown. The two houses shown on the 1913 map by the letter E in Muswell, were Blymhill Villa and Newport Villa. From a sentence in another lease which talks of restrictive covenants to a house built in Tetherdown and the fact that the cottages next door bear the same date, we can assume that the two houses were built in 1876. Kelly's Directory for 1912 shows that Newport Villa was used as a convent for St Martin of Tours nuns, but both villas were sold to Tollington School. In 1913, Newport was demolished, Blythmill became the Headteacher's house and an extension was built to form a Boarding House for the school. A pupil's drawing of the conversion plans shows the layout.

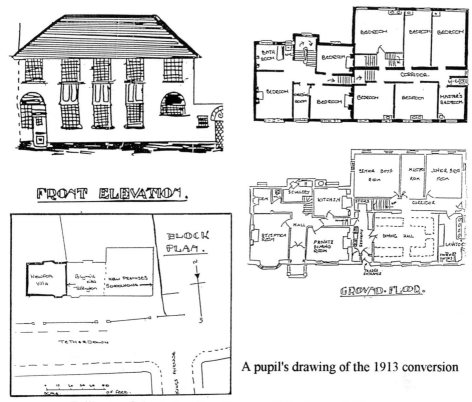

A pupil's drawing of the 1913 conversion

Tollington School Boarding House and Headmaster's House

During the First World War Campbell Brown found it difficult to run his school[6]. Food prices were rising and there seemed no way of increasing fees to cover these and other expenses. On 12th December 1917, he wrote to the Secretary of the Higher Education Committee for Hornsey:-

Sir,

I venture to submit for your consideration the present circumstances of the Tollington Schools. For some time past it has been a matter of the greatest difficulty to carry on the work of these two schools, which are privately owned and are without endowment or assistance from the public funds.

You will observe from the schedule (enclosed) that 640 children, almost all from the Borough of Hornsey, are being educated in the schools. A glance at the accompanying records and the knowledge which your Committee probably have of the general reputation of the schools, will satisfy you that the the standard of education favourably compares with that of the other secondary schools of the County.

The capital sunk in these schools amounts to some £25,000, £10,000 of which is still on mortgage. The Balance of the last year's working expenses shews a margin of £12 only on the Boys' School, and £364 on the Girls' School. This is after paying interest on the mortgages, but nothing whatever for my remuneration, apart from the provision of house room.

Having founded the schools and spent some years of my life in bringing them to their present state of efficiency, I have inevitably considered the welfare of the schools to the prejudice of my own private interests. Further, having regard to the nature of the district and the status of the children attending the school, it would not be to the public interest to raise the fees to the extent that would be necessary for the continued efficient working of the school.'

———

Campbell Brown then asked the Committee to consider taking over, in the public interest, the management and control of the schools. The subject had been raised.

By the end of the First World War the situation had become impossible. To provide the education expected of a good secondary school, Tollington needed new Science Labs, new Art, Woodwork and Metalwork Rooms and a Hall, all of which were beyond Campbell Brown's pocket. In 1919 he sold the school to the Middlesex Education Committee for £13,500 and retired to Brighton. At the same time the Committee rented land for a playing field from the Ecclesiastical Commissioners for £38 per annum. Five acres round the Gravel Pit was converted and the erosion of Coldfall Wood had begun.

The Boarding House became a Boys and Girls Preparatory School (Tolly Prep.) for the two Tollington Schools. The Boys' School was considerably enlarged. A new block was built alongside the earlier Tetherdown building, with a Hall on the ground floor, Science Rooms on the first floor and Metalwork, Woodwork and Art Rooms at the top. The Art Room had an extensive view to the north as far as Barnet. This room had plenty of light, but the new hall was so jammed against the older building that it turned the ground floor rooms of the older building into cellars, dull and gloomy. A light well would have made all the difference.

The layout from the 1928 Bazaar catalogue on page 60 gives a good idea of the school in the 1939s. C D G H L represent the original Thornton House. E & F are the corrugated iron gym. The four Bs are the old school, built when the school was opened, with its windows to Tetherdown; while A was the new Hall with its stage (not shown) at the north end.

During the Second World War pupils of all the schools were evacuated. Tolly Prep. School went to Woolverstone, in Bucks, and various other places, but many pupils returned and sometimes were evacuated once again. This meant that the school numbers fluctuated, but were always small. During the period of the doodlebugs, the small pilotless planes which caused so much destruction, a special watch was kept from the Fire Station tower in Fortis Green. The children had their lessons at strong tables in the dining room on the ground floor of the Prep School. At the alert the children continued with their lessons, while a second teacher went into another room from where she could see the fire station tower. The Fire Station was in Fortis Green, next to St James's School and is marked with an F on the 1932 map on page 59. The tower was clearly visible fron Tollingon Prep School over the rear gardens. When a doodlebug appeared, the fireman hung a white sheet over the edge of the observation platform and the teacher ran to warn the class, who immediately crouched under the tables until the danger had passed[49].

Tollington Preparatory School had always been fee-paying. All the pupils wore green blazers with the initials TPS on the pockets. With the passing of the 1944 Education Act, and its promise of better and free education for all, schools like Tolly Prep. were in limbo. Nobody knew quite what would happen. Some private schools, with huge fees, determined to stay private, but the smaller schools with modest fees found the problem difficult. New parents were unsure whether to register their children for admission, so numbers fell. Many private schools closed at this point.

In the end Tollington Prep became a State Primary School to take all the local children who wished to attend. There were no fees but the parents were still willing, indeed anxious, for the children to continue to wear the green blazers. The search was for a new name. All the equipment, including all the gardening tools, was marked with the letters TPS, for Tollington Preparatory School, and the staff wanted to keep these initials. They thrashed around until some inspired person suggested Tetherdown Primary School, which was immediately accepted.[49]

As the school numbers increased with the baby boom after the war, several huts had to be erected in the playground until the whole site became overcrowded. In 1958 William Grimshaw School was opened as a Mixed School in new premises in Creighton Avenue. This freed the Tollington Girls' School site in Grand Avenue, so Tetherdown Primary School moved in.

The premises were not ideal for Infants and Primary pupils but it became a very successful and popular school. Once again extra hutted classrooms had to be built on the playground to accommodate the extra children.

Over the next few years the old Tollington Prep building was used for various purposes, but in the early 1970s a Tutorial Class was opened there. In 1977 this became a full-time Tutorial Unit for children who needed particular help with their education. This was called Tetherdown Tutorial and helped a lot of children over the years.

In 1994 the Unit moved to 28 Philip Lane, N 15, but retained Tetherdown as a name. This name will be a complete mystery to the next generation of pupils in Tottenham, unless they read this book. To sum up, there is a Tetherdown in Grand Avenue and another in Philip Lane, neither of which is in its proper place.

Since 1944 all secondary schools have undergone many changes of name and nature as educational ideas have altered and pupil numbers have fluctuated. The way the different schools amalgamated and changed direction is too large a subject to consider here. Perhaps someone will write a complete history one day.

Nineteenth Century Fortis Green

The road from East Finchley to Muswell Hill has always run along Fortis Green and Fortis Green Road, on the ridge of glacial debris left by the last Ice Age. Milnes's map shows that in 1800 it was still a track through a wide expanse of 'Waste', the common land where local people had the right to graze their animals. Colney Hatch Lane, Muswell Hill Road, St James's Lane and Tetherdown are also old roads, but almost all the rest are newcomers, at the best about a hundred years old. Fortis Green, high up and quickly drained, had wide prospects to north and south, now largely obscured by houses, but from the top of each road one can still imagine what it was like towards the end of the nineteenth century.

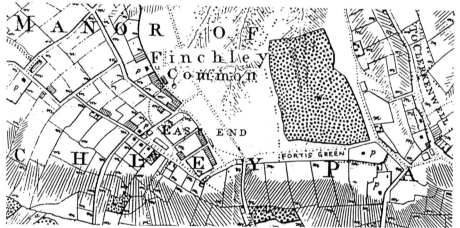

The Milne Land Utilization Map of 1800 showing Fortis Green as a track through a wide belt of unclaimed Waste.[45]

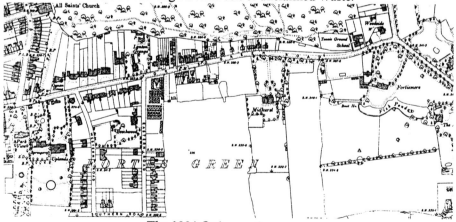

The 1894 Ordnance Survey

The Finchley end of Fortis Green was part of the land held by the Bishop of London. His 'Great Park' extended to about where East Finchley Underground Station now stands, with a curving boundary to The Spaniards Inn and The Gatehouse, Highgate. Bishop's Avenue was within the Park. Bordering the Great Park were certain freehold lands belonging to the Bishop of London who was Lord of the Manors of Finchley and Hornsey. These included the Waste along Fortis Green and a field running along the High Road, between Fortis Green and Cherry Tree Woods. The eastern side of the field ran about where Park Hall Road now stands, to give a total area of about twelve, or thirteen acres[12]. In the 1820s, Nevil Smart, a developer, built four houses on this field.

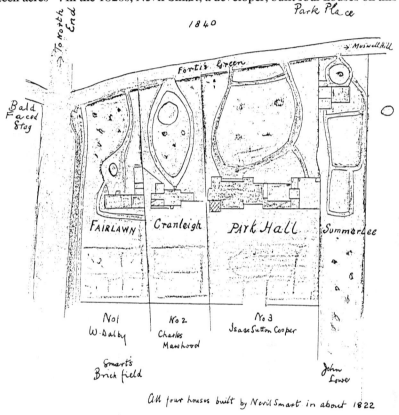

Nevil Smart's houses, built about 1820

The first house Nevil Smart built was No 1 Park Place, at the corner of Fortis Green and the High Road, where Barclays Bank now stands. No 2 he sold to Charles Mahood; No 3 went to Isaac Sutton Cooper, who himself became a developer later; and No 4, built in 1822, to John Lowe. Most houses had about one and a half acres of land, but No 3 was larger. Sutton Cooper later acquired No 4 as well and the whole became known as Park Hall. It was described as a very fine building, but unfortunately we know little about it as the auction particulars were destroyed when the Guildhall Library was bombed, in 1941.

Nevil Smart also built the house in the High Road, next to Cherry Tree Woods which used to be known as Doctor Dick's House and is now the site of Park House (how these names persist) and No 2 next door. Between these houses and No 1 Park Place, near the site of the Phoenix Cinema, was Smart's brickfield.

Anthony Salvin

The next two houses along Fortis Green were built by Anthony Salvin, a very famous architect. He was almost forgotten until quite recently when Jill Allibone wrote a splendid biography.[10] In his day he had an enormous practice all over the country, so big that one year his business income reached £24.000 - perhaps half a million pounds at today's prices. He became Vice President of the Royal Institute of British Architects and, in 1862, was presented with the Queen's Gold Medal.

Anthony Salvin was one of the many Victorian architects interested in Gothic architecture. Horace Walpole had built Strawberry Hill in the Gothic Revival style after 1747, and Beckford built Fonthill from 1796, but these were a sort of 'wallpaper gothic'. They were more like elegant and fanciful stage scenery than solid architecture, so insubstantial indeed that Fonthill actually fell down. Salvin's Gothic was far more serious and historically accurate. This book is no place to go into the architectural controversy which raged for years between the Palladian architects who worshipped in Greece and Rome, going back to the classical tradition, and those who wished to return to the Gothic ideas of the great cathedral-building age of Northern Europe. Pugin rebuilt the Houses of Commons in Gothic: Palmerston said that Gothic was barbarism and insisted on a Palladian Foreign Office and got, in fact, a Palladian front on a high-tec Victorian building, as up to date as any Victorian railway station. The battle of the T squares was fought for years, with each side claiming the moral high ground

Instead of being involved in this sound and fury, Salvin studied early architectural styles very carefully, restoring, rebuilding, and building afresh, in a sympathetic way which fitted in with old buildings and did not shock. Others took a piece from this period and a piece from that, to produce a hybrid style never seen before or since, not unlike our present Post Modernist phase. Salvin did not go in for the Gothic town halls and railway stations which became so popular in Victorian times, but continued to build Tudor or Jacobean houses and Norman, Early English, or Decorated churches, built in traditional materials, using traditional craftsmanship. He would no more have thought of introducing wrought iron piers and braces into Gothic churches, as Violet-le-Duc did, than of using corrugated iron for his restoration of the Tower of London.

Salvin's practice had developed in a different way, through the restoration of old buildings. The story of Anthony Salvin and his cousin William Nesfield is closely linked with Fortis Green and East End Road, so a sketch of the two may be of interest.

William Nesfield, who was twelve years older than Salvin, had been commissioned in the 95th Foot and fought in the Peninsular War. All officers were taught to make topographical drawings and maps. During this training at Woolwich, where he would have been taught by Thomas Paul Sandby, Nesfield found that he had a talent for watercolour painting. At the end of the Napoleonic War, in 1819, Nesfield was put on half pay and resolved to become a landscape painter. Anthony Salvin often used to stay with his uncle, Nesfield's father, who was rector of St Brandon's Church, Durham. The rectory was within a few hundred yards of Brancepeth Castle, which was then being restored. This large-scale restoration, employing at one period 300 men, so excited

Salvin that he decided to become an architect. His father, a colonel, had intended his son for the Army, which was a profession for gentlemen, while architecture at that time was not. However Colonel Salvin had lost one son in the fighting and finally agreed that Anthony Salvin should be placed as a pupil with Paterson, the architect at Brancepeth.

Paterson knew very little of architectural detail and had no respect for the past. He built on vast reception rooms, created a huge barbican where there had been a mere gate, and would have done well as a set designer for Ben Hur. However, the restoration had been enough to fire Salvin's imagination, but his work would be far more sensitive.

After a short time, Salvin and William Nesfield moved to London, taking lodgings in Newman Street, behind Oxford Street. Salvin went to work with John Nash at the period when he was building All Soul's, Langham Place, and the Regent's Park Terraces.

Clearly his early experiences at Brancepeth had turned his ideas to the problem of careful and discreet restoration of old buildings. Some people wanted to leave things as they were, allowing buildings to decay naturally. Others advocated ruthless renovation and rebuilding, without regard for historical accuracy. When Salvin was asked to restore Norwich Castle, which was becoming dangerous, he was in a dilemma, because Norwich Castle was also a prison. If he left things to rot, the walls would fall down, killing half the prisoners and allowing the rest to run away. In this case restoration was essential, but should be as sensitive as possible. This and similar work led him to study old buildings and castles closely, so that he developed a deep knowledge of styles, materials and methods. All his life he made watercolours and drawings of buildings, trimming and mounting them in albums, to build up a library of authentic details for further study. Many are now in the RIBA Drawings Collection, but wheel-barrows full were burnt after his death and are completely lost.

His close study of old buildings allowed him to build successful new houses in old styles. One example of many is Thorsby Hall[11]. The house was begun in 1864 for the 3rd Earl Mantravers who had succeeded to 38,000 acres and £50,000 a year. He

The magnificent 182 ft expanse of Thoresby Hall's south front displays Salvin's brilliance in re-creating an Elizabethan mansion

commissioned Salvin to build a house to rival the great whig palaces of the eighteenth century. It was completed just before the agricultural depression of the 1870s, and sold off by the Coal Board in 1988, an enormous pile for which a new use has to be found.

Anthony Salvin married his cousin, William Nesfield's sister Anne, to whom he had been secretly engaged for some years. By 1833 they had two children. They had to move into the country for the sake of their son's health and chose Finchley because Salvin needed easy access to rapid coach travel. The Bald Faced Stag was then a coaching inn and from here Salvin could travel quickly to town, via the new Archway Road, or north to his many prosperous clients.

Salvin took a sixty year lease at £100 a year on a large house in East End Road, called Elm House, later renamed Elmhurst. It had a ten acre paddock and a large garden looking over Bishop's Wood, stables and a coach house. The house probably dated from the sixteenth century, but had been substantially rebuilt and extended. Salvin immediately built on a new drawing room and dining room, making a total of twenty-five rooms.

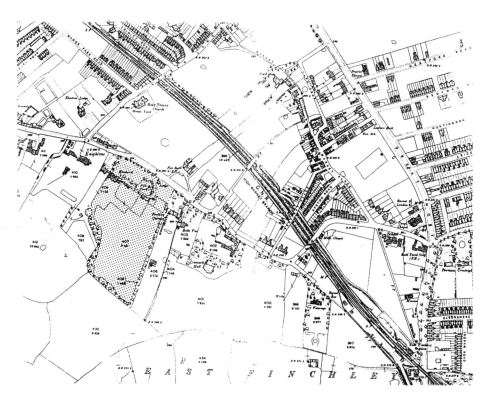

The 1894-6 Ordnance Survey with Elmhurst tinted [2].
East End Road was then still much as it was when Salvin knew it.

Elmhurst, photographed in 1939 [2]

During his time in Finchley Salvin bought and sold various pieces of land in the area. In 1835 Salvin and Nesfield, who was also married, bought adjoining plots of land in Fortis Green, next to Nevil Smart's fourth house, Summerlee, shown on page 65. There Salvin built two semi-detached houses in an Italian villa style [1,46], while Nesfield laid out the gardens as one landscaped unit and kept sheep in the field below. They called the houses Colethall and Springcroft Lodge and, since the dividing line between the two houses was probably about where Springcroft Avenue now lies, the name was passed on. Salvin let his house. Later Colethall was re-named Uplands. Both houses were still shown on the 1894 map, but by then Park Hall had been redeveloped as Park Hall Road. Salvin's two houses were then demolished as the start of Summerlee Avenue.

In 1840 Loudon, the great encyclopedist, published an article on Nesfield's villa in his Gardeners' Magazine. It described how Salvin and Nesfield had bought a field of about 8¼ acres which sloped down gently, so that the bottom fence was perhaps fifty feet below the level of Fortis Green. The field was south-facing, with splendid views across the valley to Highgate Church and Kenwood. Hints of this view can still be seen between the chimney pots, from the top of Springcroft Avenue.

If Nesfield had divided the site into two narrow strips, in the normal way, the view from either house would have been restricted. Instead, he gave each house a large, enclosed front garden, placed the houses well down the slope, and divided the rear land crossways, by a wire fence. From the houses the wire became almost invisible, allowing both houses to enjoy a wide prospect of the valley and ridge beyond.

The magazine shows Nesfield's house only, but presumably Salvin's one was very

69

Entrance Front of Fortis Green.

similar. A close-boarded gate and thick hedge to Fortis Green, gave privacy and then a long, steeply sloping entrance-drive to the house. Because Nesfield wanted to preserve the rear panorama, the kitchen garden and orchard were placed in front of the house, not behind. They were hidden behind dense laurel hedges, cut almost vertical, with dug ground and plantings beside the carriage entrance. Close to the house were flower gardens with the elaborately shaped beds which we associate with the Victorians, while the open landscape seen from the back of the house looks back to the eighteenth century. The boundary line and side path (8) were heavily screened by a thickset hedge and trees, sculpted into irregular curves.

The Gardeners' Magazine goes into great detail about rearing sheep in the field below the house. Of Nesfield's 4¼ acres, 3 acres were devoted exclusively to sheep. With this amount of land he could buy 9 ewes in lamb at 25 shillings each in September. These

View from the Lawn Front of Fortis Green.

70

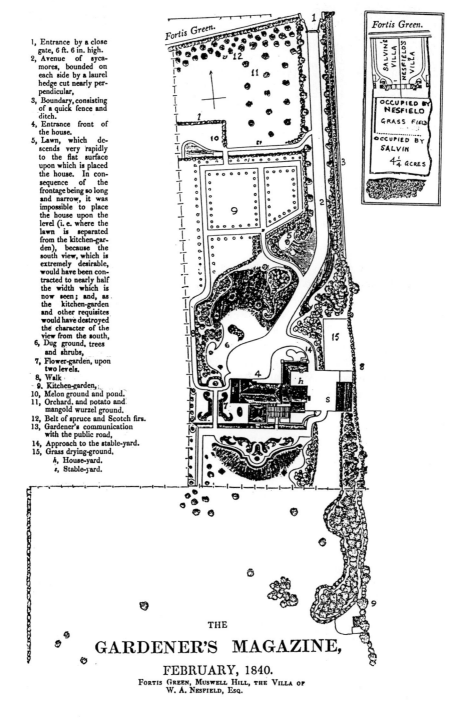

1, Entrance by a close gate, 6 ft. 6 in. high.
2, Avenue of sycamores, bounded on each side by a laurel hedge cut nearly perpendicular,
3, Boundary, consisting of a quick fence and ditch.
4, Entrance front of the house.
5, Lawn, which descends very rapidly to the flat surface upon which is placed the house. In consequence of the frontage being so long and narrow, it was impossible to place the house upon the level (i. e. where the lawn is separated from the kitchen-garden), because the south view, which is extremely desirable, would have been contracted to nearly half the width which is now seen; and, as the kitchen-garden and other requisites would have destroyed the character of the view from the south,
6, Dug ground, trees and shrubs,
7, Flower-garden, upon two levels.
8, Walk
9, Kitchen-garden,
10, Melon ground and pond.
11, Orchard, and potato and mangold wurzel ground,
12, Belt of spruce and Scotch firs.
13, Gardener's communication with the public road,
14, Approach to the stable-yard.
15, Grass drying-ground,
    h, House-yard.
    s, Stable-yard.

THE

GARDENER'S MAGAZINE,

FEBRUARY, 1840.

FORTIS GREEN, MUSWELL HILL, THE VILLA OF
W. A. NESFIELD, ESQ.

71

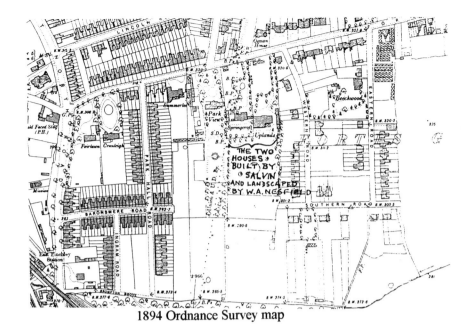
1894 Ordnance Survey map

would produce from 12 to as many as 18 lambs in February, which would be sold in May or June for 27 shillings each. The clear profit per acre was expected to be about £18. Presumably this pattern of keeping a few sheep in a field behind the house was common in Finchley and Muswell Hill at the time, but for Salvin and Nesfield it was probably only a hobby, as they had much more important sources of income. Nesfield, for example, was collaborating with Decimus Burton in planning the Royal Botanical Gardens at Kew.

Nesfield remained in Fortis Green until 1840, when he was appointed art master at Eton. Salvin's daughter, Eliza Anne, wrote that,

'There were many godless people in East End Village. There were prize fights at the Five Bells Tavern, foot races, steeple chases, etc. which caused so much confusion and gave rise to much that was bad. Drunkards abounded and there was no moral restraint, no orderly rule, no wholesome supervision.'

As a result Anthony and Mrs Salvin began raising money for a church which Salvin later built.

At Elmhurst the Salvins continued to live a warm family life, despite the fact that he was often far away on business. Salvin was a man of irrepressible energy, with a multitude of local interests and Anne was very competent. He bought and sold land in the district, had a farm near the High Street and kept a bull in Fortis Green. The family diaries of holidays with his wife are epics of endurance, seeing three major churches a day, going without food for twelve hours, all borne cheerfully without complaint. The whole family give an impression of unbroken cheerfulness and commonsense.

Salvin's commissions read like the inventory of the castles and large houses of England - Alnwick Castle, The Tower of London, Thorsby Hall, Perkforton, the big house in Cheshire - careful restorations of old buildings and the creation of new - the list published in the Builder obituary, 31 Dec. 1881, goes on and on. His twenty-five churches, included Holy Trinity Church, East Finchley.   There he became Vicar's Warden, his wife played the organ and his daughters taught in the Sunday School.

He built many small schools, including St James's School in Fortis Green, 1850, which was demolished in 1970 but unfortunately no records seem to survive; no plans or photographs except the glimpse of one gable. At about the same period Salvin built schools at Northbourne, Kent; Highgate National School 1850-52; Salisbury Schools, 1850; High Legh, Cheshire, 1853; Limpsfield, Surrey 1853; and others. Each of these and every other commission would have involved several personal visits, so he was always on the move.

A DESIGN for a CHAPEL .   A DESIGN for a SCHOOL .

Salvin's interchangeable design for a school or chapel.[10]

His drawings for a village school and a church, reproduced here, show the scale and simplicity of the buildings. There was no proper design for a school, of course, until the 1870s when London School Board completely re-thought the problem of how children should be taught. Until then pupils had sat on forms in ordinary rooms, or churches, so the same design did for both. The original part of St James's, built by Salvin, was equally simple, but the windows were larger in my memory. St James's is not listed among his works in 'The Builder': perhaps he designed it as an act of charity and it did not appear in his office accounts. Mr Plant, the Headmaster, who says that Salvin built his school, must have found the detail embedded somewhere in the Church records.

Salvin liked to travel in the front seat of the coach next to the driver, until one day he was involved in a collision and seriously hurt. He recovered, but some time later was persuaded that the travelling was becoming too arduous. Having lived in Finchley from 1833 to 1857, the family moved to Hanover Terrace, Regent's Park, near to William Nesfield, who had moved to York Terrace some years earlier.

In the 1850s, Elmhurst became a 'first-class Boarding School for Girls' and was still advertising at least as late as 1904.[2] Then the school 'prepared pupils for University if required and special attention was given to languages, under resident foreign mistresses.' Elmhurst was described as 'most charmingly situated in secluded grounds consisting of eleven acres including gardens, lawns, some finely timbered trees and a field, six acres in extent, for games.'

Later the house became the home of Alderman Samuel Pulham, Mayor of Finchley and was demolished, as we shall see. That was over a century after our next detail.

In 1815, immediately after the Napoleonic Wars, the Hornsey Enclosure Act extinguished the common rights and turned the Waste into pieces of private property. The Enclosure Map[4] shows how the land was divided up, the number of each plot and, where there is room, the areas in acres roods and perches. A Schedule accompanying the map gives all details and the names of the lessees. often the same plot shapes can be followed right up to today.

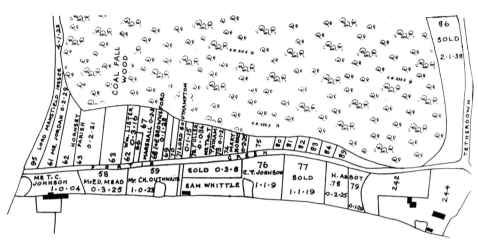

A detail from the 1815 Enclosure Map of Fortis Green.[4]

Several houses were built along Fortis Green soon after 1815. We have already considered Salvin's two houses, which were built in an Italianate style, while others were Gothic Revival.

Various conveyances and assignments which tell the stories of the sites are full of interest and their extraordinary language is worth quoting. A typical lease of this period said:

'The Court Baron of the Right Honorable and Reverend Father in God William by Divine permission Lord Bishop of London at the aforesaid Manor held at the House known as the Gatehouse at Highgate 31st October 1816 before Thomas Dickens Esq Steward of the Manor.

Wheras the commissioners named by a certain Act of Parliament passed 17 June 1816 Did award and allot into the devises of Josias Lister Esq. deceased, late one of the copyhold or Customary Tenants of the said Manor --- and so we also Award into the Devises of Josias Lister Esquire deceased All that allotment of Waste land containing 3 roods and 16 perches copyhold on Fortis Green bounded on the South East by Fortis Green and North West by Coldfall Wood. William Lister and Thomas Andrews prayed to be admitted to the said allotment of land and premises --- at the yearly rent of sixpence payable on the Feast Day of St Michael and such services as the said Copyhold Tenants are wont to perform.'

The houses must have been built fairly soon after 1815 as a vellum indenture, dated 2 August 1822, records the lease of one of them for one year to Mr J.P. Woolley. The drawing on another indenture dated 1901, reproduced here, shows three houses built on

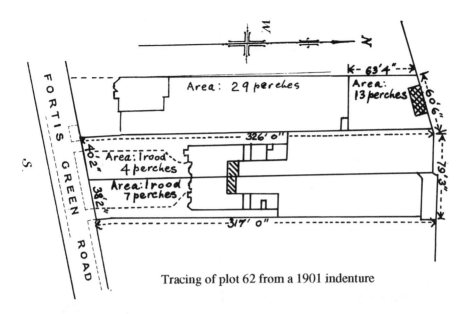

Tracing of plot 62 from a 1901 indenture

A typical 1820s house

lot 62 to which I have added measurements. Their combined areas total 3 roods 15 perches, which compares very accurately with the 3 roods 16 perches on the 1815 map. The various indentures and conveyances each add some extra detail, either describing a house, or explaining how it was owned. In 1865, for example,

'the dwelling house and premises, with the Chaise House, Stabling and gardens, together with the spring water pump jointly with the occupier for the time being of the adjoining premises, were assigned for 21 years at an annual rent of £45.'

By 1880 the rent had become £71, and by 1902, £85. A very modest inflation compared to modern times. Many of the houses persisted until the 1960s when some were demolished and replaced with flats. Soon after 1945 I had the pleasure of visiting one of these and a 1902 indenture brings it all back. It is very detailed, starting with the front bedroom which contained, 'a stove with a broken fixed back, a cupboard at side of Fireplace with shelving', - through each room of the house, describing the Venetian blinds, the fixed ironing board, the larder with slate shelves and the wine cellar with wooden bins, a complete stable, 2 mangers, 2 hay racks, a ladder to the loft, bell pull to side gate, the conservatory with 6 shelves, trellis work to the Outside WC and mahogany shelf, Fowl house and Green house.' One could almost rebuild the house from the description.

One feature of the house was surprising. The larder, which led off the kitchen was at ground level and yet had a barrel-vaulted roof as if it was in a cellar. It was very cool; a generous, walk-in larder at a temperature which one would expect to find below ground, so that the sudden change of temperature always came as a surprise. Presumably the space above the vault had been filled with broken brick, or shells, or some other traditional insulation to give coolness, and the barrel-vault was necessary to hold the weight.

This was a Jane Austen house. They say that Jane Austen herself never lived in a house with a ceiling. Instead, the joists in her houses were open, exposing the floor-boards of the room above, which must have been very convenient for a novelist storing overheard conversations for future use, but she had visited plenty of houses like this Fortis Green one and her characters would have felt at home in those rooms. Pride and Prejudice could have been filmed in this house, with the front dining room converted into a small library where Mr Bennet would fritter away his time, while Mrs Bennet bustled and complained in the main double drawing room.

The house was an excellent example of its period, modernised to an extent, but with the old doors and door frames, small cornices and original windows. There were front and back stairs, for this was a house to be run with plenty of servants, with bell-pulls in

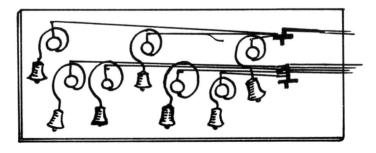

Fortis Green, c. 1910[92]

every room and an array of bells in the kitchen, each tuned to a different note. One can imagine the house full of children, one stationed by each pull, all ringing them at a signal and rushing down into the kitchen to hear all the bells pealing at once and the cook, driven to distraction, rushing away up the back stairs in hysterics.

Lynton Grange, opposite the end of Eastern Road, was another house which has since been demolished and replaced with flats. The grounds were once much larger, including all the adjoining land which is now the petrol garage. In one window of the house was a stained glass roundel with the initials J.H.S. The same initials were cast in plaster in the pediment outside, with the date 1867. The Revd. Robert Dawson once lived in the house so I thought that the initials were IHS, the Greek for Jesus, but Dawson was there in 1901, many years later. It appears that 1867 was the building date and JHS the initials of Smith, who is said to have been the owner. The house was registered with Palmer's Insurance Company, the fire company, who had their plaque on the outside wall.[56]

For many years, certainly from 1935 and perhaps even earlier, Lynton Grange was the home of the local Vets. All the neighbours with pets knew this house when Mr Taylor and then Mr Andrewes practised from the house and had animals of various kinds in pens in the garden.

Lynton Garage site was once occupied by Walker's Coach Hire firm, which let out horse-drawn carriages and traps. One lady who lived in Shakespeare Villa, in Southern Road, before Baronsmere Road had been made, remembered when it was too far for a little girl to walk to East Finchley Station. Instead, a pony cart was hired from Walker's to carry the family up Eastern Road, along Fortis Green and down the High Street to the railway Station, to catch a steam train. [56]

For nearly two centuries there have been houses in Fortis Green; the Great North Road saw to that. People with incomes lived in the generous brick and stucco houses which can still be seen, well set back from the road and with good gardens behind. Some houses have gone, but enough remain to give the picture of a leafy country road still in the country. A row of ten old houses between Eastern Road and Western Road, where Coventry Patmore used to live, have all been listed. They are varied in design, all well kept, with huge trees over-arching the road, so that this part of Fortis Green is as I remember it years ago.

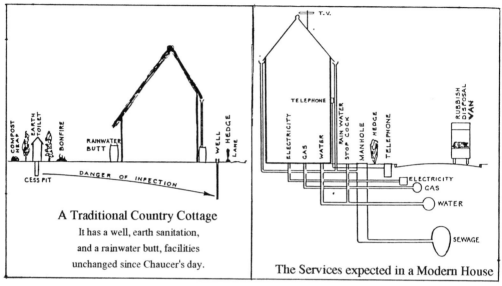

A Traditional Country Cottage
It has a well, earth sanitation, and a rainwater butt, facilities unchanged since Chaucer's day.

The Services expected in a Modern House

The hamlet near the Clissold Arms, a beer house and brewery with a long history, housed carpenters and gardeners and other modest people. Anyone who has canvassed along that road in an election will know how difficult it is to find the houses. Narrow lines of cottages, at right angles to the road, are tucked away in hidden corners, with small cottages slotted into the back entrances to fields, and behind shops.

Early Fortis Green cottages would have been very different from modern houses. The two illustrations above show how great the change has been. A description of life in a Sussex village in 1912, written by Leonard Woolf in 1972, comes as a shock today.

'In the fifty years since we had Asham House, the physical basis of life in the English countryside has been revolutionized. Conditions in 1912 were pretty primitive and our daily life was probably nearer to that of Chaucer's than of modern man with water from the main, electricity, gas, motor buses, telephone, wireless. When we went down to Asham, [their country house in Sussex] for a week-end we sometimes got a fly, which the dictionary tells us correctly was a 'one horse hackney carriage', from Lewes: but more often than not, wet or dry, we walked the four miles along the river bank and across the fields with knapsacks on our backs. All the water we used in the house we had to pump from the well. Sanitation consisted of an earth closet. We cooked on an oil stove or a primus; at night we used candles and oil lamps. Even in 1919, when we bought Monks' House and moved across the river to a house in the middle of the village, conditions were just the same, no buses, no water, no gas or electricity and the only 'sanitary convenience' an earth closet discreetly, but ineffectively hidden by a grove of cherry laurels in the middle of the garden.'

From 'Growing', by Leonard Woolf, written 1972.

78

The drawings opposite show some of the changes which have come about in a very short period of time. Perhaps the house should have a dish aerial, or cable television as well: they may become standard fittings in a few years' time, just as running water to all floors, gas and electricity, each in its turn became taken for granted.

When the Fortis Green houses still had traditional earth sanitation, like the cottage in the first illustration, night soil men used to remove the ordure from the cess pits at intervals. It was stored in Dirt House Wood, the old name for Cheerry Tree Woods. Each morning nursery gardeners brought their vegetables and flowers along the Great North Road to sell them in London. At that time The Old White Lion, now so handsomely rebuilt, was known as The Dirt House because, on their return journey, the market gardeners used to stop there for a drink. Then they collected the night soil from Dirt House Wood opposite and carried it away to manure their fields in the same carts as they carried their vegetables. The dangers of cross infection do not bear thinking about.[28]

79

Harwell Park Estate

In the middle years of the nineteenth century, two men, Thomas Morland and Conrad Wilkinson, bought the land which now contains Eastern, Western and Southern Roads and planned to develop it as Harwell Park Estate. The site corresponds to the dark outline on the 1865 Ordnance Survey below, with Salvin's land to the west. A Deed Poll was executed on 4th January, 1853 and the Poll Map, opposite, shows the land divided into house plots, most of which were not to be developed for years.

At this time there were no planning laws to control the type of buildings which could be erected, or their use. If one wished to live in a genteel neighbourhood, with congenial neighbours, and not have a glue factory built at the end of the garden, everyone had to agree to behave in an acceptable manner. The deed poll was a device to ensure that restrictive covenants were enforcable on all the purchasers. Everyone buying a plot of land had to agree to covenants controlling the type and minimum value of the houses, the use of the buildings, etc. These covenants would continue to be binding on all later owners and tenants.

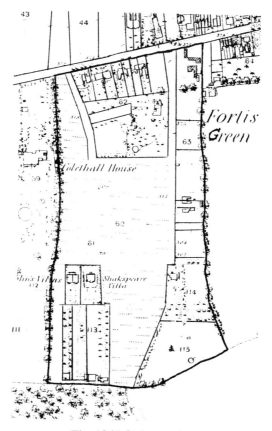

The 1865 Ordnance Survey.

80

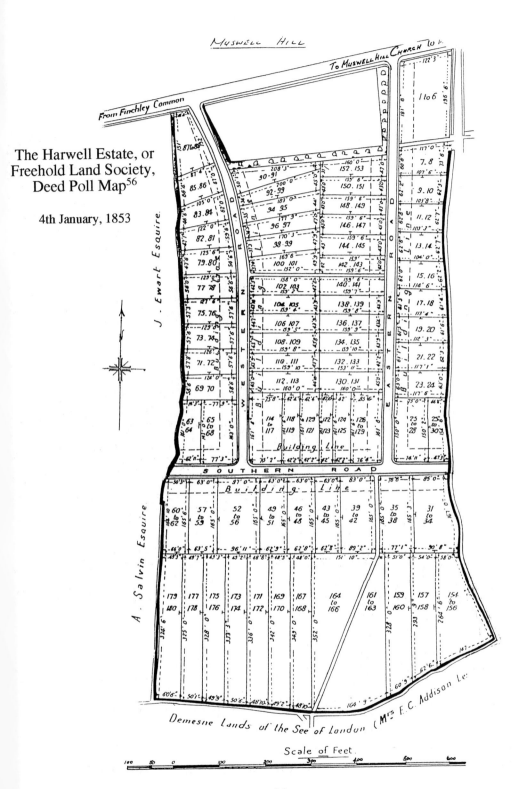

MUSWELL HILL

To MUSWELL HILL CHURCH to h.

From Finchley Common

The Harwell Estate, or
Freehold Land Society,
Deed Poll Map[56]

4th January, 1853

J. Ewart Esquire.

A. Salvin Esquire

WESTERN ROAD

EASTERN ROAD

SOUTHERN ROAD

Building Line

Building Line

Demesne Lands of the See of London (Mrs F. C. Addison Le.

Scale of Feet.

81

The covenants in this Deed restricted the value of the houses, their use, and the protection of views. Houses were to cost not less than £250, which sounds ridiculous today, but was a substantial sum in those days. Houses had to conform to regular building lines. These were easy to enforce. However, another covenant about land use was to become very relevant and contentious later, as we shall see.

The 1865 map shows that building progress was very slow. Eastern and Western Roads have been started and a few new houses are shown, although the map does not show the full position. Fourteen properties of the 1850s period can still be seen, including two pairs of semi-detached houses in Southern Road, but building was so slow that hardly two houses are to the same design. The varied styles and dates show how hesitant people were to venture so far into the country. A couple of houses were built, but by the time the next builder started work the style had changed.

Southern Road

These Southern Road, semi-detached villa-style houses were built about 1853. Each house has two principal rooms at ground and first floor, with a rear extension forming an 'L' plan. Athough Queen Victoria had been on the throne for some sixteen years when the houses was built, they are more Georgian in style than Victorian.

Quite plain, without the multi-coloured brickwork and fancy decoration which the later Victorians favoured, it is built of London stock bricks, with a shallow slate roof and some classical details for the entrance porch. In the corner house, advantage has been taken of its position to add large windows on the flank wall as well as the front, so that this house is particularly light. It also has a fine contemporaneous garden wall with a curved corner.

The wall construction of these houses is unusual: 9" brick walls have 2" thick vertical wooden battens nailed to them internally and on these are nailed wooden laths, which are plastered and decorated. Thus these are solid brick walls with a stud lining inside, creating a cavity to keep the house dry and free from the condensation which is often found on cold external walls.

The windows are sliding sashes and the ground floor ones in the main rooms have a most unusual feature. Many houses of this period had shutters which folded back

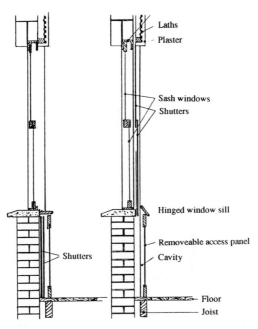

Laths
Plaster

Sash windows
Shutters

Hinged window sill

Removeable access panel
Cavity

Shutters

Floor
Joist

Window shutters which rise and fall like sash windows.
Southern Road, circa 1853.

across the windows internally, as security against burglars. These ones do not hinge, but slide. Internally each window has two counterweighted wooden shutters which rise and fall like sash windows. The sill of the window hinges upwards to reveal the top edges of the shutters, which are then raised into place at night for security and warmth. The shutters are housed in the increased wall thickness and, instead of lath and plaster, the 'apron' below the window has a removable timber panel for access to the shutter guides and weights.

In 1873, plans were submitted under a new public health act for a water closet to be added at the rear of the house, with access externally, and for the drain run to connect it with the new sewer in Southern Road. Later a larder with slate shelves (now a utility room) was added alongside.

This is an extremely interesting area to walk round because of the great variety of house styles. Hardly two houses are in the same style. Brick types, roofs, porches, all vary according to the fashion of the period when they were built and the whims of the particular builder. In 1936 Shakespeare Villa was demolished and the half-timbered houses of Shakespeare Gardens were built on its grounds. At the same time Billy Collins was building the Neo-Georgian houses at the top of Eastern Road, on the old greenhouses where I used to watch men taking geranium cuttings. Houses spanning more than eighty years can be found in these 'compass' streets and, with modern additions, people have been building here for nearly a century and a half, creating a charming jumble.

Circa 1880

Circa 1905

Circa 1935

Three more Southern Road Houses

These and the one illustrated on page 82 are only a few of the wide variety of periods to be found in the surrounding streets. Compare this with the uniformity of date and style to be found in the Collins and Edmondson estates.

The Harwell Estate in the Nineteen-nineties

In 1994 an application was made by Kennet Properties, which is the property arm of Thames Water, to build 27 houses across the Water Board land, from Southern Road to the edge of Fordington Road. Local people protested at once. There had been internicine war between local residents and the Water Board for years as The Board sought to build houses on the land and, about 1978, local residents had formed HORS (Hands Off the Reservoir Space) as a defence. At first the Water Board had said that the planned houses were for their employees, and they did succeeed in building a few at the back of Lauradale Road, but their object was far wider than this. Plans to build on the Football Field in Woodside Avenue were defeated after vigorous protests. Now here was a further stage in the battle.

HORS declared that the proposed development of 27 houses was illegal as Covenants under the Deed Poll of 1853 restricted the use of this land, south of Southern Road, to paddocks and no other buildings but stables for horses and summerhouses, were permitted. No building with sleeping or living facilities for people were permitted and these could not be more than twelve feet high. Clearly the original Poll members had wished to retain their unobstructed view across the valley to the south. Nearly a century and a half later, HORS was citing the covenants to restrict further building.

In the 1970s here had been a rush to find potential sites for new housing and, in this atmosphere, Haringey had marked the land as space for development. However, with the loss of so much open land, local opinion had changed drastically. Protesters were vocal in their opposition.

Haringey Council refused the original planning application, but Kennett Properties Limited persuaded the Secretary of State to override them and allow the scheme to go through. The developers moved bulldozers into the site, laid foundations for buildings and the beginning of a road to be called Cherry Tree Lane. By the end of 1994 one house at the Southern Road entrance had been built, with the rest pending.

In April 1994 Kennet Properties Ltd applied under the Land Tribunal Act 1949 to have the Covenants discharged, or modified. They wanted to wipe out the Covenants for good. They noted that the covenants forbade building any dwelling houses or buildings other than a summer house and without any sleeping or dwelling room therein within 200 feet of any of the lots numbered below 154 on the map (page 81). Thus the southern section of the site should not have been built on, but the covenant had been broken. The Covenants restricted building on the other sites to dwelling houses and also set out the building lines.

The application then listed no less than thirteen cases of buildings which, they claimed, breached the covenants. Shakespeare Gardens and other houses had been built on sites above no 153, where building was not permitted: various building lines had been breached: glasshouses had been built where only semi-detached houses were permitted: greenhouses had been replaced with houses: a new road had been laid on sites 15 and 16 which should have been used only for houses. So the list goes on.

Against this HORS says that the fact that covenants have been breached in the past is no justification for doing so again. Muswell Hill in 1995 is not Muswell Hill in the 1850s. Then there was lots of open space, while today the Water Board land is a unique stretch of open field land, used traditionally for archery. These fields are now an even more valuable amenity than they were before.

Local householders, especially those in Southern Road and Shakespeare Gardens who backed on to the proposed development, protested to the Land Tribunal. They said that the covenants are not obsolete because they secure practical and substantial benefits. In particular, they preserve valuable open space and amenity, provide quiet and light from the open field, and prevent visual intrusion. Houses in Southern Road and Shakespeare Gardens cannot be overlooked, so they are secluded and free from nuisance. Money would not be adequate compensation for the loss of these amenities. One typical house-holder claimed compensation, if development was permitted, equal to 5% of the value of his house.

The Inquiry is due some time in 1995.

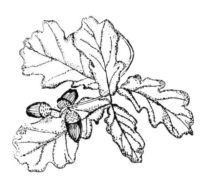

The County Roads

Durham Road and the first Victorian terraces appeared in time for the 1894-6 map. That whole development of the County Roads, from Lincoln Road to Hertford Road, and the development of Park Hall Road and Baronsmere Road south of Fortis Green, was a prophecy of what was to come.

The remaining portion of the Park Hall Estate was offered for sale at the Bald Faced Stag in 1892.[2] It consisted of land with frontages to Bedford, Hertford, and Durham

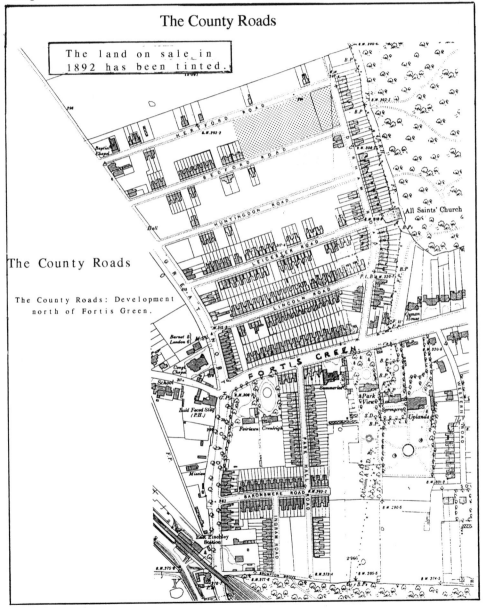

The County Roads

The land on sale in 1892 has been tinted.

The County Roads

The County Roads: Development north of Fortis Green.

All Saints' Church

Ordnance Survey 1894-96

87

Roads. A duplicate system of drainage (to take surface water and sewage respectively) had been installed by the ground landlords and the sewers connected to the main drain. As an inducement the vendors offered payment by instalments and free conveyances. Clearly the ground landlord had had to lay out the roads and drainage at his own expense and was not finding it easy to get his money back.

By 1894-6, Durham Road and Lincoln Road were complete, with odd, unrelated houses dotted along the the other roads as if scattered without sense. Presumably small-scale builders took options on small plots and the map makers were there to notice which builders were the first to rush their houses to sale. This sort of development relies entirely on the mood of the market. Buy land a few hundred yards too far from the main road and your plot will stand empty. Find a customer with ready money and his house can be finished in six months. He moves in with the plaster still wet and is surrounded for five years by empty building lots, full of purple willow herb and exploring children. The slow and spasmodic development of the County Roads probably reveals a great deal of worry: small developers with a house half built but no takers, biting their nails as the danger of bankruptcy increased each week.

The Diary of a London Schoolboy, 1826-1830[9], tells the remarkable story of a builder's son, about thirteen years old at the time, picking up his education in one of the small Marylebone private schools as and when his parents could afford a term's fees, caught up in the anguish of his father's speculative building on the edge of St John's Wood; walking in search of his father, with a message, from Edgware Road to the City, failing to find him and walking back again without complaint. His father's houses were just too far along Edgware Road for them to sell at the time. Today they are worth untold sums, but in the 1860s there were no buyers. First the family had to let one half of their own house; then his father was imprisoned for debt, like the father in Our Mutual Friend and the family had to hide this disgraceful secret from the world; then his father became ill and a barge full of bricks in Paddington Canal Basin had to be sold. The job devolved on the boy, but while he was negotiating, running backwards and forwards from the customer to his father ill in bed, the barge sank. Finally his father died and the boy went off to South Africa, later to become a homeopathic doctor. It is one of the most telling accounts ever written of the difficulties faced by small speculative builders. How many mute inglorious East Finchley schoolboys were worried by the iregular development shown by the 1894 map?

The same type of slow development is to be seen in Eastern and Western Roads by looking at the houses. In 1865 development had started, but instead of a uniform

The Cedar of Lebanon which stood at the entrance to Fortis House, on the corner of Princes Avenue and Fortis Green Road.

development such as we shall see in the Collins and Edmondson Estates later on, the houses in Eastern Road, Western and Southern Roads reveal a wide variety of styles and dates. Almost every house is different.

Going towards Muswell Hill, many of the large estates persisted to the turn of the century. Walk a couple of hundred paces from Fortis Green along Fortismere Avenue, for example, and you are standing on the site of the elliptical carriage entrance to Fortismere, with one large house facing you and another to your right, both called Fortismere on the 1881 Census form. Today there are rows of houses on either side, with a steep slope ahead, looking down into the valley where the Waterboard buildings now lie, with Highgate Woods rising up and crowning the opposite hill. The view of fields and hedgerows must have been stunning; south facing, clear of houses, an ideal place for an estate owner to build his house.

To the west was Midhurst, in smaller grounds but with a similar prospect over the valley below to Highgate Woods. On the other side of Fortismere, looking more to the east and the distant view of the Thames Valley, was Firs. Slightly lower down the slope, at the top of Muswell Rise, that sharp, curving hill from Cranley Gardens to St James's Church, were Highfield and The Hall. These houses looked more directly than Firs over the expanse of the Thames.

Beyond Firs, where Fortis Green Road turned into Muswell Hill Road at St James's Church, the roadway skirted the very edge of the cliff to reach the top of Muswell Hill. That angle made by Fortis Green Road and The Broadway was occupied by two large estates, with Fortis House, at what is now the end of Princes Avenue, and The Limes which occupied most of Queen's Avenue and stretched down the hill behind Colney Hatch Lane. The Limes, which was on the sites of the present Public Library and Barclays Bank, was later bought by Edmondson and developed, with other estates, to form Queen's, Princes' and King's Avenues, and all that fine parade of shops along the north side of Fortis Green and the Broadway, with their their characteristic arched fronts.

Shops in Fortis Green Road and the Athenaeum (demolished).[92]

89

Muswell Hill Road

Muswell Hill Road was gravelled until the 1930s, with the same houses and woods as it has today, but with few private cars and little traffic. Almost everyone travelled on the No 43 bus, the only one serving the route, or else we walked. Most commuters travelled by train, for it was the train which had opened up Muswell Hill.

Today it is difficult to imagine how remote Muswell Hill must have seemed even earlier at, for example, the end of the eighteenth century. From the City and West End, it appeared to be perched among the Northern Heights as if it was an Italian hill town fortified against attack. To travel from the City one had to walk through the city wall at Moorgate, walk up the long steady climb to The Angel, Islington, along Upper Street, Islington, along what is now Holloway Road to the bottom of Highgate North Hill. Then one could either turn right and go through Crouch End and up Muswell Hill, or climb straight up Highgate North Hill to Highgate Village and turn down Southwood Lane to Muswell Hill Road. Travelling from the West End, the route was through Kentish Town, along Dartmouth Park Hill and along the Hornsey Lane ridge

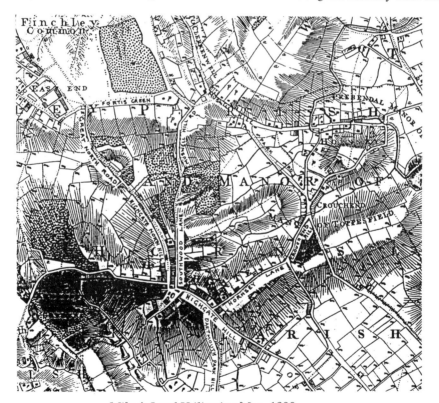

Milne's Land Utilization Map, 1800.

Symbols:- *a* arable, *m* meadow and pasture, *p* paddock.

90

to Crouch End Hill. There was no easy way to Muswell Hill, because Highgate Hill and the Hornsey Lane spur barred all progress. No wonder Dick Whittington turned back: he was too tired to tackle Highgate Hill.

Both Muswell Hill and Highgate Hill had slopes of 1 in 10 or so, which was just acceptable for pedestrians, or on horseback, but it was a major problem for wagons. A much more gentle gradient was needed. From Shepherd's Hill today one looks along Archway Road towards London down a narrow gorge, with Archway Bridge sailing across the skyline. In 1800 however one saw a long, almost level view of fields, with Hornsey Road running across in the distance. Beyond, and out of sight, was a steep drop, even sharper than Highgate Hill itself.[2]

Robert Vazie was a mining engineer who had tried to cut a tunnel below the Thames

Cutting through the Hornsey Lane Ridge to build Archway Road[83]

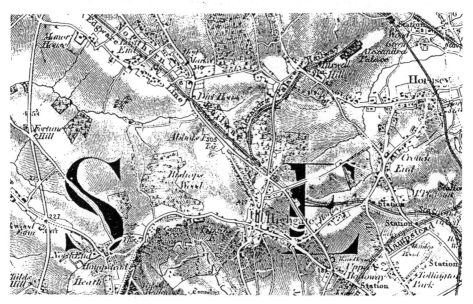

The 1822 map with railways added later.

at Rotherhithe, nearly forty years before Brunel achieved this task. In 1808, believing the soil in the area to be even and solid in formation, he proposed to build a tunnel through the hill. From Shepherd's Hill one would have seen the same fields as before, with Archway Road sloping down between the fields to a tunnel mouth, with an unchanged Hornsey Lane running high above. A Turnpike Trust resolved to follow Vazie's advice and by-pass Highgate Hill by building a tunnel below Hornsey Lane, through the escarpment. After a long, steady climb the road would skirt Highgate Hill along the dip at Shepherd's Hill as it does today, and then it would go on to meet the old North Road at the Wellington.

The Seal of the Company[6]

An Act of Parliament was passed, allowing work to be started but by 1811 Rennie, as consultant, was expressing doubt about the quality of the brickwork. On 13 April 1812 disaster happened. The tunnel fell in below Hornsey Lane with a crash like thunder and the road became impassable. Underground water and the unstable joint between the clay and the loam lying above it, probably caused the collapse. It is said that the workmen had been predicting trouble for a fortnight, but fortunately nobody was hurt in the collapse. A crowd of 800 people came on Sunday to view the ruin.

Within three days the Directors of the Highgate Archway Company had resolved to build the road as an open cutting, with a stone arch to support Hornsey Lane. The architect for the bridge was John Nash, who may also have buttressed the flanking walls. The structure consists of a series of race-track arches supporting the central arch on either side. Thus the round road tunnel was only one of a number of very similar arches and Hornsey Lane was supported like a canal viaduct spanning a valley, except that only the central arch was open and all the rest were buried in the surrounding earth. The structure could equally well have suited a viaduct carrying a canal across a valley, or a railway, or a road.

The foundations of the bridge were completed by November 1812 and Hornsey Lane was re-opened to traffic in August 1813. Archway Road had a gradient of 1-23 to 1-33, much easier than Highgate Hill, but the road surface was so bad for a time that some hauliers changed back to the Highgate Hill route. It was only when Telford dug out the old road surface and laid new drains and a concrete foundation, that the road became really popular. Archway Road made history by being the first road with the thick concrete foundations, consisting of gravel and Roman cement, which we take for granted today.[23] Before this roads had been made of crushed stone and had none of

Nash's original Archway Tunnel

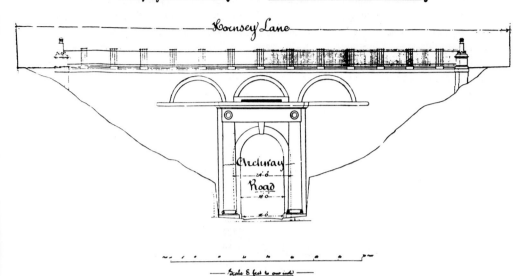

Highgate Archway —— *Elevation of Present Archway* ——

Hornsey Lane

Archway

Road

Scale 8 feet to one inch

HORNSEY LOCAL BOARD

DETAILS OF HIGHGATE ARCHWAY

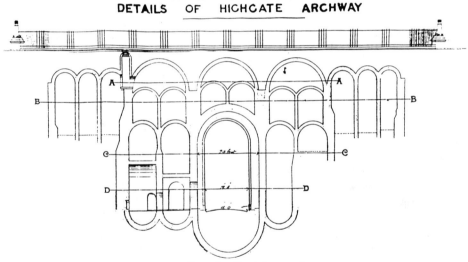

Longitudinal Section[4]

the firmness which is given by concrete.

By 1890 the 18 foot width of the roadway had become far too narrow for the traffic. Path-ways for pedestrians were opened up through the side arches, leaving the centre one solely for traffic, but this was still too narrow. Eventually the present bridge was built a few yards to the north to a design by Sir Alexander Binniee of the London County Council staff. Dated 1897, to celebrate Queen Victoria's Jubilee, it was not in fact completed until 1900.

The original Archway Bridge[18]

When the old Nash 'tunnel' bridge was removed, the modern view from Shepherd's Hill was at last created: a long, straight road through a man-made valley and the bridge floating high above, against the sky. Cutting through the edge of the escarpment had been a massive task, equivalent to breaching the walls of some medieval castle. Step after step of soil had been removed by hand, but when completed and the road surface improved, the road was like a new motorway or a high-speed rail link. Eventually Archway Road helped to open up the countryside to building development: as an immediate result, Muswell Hill Road found itself on the edge of the new by-pass. One could now reach Muswell Hill easily from the new road by way of Muswell Hill Road, or else go on to East Finchley and along Fortis Green.

Binnie's 1897 bridge

The Bishop of London's Hunting Park[30]

Before continuing with the story of Muswell Hill Road we must say something about the Bishop of London's Hunting Park as this had a profound effect on the later history of the whole district.

The Hunting Park included all of Highgate Wood but not Queen's Wood. Muswell Hill Road ran just outside the park, so that the narrow strip on the west side of the road, which became part of the Woodlands estate and now holds houses and shops, was the verge of the road, with the park behind it. The hunting park boundary continued between what are now the houses on Muswell Rise and Woodside Hospital and turned along the back fences of Grand Avenue, behind Tetherdown School, along the northern edge of the Water Board land to the corner of Cherry Tree Wood, across Edmund's Walk, along the back garden fences between Brim Hill and Abbot's Gardens, curved south west across Lyttleton Road and the Playing Fields, down the boundary of Hampstead Golf Club to Turner's Wood, along to the Spaniards and from there to Highgate Gatehouse.

All the Woodside Avenue, Lanchester Road and Fordington Road block of houses were inside the park, while the Fortis Green and Muswell Hill Road developments were just outside it.

The hunting park would have been surrounded by a hedge and ditch strong enough to keep the deer and other game in so that they could be hunted, no easy task before the

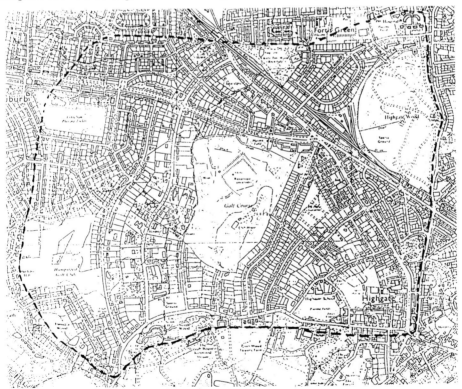

The Bishop of London's Hunting Park
imposed on a modern map[30]

95

invention of barbed wire. The remains of three thirty-yard stretches of the border hedge in Lyttleton Playing Fields, were examined by G.H.Musgrove of the Hendon and District Archaeological Society. By using methods of hedgerow dating developed by Dr Max Hooper of Nature Conservancy, the hedges were given an approximate date of 725 years, thus taking them back to the mid-thirteenth century. No doubt this date applied to the whole hedge. Since a boundary hedge has no value if there are gaps in it, presumably there was once a hedge dense enough to hold back wild animals along the back fences of, for example, Grand Avenue and Muswell Hill Rise. [23]

Old hunting parks were built not only to keep deer in, but to attract deer from outside and trap them. This was achieved by choosing a place on the boundary where the outside ground was higher than the inside and creating a leap. The deer found it easier to leap down than to escape by leaping upwards, so they were trapped. Thus the higher ground along Grand Avenue and across the hillocks of the Water Board land, may perhaps have been the start for building this type of ditch and leap to trap deer from outside the park. Pure speculation, but it is extraordinary today to imagine rutting deer running down Midhurst Avenue and leaping into the Bishop of London's stew-pot.

Besides the Hunting Park, the Bishop of London held lands as the Lord of the Manors of Hornsey and Finchley, so his powers extended well beyond the hedge line, so Southwood Hall would have been well within his jurisdiction.

In the 19th century, Muswell Hill Road was far out in the country. Southwood Hall stood at the top of the hill, on the corner between Muswell Hill Road and Wood Lane, commanding a view of the Thames Valley and all the air that blew. When it was sold in 1832, it was advertised as:-

'A Castellated Mansion of the Olden Time. The design is pure Gothic, combining the chaste, the simple, and the beautiful, and (which is not so often found in this style) in an eminent degree the cheerful. The principal Chambers are adorned by some very fine specimens of Tapestry and a profusion of Painted Glass. The Pleasure Grounds and land include in the whole about four acres. Their disposition is most happy and so arranged that the picturesque always prevails. The natural advantage of an irregular surface has been so far improved by Art, that at no point is the extent developed and the most luxuriant trees ornament this favoured spot in every direction. Some beautiful Specimens of Sculpture adorn the house and grounds and it may be safely pronounced that for any gentleman of Taste and Opulence a Suburban Retreat so every way desirable, could not easily be found. The situation is dry, the air remarkably pure and healthful and there is an abundance of the finest water.'

Clearly the garden designer had chosen not to exploit the distant views, but to create an enclosed world within a thick shelter belt of trees.

The 1815 Enclosure Map (overleaf) shows that Southwood Hall was built on the two plots owned at that time by Jaques and Jones. In 1815 there had been two houses on the site but presumably these were demolished, more land was bought to extend the grounds right up to the Wood, and a new house was built.

The Estates Map shows the original four acres mentioned in the 1832 sales documents, which is much larger than the Jaques and Jones property had been. Thus by this time Southwood Hall estate must have extended right up to the stream and ponds on the edge of Queen's Wood, a natural boundary, and been enclosed on two sides by Queen's

Engraving of Southwood Hall [1,7]

Wood and King's Woods. The third side was open with fine views over the Thames valley.

Today Southwood Hall has been demolished and blocks of red-brick flats erected, but before this was done about three-quarters of the original site had been sold off for development and the estate reducued to about its 1815 size. The three acres sold now contain Bond & White's Yard, full of building materials, and Summersby Road.

Queen's Woods extended beyond, as they do today, and beyond them again, right up to the site of St James's Church, were the fields of Upton Farm. Milne's Land Utilization Map of 1800, on page 90, shows them as 'pasture and meadows', for Upton Farm was one of the belt of farms surrounding London which supplied milk and meat and grew hay for the horses. When the farm was sold in 1885, the five lots totalled 42 acres 7 perches, providing house sites from Connaught Gardens to St James's Church and round the hill to the edge of Collins's Rookfield Estate. Room for street after street of houses.

Woodlands

Woodlands was a large T shaped estate of seven acres, which straddled Muswell Hill Road. The 1890 estate plan, on page 100,shows that the house and grounds stretched in a long strip down what is now Woodland Rise and Woodland Gardens, while on the other side of the road, where there are now houses and shops, were stables, large and productive kitchen gardens, with a gardener's cottage, all cut from the Waste which used to line Muswell Hill Road on the edge of The Bishop of London's Hunting Park, which became Highgate Woods.

It was here, in 1863, that Frederick Lehmann had a fine house and began to hold a literary and artistic salon. When the Lehmanns first rented the house from its owner, Mr Cameron, it was a newish house but it is not clear exactly when it had been built. They soon decided to buy and it became their country reteat.

97

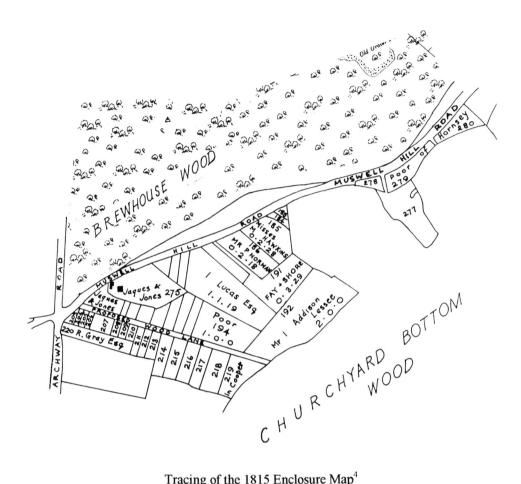

Tracing of the 1815 Enclosure Map[4]

Tracing from the 1815 Enclosure Map of Hornsey [4] showing
part of the Woodlands Estate west of Muswell Hill Road. [6]

Two brothers, Frederick and Rudolph Lehmann, sons of a miniature painter from
Hamburg, had come to Edinburgh where they married the two daughters of Robert
Chambers, the publisher and founder of Chamber's Journal and Chamber's
Encyclopedia. It was a highly talented family, producing creative musicians, writers
and actors. Rudolph had two daughters, one of whom was Liza Lehmann, the
composer and singer. Frederick and his wife were talented musicians, he playing the
violin and she the piano.

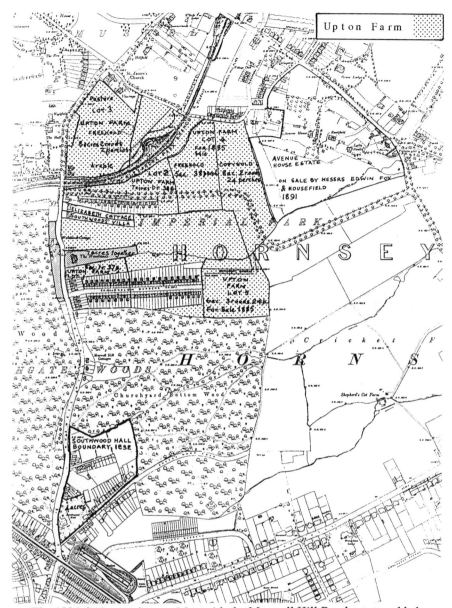

The 1894 Ordnance Survey Map with the Muswell Hill Road estates added

Frederick's son, called Rudolph Chambers Lehmann, was born in 1856, a great sportsman and oarsman, became a Liberal MP in the 1905 landslide, was editor of the Daily News, wrote for Punch and often edited it. He had four children, Helen, Rosamund the novelist, Beatrix, the actress and John, publisher and writer.

This last generation would not have known Woodlands, for the house was sold in 1890, and they were brought up in a house on the edge of the Thames, but John Lehmann records that when young, his father had had glimpses of Dickens, Wilkie Collins, George Elliot, Bulwer Lytton, Browning and dozens of other literary and

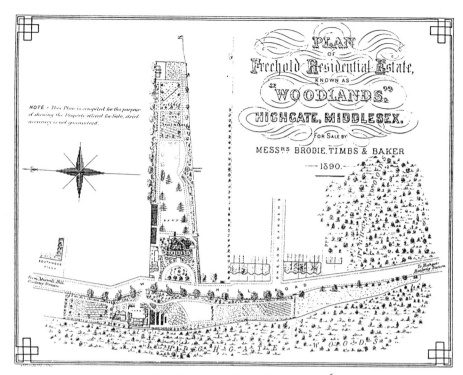

The 1890 Sale Plan of Woodlands[6]

artistic friends of the older generation, at Woodlands and elsewhere.

Besides Woodlands, Frederick and his wife Nina had a house in Berkeley Square and later in Westbourne Terrace and later still, off Piccadilly. In all their houses they held brilliant literary and musical parties, with the foremost writers and musicians, but Woodlands was always the place to which Nina retired for peace and beauty. Some of

Woodlands.[6]

FRONT VIEW OF HOUSE.

100

her letters are quite lyrical about it.

'If I could only give you a picture that could convey an idea of the brilliant beauty in which Woodlands bathes this morning! The atmosphere is so clear the we see to the Essex Hills, over the terraces of trees, the ivy covered tower of Hornsey, the lines of delicious green fields dotted with white houses - sheep - horses - cattle. In front our own delicious lawn, with its graceful Deodars waving slightly in the crisp yet mild morning breeze, the warm sun shining over all---'.

Frederick was a successful business man who travelled widely and his wife continued to entertain and meet people in London, so their letters gave a lively picture of life in London, America and Japan. These John Lehmann used later in a delightful book called Ancestors and Friends, well worth reading. [16]

Woodlands was sold for development in 1890[6]. The Key Plan, on page 102, shows the railway with stations at Muswell Hill and Alexandra Palace, but before that the trains ran through open fields and there was no Cranley Gardens Station. When it was built it opened up a huge tract of land to builders and commuters.

HIGHGATE,

Midway between Highgate and Muswell Hill Stations on the Great Northern Railway.

Particulars, Views, Plan and Conditions of Sale

OF THE

HIGHLY CHOICE AND VALUABLE

FREEHOLD RESIDENTIAL ESTATE

KNOWN AS

→ "Woodlands," ←

DELIGHTFULLY SITUATE IN

MUSWELL HILL ROAD,

Commanding Grand Views over the surrounding Country, and embracing the well-built and excellently appointed

HANDSOME FAMILY MANSION,

DELIGHTFUL PLEASURE GROUNDS,

SPLENDID RANGE OF GLASS HOUSES.

LARGE AND PRODUCTIVE KITCHEN GARDENS,

CAPITAL STABLING,

GARDENER'S COTTAGE and other OUTBUILDINGS.

THE WHOLE COMPRISING AN AREA OF ABOUT

SEVEN ACRES.

Which will be Sold by Auction by

Messrs. BRODIE, TIMBS & BAKER,

A Mr R. Metherell built typical houses in Woodland Rise, solid substantial Edwardian houses, with two storeys at front and three behind, with the rooms filling the roof space. Unfortunately the front elevation has not survived, so the drawing reproduced on the next page is incomplete.

In 1905 Metherell was advertising houses for sale from £550 or at £50 a year rent. In the same issue an estate agent at Cranley Gardens advertised houses with eight rooms, baths and offices to rent at £38 a year.[82]

W.J.Collins bought part of Lot 3 from the Upton Farm sale from the railway company and built Church Crescent, while the Imperial Property Company built on the other side of Muswell Hill Rise, so that within a few years red brick houses stretched right up to St James's Church.

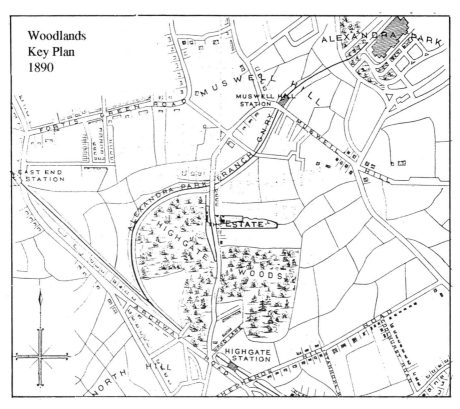

The Woodlands 'Key Plan', before Cranley Gardens Station had been built.

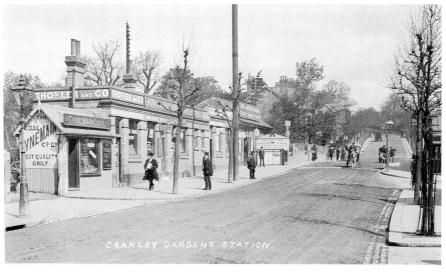

CRANLEY GARDENS STATION, c.1912

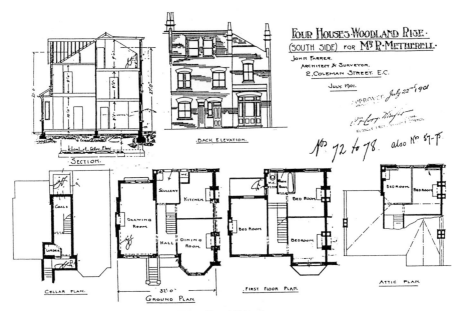

Woodland Rise houses.

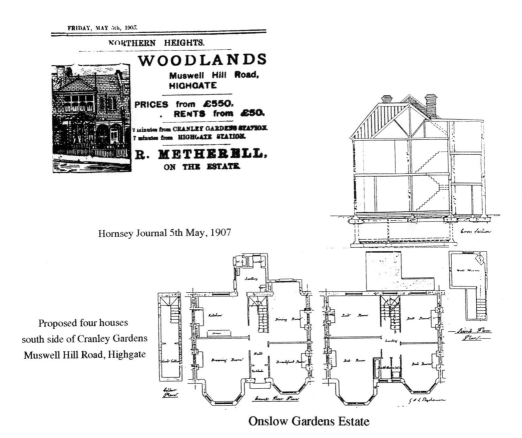

Hornsey Journal 5th May, 1907

Proposed four houses
south side of Cranley Gardens
Muswell Hill Road, Highgate

Onslow Gardens Estate

Fortismere

Fortismere was a large estate stretching from what is now Birchwood Avenue, to the edge of the playing field in Woodside Avenue in the south and to Collingwood Avenue in the west. Some of the trees along the back garden fences of Grand Avenue and Collingwood Avenue may be the ones shown on the 1865 map, not shown here. A narrow, sinuous lake lay about half way down the slope between Fortis Green and Grand Avenue. Nearly five hundred yards long, it stretched from the west side of Firs Avenue to the east side of Leaside Avenue, with an island in Birchwood Avenue and a boathouse on the back fence between Leaside Avenue and Fortismere Avenue.

This was a considerable area of water, yet it was almost at the top of a hill. Where did the water come from? Presumably the lake was fed by springs produced as a result of the ice action ten thousand years ago. The ice brought a mixed deposit of stones and sand from far afield and laid it on top of the London Clay. Long before the ice had deposited its debris, rivers and streams had run on top of the London Clay and laid down gravel beds. Thus the glacial drifts now rest on clay and irregular patches of

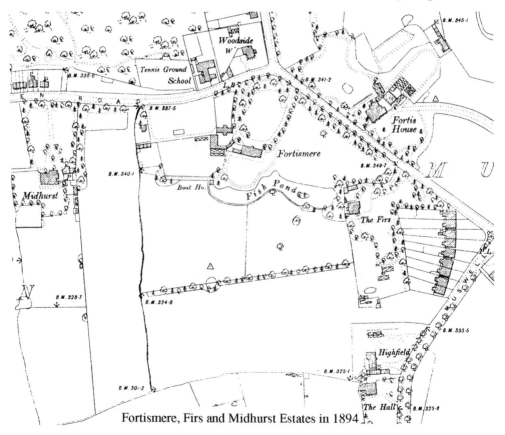

Fortismere, Firs and Midhurst Estates in 1894

104

gravel. As I was told so long ago, sitting in St James's School, the bench of mixed debris left after the Ice Age runs from Alexandra Palace to East End Road. Any gravel pockets left in it are permeable, allowing rain to pass through and emerge as springs where the water reaches the clay joint. The stream in Coldfall Woods starts as two springs on either side of Creighton Avenue, at about the same height as the lost Fortismere Lake, and flowed northwards through Southgate. Springfield Avenue, again a few metres below the top of the hill, was not given its name for nothing. A stream arose south of Fortis Green, flowed south to about Woodside Avenue and then east, along the line of Fordington Road. From there it went through watercress beds in the unfortunately named Dirthouse Wood, which we now call Cherry Tree Wood, under the Great North Road and Bishop's Avenue to join the Mutton Brook.

For centuries this drainage pattern continued, but perhaps one day some early owner of Fortismere called in a 'Repton' to make his estate more picturesque. Who he was, where he came from, or how he came to own the estate, we do not know, but the evidence of the map is clear. The lake in the 1894 map is artificial, for no lake of this shape, in this position, could have been formed naturally. Nor when formed, could it have survived for long. The natural flow of the spring would have cut through the bank and drained the pond, since the force and persistence of streams are often astonishing.

Hampstead Ponds were formed to provide drinking water by damming a similar stream and digging out reservoirs. When no longer used for this purpose, a brickfield was dug higher up the slope, with stepped ledges all round where the clay was cut. The brickfield was abandoned and vegetation took over, producing, with the aid of judicious planting, a beautiful 'natural' pond, now called the Bathing Lake. By the 1980s it was becoming shallow, filled with decades of silt, so it had to be demudded. The water was drained out into a lower pond, floundering fish captured in nets and transferred to a safe enclosure, and the bottom silt was revealed. There, running through the centre of the pond as it had done for centuries, was the old stream, cutting a clean path through the bordering mud. If the Bathing Lake had not been demudded, the silt would eventually have completely filled the pond and the stream would have reappeared on the surface.

The Fortismere Lake could not have been natural either: nor could it have survived for long without perpetual renewal. It has all the hallmarks of the romantic improvements so popular in the eighteenth and early nineteenth centuries. Probably whoever created the lake as a long narrow ribbon along the contour, half way down the slope, also planted a long screenline of trees near the bottoms of Birchwood, Fortismere and Leaside Avenues. This line of trees, which is shown on the 1894 map, is more than a normal field hedge: in the centre is a circular interruption, perhaps a semicircular seat with a sundial in the middle, or a round summerhouse set in a clipped hedge. This semicircle is surely artificial, while the trigonometrical point nearby, shown as a triangle on the map, cannot be older than the first Ordnance Survey about 1790, and may have been the reason for placing the semicircular feature just there. However old the pond may be, the screen of trees is surely an 'improvement' which Repton could have designed. He drew landscapes for his clients in his famous Red Books. A drawing showed the existing view with a folding flap to show what it would look like after the work was done. With these drawings he would beguile his patrons into spending untold sums of money to remodel their estates. The sketches shown on the next page can be seen as an imitation 'Repton', showing Fortismere before and after the lake was created.

The first drawing shows the view looking south from Fortismere towards Highgate, with fields down in the valley and the trees of Highgate Woods rising up the opposite hillside. Muswell Hill Road drops down and then rises up as it still does today, but the view was wider then because there were no houses to obscure the slopes of the hill. The second drawing shows the same view with the lake dug and a tall screen of trees planted beyond.

Landscaped, it would have created a wide, peaceful vista. Below the lake was an open field reaching to the southern edge of the estate, along what are now the back garden fences of Grand Avenue. Beyond that were more fields. With the tree screen in place, all this pasture land would have been hidden by the mature trees, while their crowns reached up to the bottom edge of Highgate Woods on the opposite hill. From the windows of Fortismere House one would have looked south over a long narrow lake stretching from the back of Firs Avenue to a boathouse in Leaside Avenue. The estate beyond would have appeared endless, stretching beyond the lake and the screen of trees, over the tops of the fields along 'Woodside Avenue', into Highgate Woods on the opposite hill and so on for ever. The lake and the line of trees would have converted the thirty acres into thirty thousand.

All this was speculation until I found the 1815 Enclosure Map for Hornsey[4]. This is enormous, and beautifully drawn, made of perhaps a dozen pieces of vellum pasted together, with wooden rollers top and bottom and dated 14 June 1816. The vellum is

Imaginary drawing showing Fortismere before the lake was cut

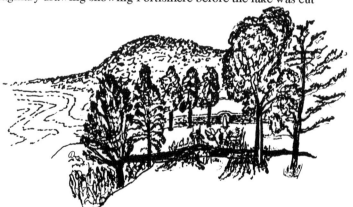

The lake and hedge line as they may have been planned.

106

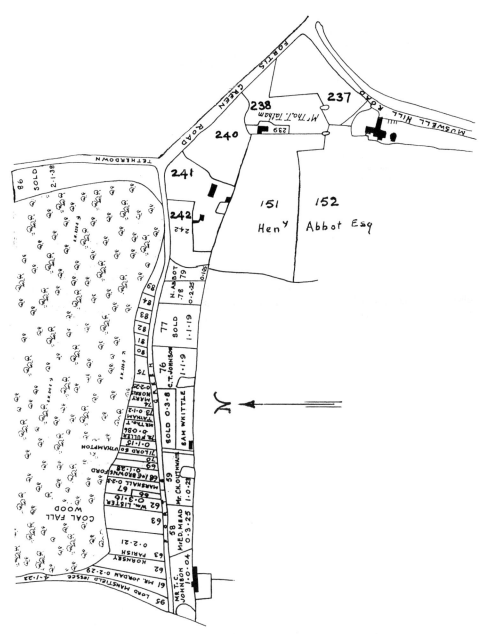

Tracing of part of the 1815 Enclosure Map of Hornsey.[4]

dry, hard as a drum head and very cockled, so that when the map is unrolled it explodes like a jumping cracker. It is certainly the noisiest map I have ever handled, causing everyone in the Map Room to look up each time I moved it.

The tracing above shows the numbered plots along Fortis Green, from the Hornsey boundary, at what is now Durham Road to Tetherdown. Each plot is numbered and all the way along there are ponds on the south side of Fortis Green. This is where the

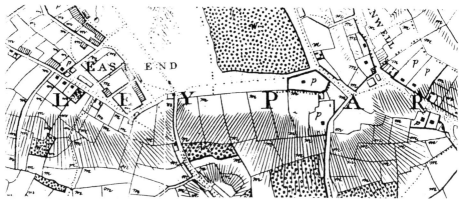

A piece of the Milne Land Utilization Map, 1800, with the site of Fortismere shown as a Park (lined in).

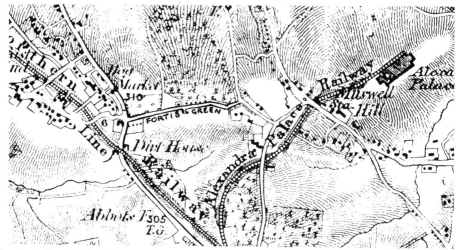

Part of the 1822 Ordnance Survey showing Fortis Green and Fortismere with two houses built on it.

villagers would have got their water. Fresh, clean water fed by a series of springs, plentiful enough to grow watercress in Cherry Tree Woods. There are no ponds north of the road but various houses there owned wells, so the gravel beds and the water were not far down.

On the Enclosure map (page 107) the plots which were to make up the Collins Fortismere estate are centred round number 241, which already has two houses on it, and Firs on 238-9. The pond that concerns us is on plot 241. It seems clear that someone created the lake in Fortismere by extending this pond into a long waterway.

The 1822 Ordnance Survey map had the railways inserted in 1890, making it slightly difficult to read as all the details except the railway are of 1822. This confirms that there were already two houses close together, behind a hedge, on the Fortismere site and a third house, which was probably Firs, nearby. No drawings of any of these houses seem to have survived.

The Fortismere Census

Everyone knows that Muswell Hill, from having been a rural area, was suddenly developed at the end of the nineteenth century. Large estates were developed, mainly by two builders, W.J.Collins and J.Edmonds. This chapter tries to describe some of the people who lived in the big estates before the expansion started. The main source is the census returns.

The first Census returns, at the start of the nineteenth century, were mere totals of the numbers of people in the district divided into four occupational groups, manufacturing, commerce, handicrafts and agriculture. Figures were collected by parish officials and gave nothing more than a few statistical details. No names were collected. The census has always been a counting operation, but gradually more questions were asked, names of people and later of houses were added, so that the schedules now released after a hundred years when all the people are dead, can tell us a certain amount about the population of Muswell Hill in the period. Many houses had no name and, as they were not numbered either, we can seldom tell where the houses stood. No doubt someone will make, or indeed may already have made, a statistical analysis of the demographic changes of the neighbourhood from census to census. Here we are concerned only with trying to trace the story of a few houses which stood in grounds large enough to interest later housing developers.

The first census returns which give names of individuals were collected in 1851, so the first pupils of St James's School which had opened the year before would have been on this census and probably formed the first school register. The first census to give house names was in 1881, so one has to start there, but by tracing names backwards we can follow the story of some houses with large grounds back to the 1871 and 1861 schedules. Even so, much is guesswork.

The 1894 map shows that Fortismere Estate had two large houses adjoining and sharing the same elliptical carriage drive. The 1881 Census calls them both Fortismere.

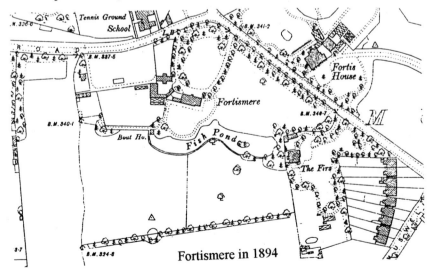

Fortismere in 1894

In 1881, the two Fortismere houses were occupied by the Soames and the Woods families, but which occupied which house we do not know. The Soames family first appeared on the 1861 census, when Sarah Soames, a widow of 68, was Head of Household. She had been born in Wapping and clearly this was a shipping family because her son Samuel, aged 31, was a ship owner. Samuel and his sister Ellen, aged 37 and unmarried, were both born in Stepney. Presumably the father had owned the ships and done well enough to move from the Thames Basin to a thirty-two acre estate in Muswell Hill. The family had a footman, a cook, two housemaids, a ladies' maid and a groom of 16. Living in the stables were another groom, aged 24, and his wife.

Ten years later, by the time of the 1871 census, old Mrs Soames had died and Samuel was shown as a commission merchant. He had married Harriet, aged 30, and they had two children, a son of 7 and a daughter of 3. What happened then we do not know, but between 1871 and 1881 Harriet died. Nor is her son (aged 7 on the 1871 census) on the 1881 schedule, so perhaps both had died, but by then he would have been 17 so perhaps he was away at school in 1881, or working elsewhere.

In the 1881 census the family appears to have been reduced to Samuel and his daughter, now aged 13. Ellen had been born in Muswell Hill and was still at school. Living with them was a nephew, George Layard. aged 24, unmarried and a BA law student, born in Clifton, Bristol. This is the difficulty with restricted records. A census form filled in on a spring night in 1881 gives tantalising clues, but only suggests relationships. Was the nephew the prospective heir, or a transitory visitor? How did this oddly associated trio get on? Were they three individuals living solitary lives, or were there warm ties? This is the province of a novelist, not a census enumerator.

To look after these three, there were eight servants; a butler, William Allsopp, aged 30 and his wife Sophia who was the cook, two years older; Emma Heathering, an unmarried housemaid aged 24, born in Totteridge, Herts; Sarah Badder, a domestic servant, was 22; Harriet Broomes, aged 25, was a ladies' maid born in London; while Harry Narroway, 45, was the coachman and his wife Elizabeth, aged 47 and born in Eltham, Kent, was a domestic servant. The Narroways, the coachman and his wife, are listed separately on this census return, so clearly they lived in a separate building.

In the second house on the Fortismere estate was a family worthy of Iris Murdoch. Thomas Wood, aged 79 and his wife Isobel five years younger, were the heads of an extended family covering three generations. He is listed as having no occupation, not surprising at his age, but he was 'the owner of land and coal', born in Lincoln. Isobel was born in Durham, so perhaps she had brought the coal with her as a wedding dowry. They had at least six children, one deceased and the other five still living at home. Perhaps there were more. There were two sons, one an army officer in the Royal Artillery, and the other a 'late lieutenant in the 14th Foot', living in the house with his wife, aged 36 born in Leicester. A daughter-in-law, widow of the deceased son, and her eighteen year old daughter also lived at Fortismere. As well, three unmarried daughters aged 48, 39 and 36, also lived at home. All this generation and the grand-daughter had been born in Durham. A 71 year old widowed sister-in-law also lived in the house. What possibilities for a novelist.

This complicated household was attended by seven servants, including a butler, John Juno, aged 41, born in London and the cook, Elizabeth Carswell, aged 36 and unmarried. There were two women general servants of 28 and 38, both born in Gloucestershire, and a twenty year old kitchen maid, born in Salop. Two young brothers, aged 18 and 17 were footman and groom. As they also came from Gloucestershire, the servants may have recruited each other whenever the opportunity arose to bring yet another person from the depressed countryside to booming London. The influx at this period was enormous.

There is no certainty about who lived in Fortismere in 1851, but from the size of his establishment, one candidate must be Edward Morgan, a stockbroker of 43, with his wife Katherine, aged 42 and their eight children from 14 to 2 years old and five domestic servants. One of these lived in a separate dwelling in the grounds, which could be the cottage occupied by the coachman Narroway and his wife in later schedules and which Collins was to put to good use fifty years later.

The Woods appeared on the census in 1881 but were not there in 1871, so who occupied the second Fortismere House before the Woods I do not know. Collins bought both houses in the last decade of the nineteenth century as his family home and began developing the estate.

The other house which W.J.Collins bought was Firs, at the top end of what is now Firs Avenue, standing in about two acres of ground which stretched down the slope. We learn about the man who lived there from a lecture on Literary Muswell Hill by Dr Draper, Headmaster of Tollington Boys' School. This was printed as a charming pamphlet, full of literary history and well worth reading today.

As mentioned earlier, the Lehmann family held a literary salon at Woodlands, in Muswell Hill Road. An anecdote about Chorley, the critic, tells us something about the owner of Firs. As Dr Draper describes it:-

> An old friend of the Lehmanns was the eccentric Chorley, literary and musical critic of the Athenaeum, who sometimes, dining at their house, behaved as if the dinner was of his own choosing and the guests invited by himself. One night at Woodlands the Lehmanns gave a dinner party at which Chorley knew everybody but a Mr Brockett, who lived at the Firs in Fortis Green Road. He was particularly taken with Mr Brockett, as a host should be, even when he isn't the host, and kept sending good things round to him. "Take the champagne to Mr Brockett please," and so on. Afterwards, in the music room, Chorley informed Frederic Lehmann: "I shall certainly ask Mr Brockett again. He is very nice." [68]

John Symonds Brockett appears on the 1871 census and, from the anecdote above, we can identify the house as the Firs. He was a solicitor, aged 38, who was living with his wife Emily, three years younger, and five children aged from seven to one year old. They had six servants including a nurse and an under-nurse, a housemaid, a coachman, groom and cook. Annie Beare, a widow, was also in the household, but who she was is not clear - perhaps his wife's mother.

By 1881 Firs was occupied by Pierre Michand, a Bordeaux Shipper from France, and his wife Gabriella, also from France. On the night of the census they had two visitors, Flossie Fiveline, a schoolgirl from Camden Town and André Beyle, aged 24, who was a clerk in an office, again born in France. Perhaps he was in Michand's London office, perhaps in an office in Bordeaux. There were three servants, a cook aged 11 according to the schedule but clearly this is wrong, a parlourmaid and a housemaid.

By 1901 Michand had moved and Firs was occupied by Thomas Wilson. Either Wilson or his landlord sold the estate to Collins soon after this. As the houses in Firs Avenue were not built until 1904, Firs was probably still occupied while Collingwood Avenue and Grand Avenue were being built. Collins had installed his foreman in the cottage which had once been occupied by Narroway, the coachman in the 1881 census, and proceeded to build the Collingwood and Grand Avenues around 'Fortismere', now his family home, and its lake.

Two other houses concern us, 'Midhurst' and 'Highfield'. Collins did not buy either, but their stories are of interest and in one case affected Collins's building strategy.

In 1861, Martha Baker, unmarried, aged 31 and a 'Fund Holder', was living in Midhurst, in Fortis Green with her three children. Walter, age 11, had been born in Devonshire, Annie, aged 6, in Islington, and Arthur, aged 3, in Fortis Green. It was rather bold in those days for a woman with three children to declare herself unmarried: it shows perhaps the confidence given by being a fund holder and able to defy the neighbours. Living in the same house was a boarder, William Arnold, aged 34, a 'Stationer - master employing 5 men', who had been born in Shoreditch.

By the 1871 census William Arnold was married to Martha Baker and was living as Head of Household in Midhurst. Arnold had given his name to Arthur, the three year old in the previous census. Martha Baker's two older children (aged 21 and 16 by this time) are not listed in this 1871 return. Incidentally, Martha's age has increased from 31 to 45 in ten years so perhaps she may have pretended earlier to William that she was younger than she was. There are four more children aged from 7 to 2, and one domestic servant who had been born in Clovelly, Devon.

In 1881 the family was growing up. Arthur, now 23, was an analytical chemist, while Rose, the baby of the family, was twelve. All the children, from Mary aged 18 downwards, are listed as scholars and the large family was looked after by a single cook from Inverness. The Arnolds seem to have drawn their servants from the far corners of the British Isles.

The local directory shows that Arnold was still living in Midhurst in 1901, but the fate of the family we shall not know until 2002 when the census details are releasd.

Highfield is referred to again on page 120, in connection with the building of Grand Avenue.

W. J. Collins before he bought Fortismere

W.J.Collins had been an estate agent and builder for some time before he bought the Fortismere Estate. In January 1898 he advertised 'high-class residences near Crouch End Station, from £850 to £2000, for investment, with low ground rents, let to first-class tenants, and paying 7-8% per annum.' These were substantial prices at that period. The northern suburbs of London were developing rapidly as a result of the railway expansion. In the same issue another agent advertised 90 freehold plots at moderate prices in Muswell Hill, Archway Road, Highgate, Wood Green, Finchley, Alexandra Palace, Edgware and Barnet.

How many of the houses Collins was advertising had been built by himself, and what proportion of his business was to act as the agent for others, we do not know. With the purchase of Fortismere Estate he certainly became a large developer in his own right.

Collins and the Fortismere Estate

Collins bought the Fortismere and Firs estates and created the modern street pattern bounded by Collingwood Avenue, Firs Avenue, Grand Avenue and Fortis Green. The edges of the Fortismere and Firs Estates ran along Fortis Green, Fortis Green Road and Muswell Hill Road. The corner opposite St James's Church, now occupied by the cinema and shops, had been built earlier, as a crescent of Victorian Gothic houses, with long narrow gardens, only two of which remain. Highfield School, on the site of the present 1930s houses and telephone exchange, was still flourishing, and about to cause Collins difficulties, as it narrowed the entrance to his estate. Thus the shapes of the two old estates, Fortismere and Firs, dictated the boundaries, while the presence of the lake explains the order in which the streets had to be built. Collins wished to occupy Fortismere as a family home and enjoy the lake for as long as possible, so he built Collingwood and Grand Avenues along the borders and gradually built towards his own house. Lay-out and strategy were clear in Collins' mind from the start, but the details were to take years to complete.

Collins houses with their warm brick and generous woodwork are justly popular in Muswell Hill as they give an attractive feeling of warmth and solidity. He was building at the end of the Sweetness and Light period which had dispersed the Victorian gloom by using big windows, warm red brick and large areas of white woodwork. Collins and his sons continued to build into the Arts and Crafts period, with its stress on using 'natural' materials in a direct, honest way. This transition can be followed in the estates. Both styles allow the houses to conform to the landscape and hug it, giving most interesting roof shapes.

Classical architects always built up their foundation walls to produce a level surface, well above the surrounding site. Then they built a symmetrical house on this foundation. Collins houses have their foundations at all sorts of levels. Collins houses are rather like a group of people lying completely relaxed on uneven ground. Some lie with their feet and heads level; some have their feet lower and some have their feet

113

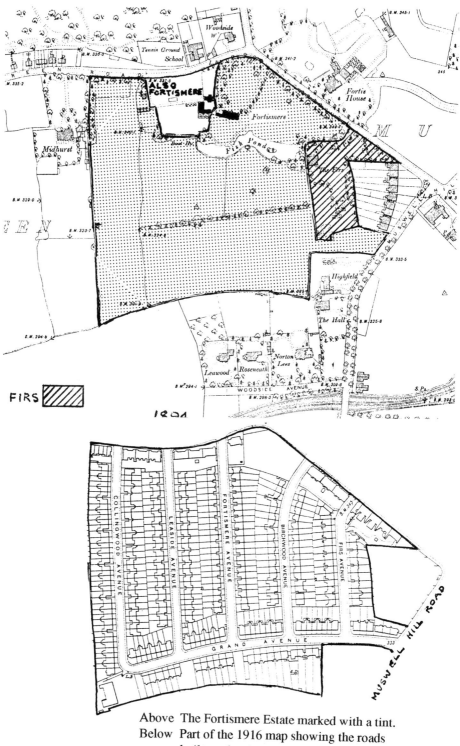

Above The Fortismere Estate marked with a tint.
Below Part of the 1916 map showing the roads
       built on the site.

114

higher than their heads. Everything depends on the slope of the ground and the way they choose to dispose themselves.

By taking advantage of the different site levels, Collins was able to reduce his excavation to a minimum. If the road is higher than the garden, then the rear of the house lowers itself to garden level. If the garden is higher, the rear rooms are reached by a few steps, or the whole front of the house is raised, with a flight of steps in the front garden and the cellar door almost level with the front garden. Each house rises or falls according to the site and this produces the varied roof lines.

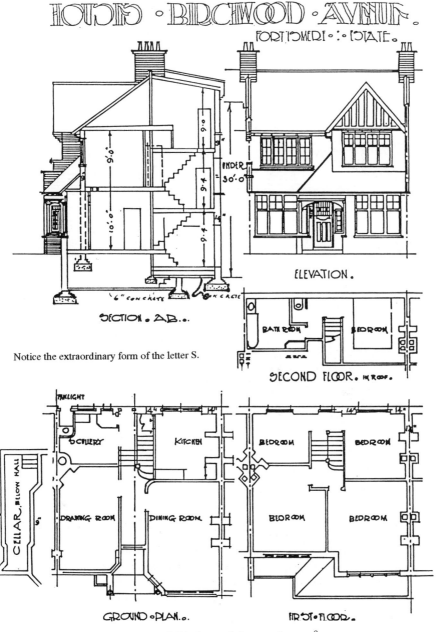

ELEVATION.

SECTION. AB.

Notice the extraordinary form of the letter S.

SECOND FLOOR. IN ROOF.

GROUND PLAN.

FIRST FLOOR.

A typical Birchwood Avenue house.[8]

115

Victorians used to build houses with back additions, a very flexible form of room arrangement which could be built with the minimum of excavation. The back addition could be above or below the rest of the house, according to slopes on the given the site.

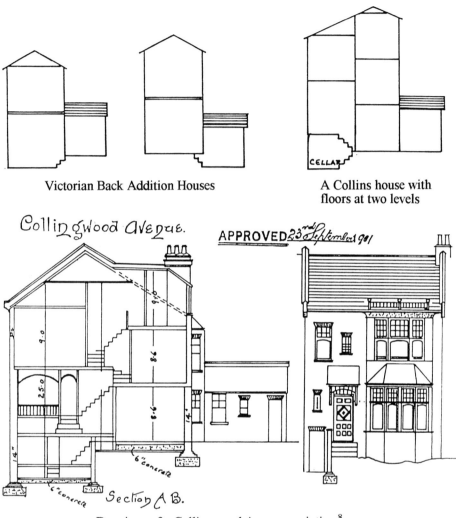

Victorian Back Addition Houses

A Collins house with floors at two levels

Collingwood Avenue.

APPROVED 23rd September 901

Section A B.

Drawings of a Collingwood Avenue variation[8]

The designs of Collins's houses were even more flexible, with the change of level within the body of the house itself.

On the previous page is a cross section of one of the houses, built as it happens near the edge of the old fish pond. In this version the coal cellar is in the centre of the house, with the access from the side entrance. The front rooms are at one level and the rear ones are half a storey lower. This has allowed the architect to add a third storey at the rear and yet make the house look quite modest from the front. By lifting the top ceilings into the roof and rounding the top corners of the attic rooms, the normal roof space has been reduced to almost nothing. Many householders have considered putting an extra room in the roof, only to find that it is impossible as Collins has forestalled them and had already filled the roof space.

This ability to vary the design from one house to the next was possible because Collins had his own experienced work force and was able to change his design to suit a particular site. The firm had a number of different designs for larger and smaller houses, single-fronted and double-fronted, two and three storey, with cellars in the centre, on one side, or across the house. On these he could play any number of variations. Almost all the design elements for the complete estate can be seen in the first few houses which he had built at the top of Collingwood Avenue by 1901, but he played tricks with these for the next ten years.

The house fronts are in a warm red brick, with many of the rear elevations in a colder white gault. Where houses turn corners, as at the road junctions along Grand Avenue, the entrance doors are in the side road, with the red brick carried round to spread the warmth.

1900 was a period of very cheap softwoods. Wonderful pine in wide boards, completely clear of knots, was flooding into the country from the Baltic and Russia. The Thames and Lee were full of boats bringing timber at prices which today would appear absurd. Cheap timber encouraged joiners to show off their skills. Elaborate porches with turned and bow-sawn decoration abound in a multitude of designs. Six of this and four of that, the patterns change as you walk down the street. White paint links them together, while the varied designs give continual interest. For any householder to paint in any other colour would spoil the effect completely, so public opinion has now made the estate into a Conservation Area, which will act as a restraint.

A series of doors with coloured or engraved glass panels.

Two typical Collins porch designs

The First Layout of the Estate

It is interesting to consider how Collins organised the development of his estate. Clearly the complete layout was planned from the start, because a well-drawn plan of the whole estate, dated November 1898 [47], shows all the roads and houses in position. It is too large to be reproduced here so a description will have to suffice. This plan shows the same estate shape as we have seen on page 114 and in the street plan opposite. Streets and house plots are all marked out with terraces of houses drawn in detail and tinted. They are not necessarily the exact houses which were finally built. In Firs Avenue, for example, several houses with fine semicircular bays are shown, but no such houses are to be found in any of today's streets. The drawing shows that the whole estate was planned from the start. The houses would be built over the years as demand allowed and finance permitted, but this plan was a confident statement of intent.[47]

On the plan is a long written statement giving details of the layout and quality of the houses such as:-

'Back fences to be in oak 4ft high and fronts of iron. Roads 40 ft wide with trees planted in the pavements. All cellars to have a double damp-proof course and be rendered outside with a vertical asphalt damp course.'

On April 7 1899 Collins agreed to all the changes which the Council had made to the plan and he was ready to start. By examining the dates of individual drawings, approval dates by the local planning authority (Hornsey Urban District Council) and local directories, the order of building the estate emerges. Some dates may be slightly inaccurate, but the order is correct. The map giving the dates of different houses shows how long it all took.

Building the Estate

The very first houses were built at the top end of Collingwood Avenue. The map shows how Collingwood Avenue was started in 1900 and not completed for several years, but before finishing Collingwood Avenue, Collins had begun on Grand, his other point of entry. One oddity about the numbering of Grand Avenue is still a puzzle, and may illustrate one of his problems. There is a gap between numbers 28 and 34, which was clearly the entrance to Roseneath, the large house in Woodside Avenue and is now the entrance to the Hospital. A second gap between 44 and 50 appears to have been the rear entrance to Leawood, then the next large house in Woodside Avenue, but why are the numbers missing? Did houses ever fill the gap? Did Nos 30, 32, 46 and 48 ever exist? Did Collins hope to buy these gaps and build across? According to the records the houses were not bombed and do not appear in any street directory I have seen. Perhaps some local resident may know. The original plan, mentioned earlier, numbered the south side of Grand Avenue from 10 - 60 with no gaps. Presumably he hoped to override the objections of the Woodside Avenue house owners and build across? We may never know.

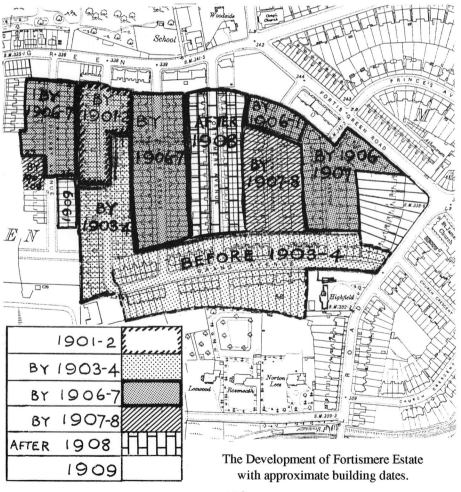

1901-2	
BY 1903-4	
BY 1906-7	
BY 1907-8	
AFTER 1908	
1909	

The Development of Fortismere Estate
with approximate building dates.

119

A bigger problem was his entrance to the estate from Muswell Hill Road where Highfield, now a school run by Frederick Newcombe MA, blocked his way. Collins could start roads anywhere he liked from Fortis Green, but access from Muswell Hill Road was very restricted. On one side was Highfield School and on the other was a crescent of houses built in the 1860s. By the 1890s these were still new, with a long life before them, so he could not buy and demolish. However he may have had some hopes of demolishing Highfield, on the opposite side of his narrow entrance.

There is a small plan dated 23rd Dec. 1901, in the RIBA collection (see below). It shows the Highfield site at the top of Muswell Rise, where new houses and the Telephone Exchange now stand. The old house is marked for demolition and the building line agrees with the one used on the opposite side of Grand Avenue. By 1901 Collins was building in Collingwood Avenue and actively planning Grand Avenue. It would have made his life easier if he could have bought the Highfield site to create a wide entrance from Muswell Hill Road, so the plan may easily be his.

The school must have been too flourishing a concern to have considered selling: perhaps the Head thought that Collins's houses would be a good recruiting area for his school and looked forward to more pupils. In any case, the school was not sold and Collins had to slip his entrance in beside the Highfield grounds, with room for a road and only one row of houses. Further along Grand Avenue, beyond Highfield, the site widened out, allowing Collins to start building on both sides of the road. Thus the entrance to Grand Avenue had houses on one side only and even this was possible only by giving the first three houses very short back gardens. As a result, the numbering pattern runs with odds and evens from 1 to 9 on the north side of Grand Avenue. Number 9 is a couple of houses past Firs Avenue. Only then do No 10 and the rest of the even numbers move to the south side, with the odd numbers continuing on the north.

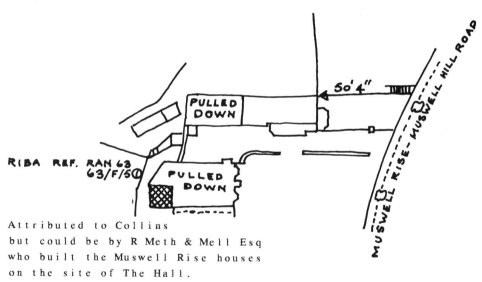

Sketch made from the 1901 plan of the Highfield School site.[57]

120

Numbers 1 to 7 Grand Avenue must have been Collins' shop window, as they were the first houses to be seen when approaching the estate from Highgate. He made them as big and impressive as he could, giving Number 1 an attractive semi-circular bay to make up for its lack of a back garden. Number 3 became Collins's estate office and was no doubt a show house.

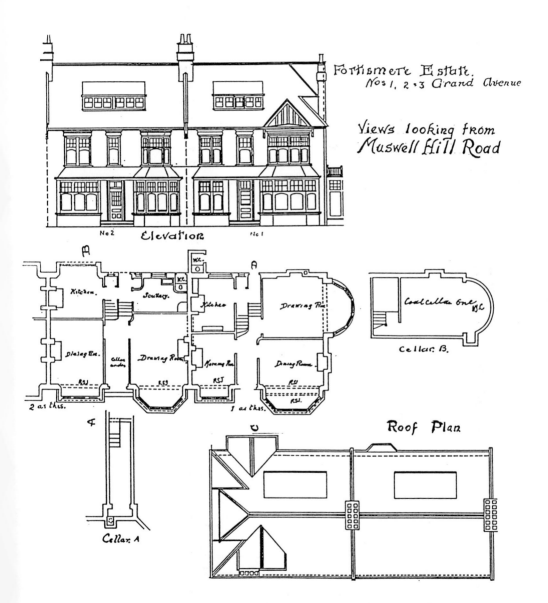

Plans and elevations of the first Grand Avenue houses[8]

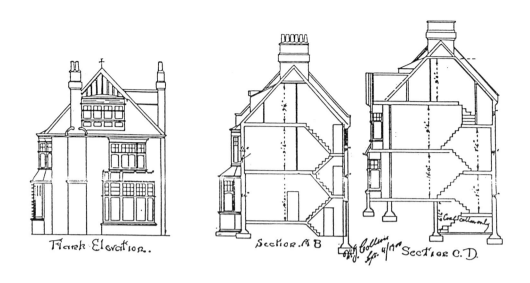

Flank Elevation.

Section. AB

H. J. Collins &c. 4/"

Section C. D.

Section through No. 1   Section through Nos .

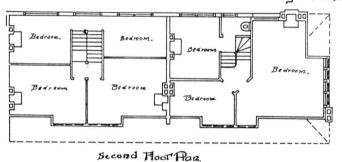

Second Floor Plan.

Bedroom.   Bedroom.   Bedroom.   Bedroom.

Bedroom   Bedroom   Bedroom.

Bedroom   Bath R   W.C.   Bedroom   Bedroom.

Bedroom.   Bedroom   Bedroom   Bath Loo   Bedroom.

Fortismere Estate
Nos 1, 2 +3 Grand Ave

First Floor Plan.

Plans and elevations of the first Grand Avenue houses[8]

122

GRAND AVENUE, c.1905

By 1903-4 Grand Avenue was complete, with the corners neatly turned ready for Firs, Birchwood, Fortismere and Leaside Avenues to be built later, although no house had been started in any of these roads. Collins had outlined his estate by building Collingwood and Grand Avenues and had reserved the whole of the valuable Fortis Green and Fortis Green Road frontages for flats and shops. Some of the flats were not to be built for more than twenty years.

Next Collins began to close in from both sides towards Fortismere House, where he was living with his family. The original Firs House was still occupied by Thomas Wilson until at least 1901, but by 1906-7 Firs Avenue, the shops and flats of Firs Parade, and the first few houses of Birchwood Avenue had all been built. In the same period, Leaside Avenue, together with Leaside and Midhurst Mansions, had been completed. Collins was finally approaching Fortismere House itself.

Fortismere must have been an ideal place to bring up a growing family and he put his bailiff, Thomas Batten, in Fortismere Cottage, the building which had been occupied by the coachman Narroway in 1881. Collins was now living comfortably in a large house with his estate rising around him.

Fortismere was not listed in the 1901 Street Directory, so we do not know how he used the second Fortismere house. He may have let it, or used it as offices, workshops and stores, only demolishing both houses at the last moment, in perhaps 1909.

It is worth breaking off here to discuss the Collins family as it shows how a Victorian/Edwardian father planned for his business to be continued.

The Collins Family

W.J.Collins' father was a successful bookbinder who founded Benjamin Collins and Sons, of London. Several of his sons entered the business, but William Jeffries Collins (1856 - 1939) became a speculative builder who bought land in the districts being opened up by the new railway lines. There he built houses for the new commuters, some for sale but most for renting.

He married Mary Martin, music teacher, and they had six children, Ada, William (Billy), Herbert, Ethel, Martyn and Ralph. They lived in Fortismere, rowed on the lake and skated on it in icy weather. Indeed the lake had become a centre for ice-skating events after Crouch Hall, the large house in Crouch End which had had a famous skating lake, was demolished in the 1880s. Billy and Herbert went to Mill Hill School, but at the age of fifteen, instead of continuing their education, they were both taken away from school and put to work on the Fortismere Estate. Billy left at Christmas 1898 and Herbert in July 1900.

They worked as carpenters alongside the men, learning in the traditional craft apprentice manner. In 1903 and 1904, Herbert, the younger son, obtained City and Guilds certificates in carpentry and brickwork, as no doubt Billy had done before him, and passed a Board of Education building construction examination at South Kensington. Thus the boys learnt to handle materials at a period of good craftsmanship and to

The Collins Family, probably at Rookfield[14]

observe all types of construction closely - good training for any future architect or builder. Herbert became an architect, Billy a designer, Ralph became a builder who organised a force of thirty men and did the actual building, but tragically Martyn, the youngest, was killed in Flanders during the First World War.

Herbert attended evening classes in architecture between 1914 and 1919 at the British Museum, the Victoria and Albert Museum, and the Central School of Arts and Crafts. Herbert also studied part-time at the Architectural Association. By the time he had completed three years there he was an experienced builder, aged thirty-four, and trading under the name of Herbert and Co.

Having passed the Society of Architects Examination he was elected a Member of the Society on 1 September, 1921. On the Society of Architects and the Royal Institute of British Architects merging, in 1925, he automatically became an Associate of the RIBA.[14,48] In his statement supporting his application to become a Fellow of RIBA, in 1940, he listed his work. This included various estates in Southampton, private houses in Hampshire and Sussex, and Village Halls in Chichester, Littlehampton, and Wood Green Village, near Fordingbridge. This concentration of village halls seems to reflect his early work at Letchworth and his friendship with Ebenezer Howard and Raymond Unwin, the town planners.

Thus from as early as 1900, the boys were exposed to other influences besides their father and his workmen. The latter, who had all learnt their skills at the end of the Victorian period, were used to building in the Queen Anne style. By the time the boys were learning, Parker and Unwin, Voysey, Baillie Scott, and Lutyens, were all building in Hampstead Garden Suburb and Herbert Collins was much influenced by them. Herbert also worked for about eighteen months on the early stages of Welwyn Garden City and was always interested thereafter in the garden city concept. In 1906 he started building the west side of Rookfield Avenue, using roughcast walls, large gables, and corner windows with small panes. The same influence can be seen in Fortismere Avenue, which is built in a completely different style from nearby Leaside and Birchwood Avenues.

Arts and Crafts houses in Fortismere Avenue, 1907.

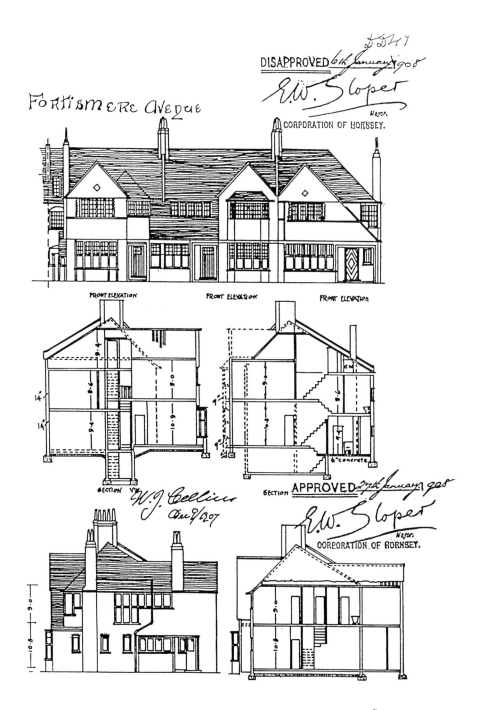

FORTISMERE AVENUE

DISAPPROVED 6th January 1908
£547
E.W. Sloper
Mayor.
CORPORATION OF HORNSEY.

FRONT ELEVATION   FRONT ELEVATION   FRONT ELEVATION

SECTION   W.J. Collins
Dec 9/1907

SECTION   APPROVED 27th January 1908
E.W. Sloper
Mayor.
CORPORATION OF HORNSEY.

Arts and Crafts houses in Fortismere Avenue, 1907.[8]

Collins had gradually brought his sons into the business. Drawings began to be signed Collins and Sons. Herbert Collins set up Herbert and Company; Billy later set up his own company to complete Rookfield Estate, while Ralph had his own building firm.

Fairport, the Arts and Crafts house at the corner of
Fortis Green and Fortismere Avenue, 1908.

The drawing of the large house at the corner of Fortis Green and Fortismere Avenue, dated 1908, is signed W.J.C & Sons and J.D.R.Mouro. It is a fine building in roughcast, with hanging tiles, square corner windows on brackets, a huge roof in rich hand-made tiles and tall chimneys. One could be in Letchworth, or Welwyn Garden City, or in large grounds in Buckinghamshire.

When Birchwood and Leaside Avenues had been completed, Fortismere House was demolished and the whole family moved to Rookfield, the large house on the Rookfield Estate, halfway down Muswell Hill, where they continued to live as they had lived in Fortismere House, but this time with the Rookfield Estate houses rising around them.

Arts and Crafts houses in Fortismere Avenue, 1907.

Having demolished Fortismere, Collins had to deal with the lake. He had built Leaside and Firs Avenues up to the two ends of the lake and had probably started to fill it with the spoil from their foundations. A detailed section drawing still exists, dated Oct 1st 1909, of the 'private street works' in Fortismere Avenue. It shows 9 inch surface and sewage pipes running down the centre of the road to Grand Avenue. No doubt the last of the lake water was directed into them.[47]

Much of Fortismere Avenue was bomb damaged in the 1939-45 War, as we shall see, but both ends of the road were untouched. Nos. 4 and 6 appear to be as Herbert Collins built them, apart from new machine-made roof tiles, while right at the other end of the road, No 48 is completely unaltered. They are typical Arts and Crafts houses, completely different from the houses in the roads on either side. The photograph below and the drawing at the bottom of the previous page appear to be identical, but the drawing is of Fortismere Avenue and the photograph is of Rookfield Avenue. Late Fortismere Estate houses were being repeated in Rookfield Avenue, as the builders moved on from one estate to the next. Herbert Collins, who designed and built both terraces, lived in No 31 Rookfield Avenue, the first house on the left in the photograph.

Rookfield Avenue, designed and built by Herbert Collins,
1906-1911

The Collins Flats in Fortis Green

The Fortis Green and Fortis Green Road flats present a history of flat building from about 1906 to the 1930s. Children have always called Leaside Mansions 'The Firemen's Flats' because of the plaster helmets still over the entrance doors. The shields bear the initials LM, for Leaside Mansions, with a fireman's helmet above, while behind are crossed flags and firemen's axes with sword-hilt handles.

Birchwood Mansions and the other blocks are fine examples of Arts and Crafts work. About 1925 came Woodside Mansions and Fortis Court which reflect the buildings Lutyens was putting up at the same time, in warm orange brick with a sandy mortar. Longridges, facing the end of Midhurst Avenue, and Twyford Court, at the end of Twyford Avenue, take us right up to the Second World War. The same orange brick was used for the small houses at the top of Eastern Road, built on the Nursery grounds. This brick was a fingerprint of Billy Collins at this period.

128

Crest from the Firemen's Flats,
Fortis Green

Rookfield Estate

This book does not pretend to consider Rookfield Estate in depth. Readers should refer to the excellent article by Anne Trevett in the Hornsey Historical Bulletin, 1988[19],but the transition from Fortismere Estate to Rookfield is relevant. Rookfield contains a history of the family building styles. At the corner of Muswell Hill and Cascade Avenue is a house which turns the corner exactly as the houses in Grand Avenue turn into Firs Avenue. They are typical of W.J.Collins, the father.

The west side of Cascade Avenue, built by Herbert Collins, copies the Fortismere Avenue houses which he had also built. These houses have the projecting party walls which were then required by the building regulations. The rules about party walls were later relaxed and the 1913 drawings by Herbert and Co, on the next page, show the effect. The party walls no longer project and the roof is one long sweep, instead of a set of separate slices.

William J. Collins, the father, lived in Rookfield until he left in 1911 to develop his Southampton estates. Then Rookfield, the old house on the estate, was demolished in its turn. In 1912, Billy Collins formed Rookfield Garden Village Ltd to complete the estate. Billy continued to build in Muswell Hill and North London for the rest of his life, while Herbert later took over the Southampton developments.

The last block of houses in Cascade Avenue, on the south side nearest to Muswell Hill, was not built until 1936 because it was a very awkward site and so left to the last. Because of the steep slope, the houses had to be built on heavy steel girders, which incidentally provided very useful air raid shelters during the War. The girders are not obvious, of course, so these appear to be typical Billy Collins houses, with their arched tunnels between each pair of houses, something never seen in the Fortismere Estate. Herbert also used tunnel-backs when he went to Southampton. In these houses the upper floors spread over the tunnels, giving space for an extra bedroom in alternate houses. Thus four-bedroom and three-bedroom houses alternate down the road.

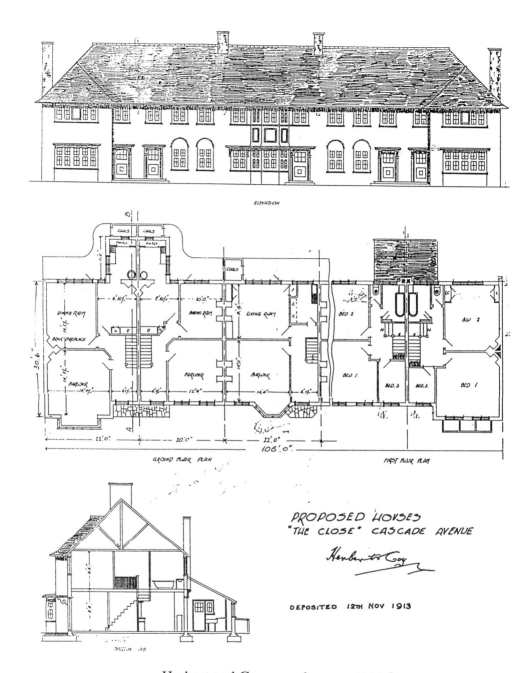

ELEVATION

GROUND FLOOR PLAN

FIRST FLOOR PLAN

PROPOSED HOUSES
"THE CLOSE" CASCADE AVENUE

Herbert & Cox

DEPOSITED 12TH NOV 1913

Herbert and Company houses, 1913.[8]

With the change in the Building Regulations the
projecting party walls have disappeared.

130

Collins' Upton Farm Estate

Upton Farm Estate runs down Muswell Hill Road from St James's Church towards Cranley Gardens and includes Church Crescent, with its views over the Parkland Walk. When W. J. Collins bought land from the Railway Company, shown as part of Lot 3 at the Upton Farm sale, he had the chance to develop one of the best views in London. Perched on the top of the hill, with the valley of the Thames spread out before him, he decided to build rather larger houses than on the Fortismere Estate. Only one side of Church Crescent would look over the valley and the view was so attractive and so marketable, that he decided to put as many houses as possible on this side. Thus the houses with the view are single-fronted, while the rest of the houses, to make up for the loss of the view, are double-fronted.

When the original steam railway was made, the company had built round the contour of the hill, producing quite a steep escarpment, so when the railway company let the land for housing, it kept control of a wide swathe of land between the line and the houses, to ensure that there should be no claims against it later for subsidence. The company let this land to the tenants at five shillings a year, providing each of them with an allotment at the end of the garden. When the railway was closed, the land was offered for sale to the householders, many of whom bought their share, to enjoy large gardens and protect the view.

Had the War come a year later, in 1940 instead of 1939, electrification of the line,

Collins' original drawing

131

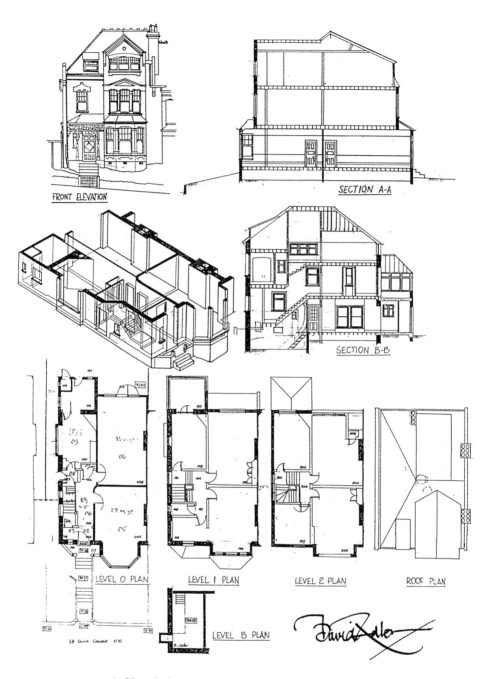

FRONT ELEVATION

SECTION A-A

SECTION B-B

LEVEL 0 PLAN

LEVEL 1 PLAN

LEVEL 2 PLAN

ROOF PLAN

LEVEL B PLAN

A Church Crescent house, built on Upton Farm land.
Drawings by David Adler

which was already well in hand, would have been completed and we should now have a flourishing extension to the Northern Line Underground system right to the Alexandra Palace. In fact, electrification was abandoned at the start of the War and never resumed. When, in 1957, the steam line had become uneconomical, the railway was closed. The line became the Parkland Walk, a much loved amenity, but perhaps some day this will become a light railway again. However, we must return to Collins.

Church Crescent houses are not only larger than most of the Fortismere Estate ones, taller, with large rooms and billiard rooms, but are in a heavier design, with echoes of Victorian Gothic and often in a darker brick. Porches have double-stepped roofs, not used elsewhere by Collins, so far as I know: there are decorative basket-weave airbricks, and many other interesting features. Houses have encaustic tiled halls, handsome wooden staircases and the rooms, as is usual in a Collins house, are built well into the roof space. Every inch of the house can be used.

The first tenants were offered gas or electricity, but not both. Thus some houses were fitted with concealed gas pipes, while others had concealed electric cables. When the second service was added later, it involved unsightly surface conduits and only more recently, as houses have been modernised, have both gas and electricity supplies been hidden. Houses had speaking tubes from the sitting room, dining room and two main bedrooms, to the kitchen. These were lead pipes with speaking trumpets at both ends and look most strange today, fossilized in the walls, waiting to summon non-existent servants. They sum up enormous social changes.

This was a prosperous development for substantial people, not so well off as the magnates in Edmondson's huge Queen's Avenue houses, but for managers of City firms and professional people. The houses differ too from the Rookfield ones, which are modelled on garden suburbs for those who wished to live in a country village, yet still be on the railway line. Queen's Avenue was for top hats and spats, Church Crescent was for bowlers, while Rookfield was for berets and sandals.

It is interesting to see the scale at which Collins worked. At one period he had the Fortismere, Upton Farm and Rookfield Estates all in hand at the same time, besides some smaller developments elsewhere. With this work well forward, he was able to leave Rookfield Estate in the hands of his sons and go to Southampton, where he was building yet more estates.

William 'Billy' Collins

In December 1975, Billy Collins, the oldest son of the founder of the firm, was in his early nineties. His memories went back to a completely different Muswell Hill, before the present St James's Church was built, in 1901. He gave an interview recalling his past and the part his family had played in building Muswell Hill to David Jones, who was living in one of the many Collins houses. I am grateful to David Jones for permission to print the interview which has not been published before.

William Brannan Collins, 'Billy', had spent most of his life transforming Muswell Hill, but he and his brother had been encouraged by their father to travel when young to gain experience. Herbert Collins spent holidays in Scandinavia and other parts of Europe and in 1910 visited South Africa.[14] Billy worked for a time in an architect's office in America before returning to the family firm. He was responsible for designing and building hundreds of Muswell Hill houses including among others, Rookfield Close in 1906, now part of a conservation area, and Twyford Estate and flats in Fortis Green. He also built neo-Georgian houses in Southway, Totteridge.

Until the age of 91 he used to drive to his office, but in the later years his health had been failing. He had been looked after by a housekeeper after his wife died in 1970. The couple had no children.[61]

The house in Sheldon Avenue, Highgate, where he had lived from 1934 with his wife, was very large and silent, so that when the door was opened by the housekeeper one could hear the clocks ticking. Billy Collins gave the appearance of living a very orderly and methodical life in a house with everything in its correct place. He wore a suit, which for a man at ease in his own home was not entirely necessary. Clearly he was very concerned with visual detail which became evident when he became animated about the roof details of his great interest, the Rookfield Estate. He was also a painter and a member of the Highgate Art Club.

The interview, written up immediately afterwards but not published before, took place in the afternoon in his large drawing room, which faced west.

Notes on a meeting with William Brannan Collins, by David Jones.

Billy Collins began, "I was fifteen when I used to lean over the fence on what is now Fortis Green Road watching the work that was going on. The work at Muswell Hill must have started around 1898-1900. It was more or less all finished by the the First World War, or actually even earlier, about 1910.

My father owned the Fortismere estate and some land north of Fortis Green where Tyyford Court and Long Ridges now stand. He also bought the land where Church Crescent is. Most of the rest of the area was developed by Edmondson.

My father built the houses in the Fortis estate - Grand, Birchwood, Firs and so on. They were mostly leasehold but sometimes they were let when he couldn't sell them. But in Church Crescent the ground rents were sold to the Imperial Property Investment

Company, something he didn't do usually. He must have needed the money or something I suppose.

The trees I think were planted by the Council. The owners probably paid extra and it was added in with the road-making which was then about £1 a foot frontage. The cost of the trees was added to that.

Straddling the Fortis estate was a fish pond running from Birchwood through Fortismere Avenue to Leaside. I remember once over lunch hanging my line in and catching two perch on one hook. One had eaten the other, or tried to. The pond was full of perch. There were numerous streams and ditches in what must have been meadow land. It was drained into the sewers at the time of building.

Below the fishpond, between it and the area of Grand Avenue was a paddock. My father was very keen on horses and he had a lot of jumps erected in that area. The pond was on the brow of the slope, I don't know quite where the water was coming from but it must have been draining in from somewhere.

The shopping centre was all built by Edmondsons except I think for one parade, the one on the south east corner of the roundabout. I can't remember who built that but it wasn't Edmondson. My father didn't do any of the shops except a row at the end of Collingwood Avenue and the row of shops from Firs Avenue to the corner. Our offices are in that row now [1975].

The man who built the United Reform Church in the Broadway was Baines. He built a lot of non-conformist churches in the area. They all look a bit like wedding cakes but they are definitely better than some. Baines also built the Baptist Church, or rather he designed it. He was the architect. That was built at the same time as the shopping centre was being built, both churches were. It must have been about 1905.

Baines also built the Ferme Park Church in Crouch End. That's gone now, but when I was a youth I remember being taken down there and meeting him. He was wearing the regulation frockcoat, silk hat and probably a monocle. I remember being right up the roof of the church and looking down into the body of the church as the work was going on.

Of course the best church is the one at the top end of Queens Avenue, on the corner with Tetherdown. That was designed by Morley Horder. I liked his work. He always wore a velvet jacket and a monocle.

St James's is a fine landmark. Of course there was a church there before the present one. That was smaller and had a wooden spire but it's gone now. I like the vicarage that was built soon after the church.

The building of Dukes Avenue I think followed on immediately after the building of the centre of the Broadway. There was no interval. Edmondson's, I think, were involved down there as they were in Hillfield Park and Hillfield Gardens.

At the time the building was going on in houses in Grand Avenue, the single fronted ones were sold for about £450 leasehold. The people who bought them were middle class but all sorts. I suppose they all had a living-in maid. I married in 1929 and we had a living-in maid for a long time - for five or six years. We came here in 1934 and had two living-in maids for some years.

My father did a lot of building in Crouch End, Crouch Hill and Stroud Green as well as Muswell Hill. I did the Fortis Court in 1925 and three blocks in Fortis Green between 1930 and 1932. These include the Twyford and Long Ridges blocks. I wouldn't call myself an architect because I am not a registered architect. I am a designer but have always been interested in architecture. I also did twelve houses on the east side of Eastern Road, in Fortis Green. They are in a style looking like early 19th Century, with hipped gables, not vertical gables.

In the Rookfield Estate I did Cranmer Way, Rookfield Avenue (east side), a lot of Cascade Avenue and Rookfield Close. In those days you always had to keep the ugly effect of rows and rows of parapet walls in mind. Under the by-laws party walls had to extend through the roof so it projected at least a foot above the tiles from the front to the back. You always were trying to draw the eye away from parapet walls with lots of gables and so forth. I tried to get the council to let me do the Rookfield Estate without party walls but they told me I would need a special Act of Parliament as was needed for Hampstead Garden Suburb. But they did accept gables in one place with a solid concrete block along the top of the gable instead.

In a lot of Victorian and Edwardian houses, the front sitting rooms are wider than the rooms at the back and the corners were rounded off instead of having a square angle. In Church Crescent my father built the houses and he thought I should learn how to use some of the carpenters' tools and I had to fix the chair rails around the corners and elsewhere.

Queens Avenue was built by Edmondsons, and Kings Avenue by Pappin. My father, W.J.Collins did Grand and Collingwood and that estate was done in four years, or maybe it was five. The front doors probably all came from Clapton Joinery Works although they didn't do the stained glass or the leaded lights. They were bought in.

21 Sheldon Avenue N6, 15 December 1975.

Billy Collins died only eighteen months after this interview and a short obituary was published in the Finchley Press on 26 June, 1977.[73]

Bond & White's

As one goes from house to house in a Collins estate one is always among familiar things, yet each house has its surprise. The same mouldings, carving and fretted panels have been seen in other houses. No house is quite the same shape as its neighbours, yet some parts may be identical, for these are real factory-made houses. In the 1960s the government announced that a revolution had struck the building industry: for the first time houses would be built in factories and merely erected on the site. A howl of laughter went up from architectural historians. What then had the Victorians and Edwardians been doing all this time? They had been building houses in factories a century before.

In 1900 there were thick pattern books for every side of the building industry. Joinery designs, flooring blocks, ironmongery, stained glass and cast-iron catalogues were on every building merchant's shelves. Macfarlane's Castings, Glasgow, who built for

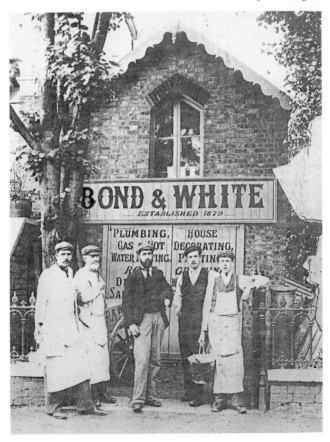

Bond & White's on the site of 19 Barnard Hill, 1901-1914
Hornsey Historical Bulletin No 20.[7]

"CLOISONNE GLASS"

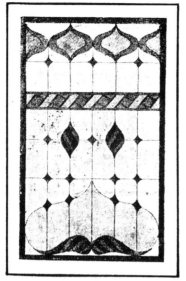

A decorative material transparent and opaque.

The CLOISONNE GLASS CO.

9F Berners St. Oxford St. London W.

prices from 3/- per square foot

1906

Typical advertisements taken from one issue of The Builder in 1906.

FLOORING BLOCKS.

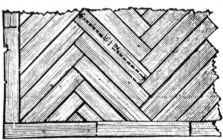

Out of 17½"×3"×3" best yellow deal, planed all round 12s. 9d. per 100; 17½"×3"×2" ditto, 8s. 3d. per 100 17½"×3"×1½" ditto, 6s. 9d. per 100.

Also in Pitch Pine. Prices on application.

Figured Wainscot Flooring with above special joint to conceal nails at following very low prices :—
1½ × 4" Wainscot Oak   at 56s. 9d. per square.
1 × 4"   ditto   at 45s. 0d.   ,,
1½ × 4" Pitch Pine   at 27s. 0d.   ,,
1 × 4"   ditto   at 22s. 9d.   ,,
These prices do not include desiccation.

IMPORTANT—

VIGERS BROS., Timber Merchants,
Head Office :—67 & 68 KING WILLIAM STREET, E.C.
Telephone, 601 and 602 Avenue

THE WOOD CARVING CO.
WINDSOR ST., Ltd.
BIRMINGHAM.
BALUSTERS, NEWELS, OVERDOORS, and CARVING of every description.

WRITE FOR ILLUSTRATED LIST.

Typical advertisements taken from one issue of The Builder in 1906.

138

everyone, had a two volume catalogue bound in heavy green boards and totalling 698 pages full of illustrations of castings of railings, stoves, fireplaces, cast-iron floor panels, staircases, street lanterns, greenhouses, railway stations, shop fronts. It appeared that the whole world could be made of cast-iron. It was the ideal Victorian material, fireproof, cheap and everlasting. Collins's houses were full of cast iron. There are cast iron fireplaces, kitchen ranges, gutterings, coal-hole covers and baths. There is even a story of an iron founder who made himself a cast iron bowler hat.

Collins' joinery too came from catalogues. The Wood Carving Company's advertisement shows what a variety was available. Grotesque as it looks, with all the designs jammed together on one short stairway, pieces of carving similar to these can be found in all the Collins houses. When the foreman went along to Bond & White's he could select any of a dozen types of moulding, banisters or newel posts. The same barley--twist half-round moulding can be found in every street. If the yard had run out of one design the foreman took another. There are houses where the design of banister changes from one floor to the next, when supplies of the original pattern had run out.

Doors were made in vast numbers, especially in the vast Canadian factories, and shipped to Britain. This was a cut-throat business. At the turn of the century, Russian timber was available in Britain at half the price of Canadian and yet Canadian joinery undercut British because of their scale of production and the proximity to the forests. However, mass production did not make Collins' houses boring. Hall doors may have been in a few familiar patterns, but the varied glass panels made each door unique. With stained glass from three shillings per square foot, a door could be made glorious for a pound.

Behind all the catalogues were extraordinary worlds of which we ordinary mortals knew nothing. Worlds of the experts who were familiar with a hundred types of brick, a thousand tiles, and house fittings of every shape: where men spent their lives making terra-cotta panels for buildings designed to last for ever: men who turned and polished granite pillars to decorate the outsides of pubs, or blew glass in rainbow colours. The men looked like other people; smoked cigarettes and groused about the weather, but then they turned round and did astonishing things.

As a young boy, standing at Bond & White's counter, waitng to buy some four inch nails, a man became lyrical about his trade. He was a glass-worker, a maker of stained glass windows, with watering eyes strained by peering at white-hot glass, suddenly talking excitedly about his work.

'You lift a large gathering of molten glass from the furnace on a steel blowpipe and twirl it so that it becomes a round, heavy ball. You blow to start the bubble and then put it in a long mould and blow very hard so that it becomes a long bottle, red, glowing, soft as butter. You cut off the pasty glass at top and bottom with huge scissors and shear down the tube from one end to the other. Flatten it out like a piece of pastry and let it fall on a flat bed by its own weight, to cool. Tap it down and let it flow flat.

'You never know what you will achieve. Colour and life vary from piece to piece - a little more cobalt, a little more iron in the furnace, give a different colour, a different shade. Thicker, thinner, the richness changes. On a dull day you can't even guess the colour. You've worked all morning and don't know if your work is any good. I can remember day after day of dull, overcast skies with the new glass squares piling up on the viewing rack and us not knowing if the colours were good or bad. Electric light's no use. You need clear, bright sunlight to see the colours. Not in the morning, not in the evening. Mid-day, The viewing rack stands against the light and then, when the sun comes out and the light is strong with every colour in the spectrum, the glass will glow. That is when you can select your colours for the different parts of the design. All the work is controlled by the sun. In the morning you blow new glass, or cut pieces you have selected earlier, but when the sun comes out you spend all your time searching for the perfect piece."

In all seriousness, as if I had been a fourteenth century apprentice learning his art in a great cathedral instead of a mere schoolboy, he said,

"Never start to make a St George until you have found the red for the dragon's eye. St George deserves something worth fighting. It must be a real dragon, dangerous and terrifying, so everything depends on the eye. The eye is the centre of the whole window, so it must glow like the brightest fire. You must find that perfect, fierce red."

Later, when I visited stained-glass studios, I was fascinated by the order and calm. Nobody moves quickly in the presence of glass. Everything is deliberate, watchful, alert for the finest splinter which might cut a finger, or cause a sudden, unexpected break in this treacherous material. Pieces of glass of a hundred colours in pigeon holes; large windows to give a flood of light; a centre table covered in green baize and part-cut glass with light flashing along its edges; a brush and pan to sweep the baize again and again to remove splinters. Men and women working steadily, measuring and marking with care and considering yet again before making a cut, Then the gentle tapping below the cut with the head of the cutting wheel to start the crack and the splitting of the glass. Straight lines, circles, curves, all shapes were possible to these artists.

Collins' houses were full of coloured and stained glass, while some of the larger ones had painted glass as opposed to stained, painted with flowers and birds as they had been in Victorian times. Some front doors were in full-blown Art Nouveau, which did not come into fashion until forty years later. This did not mean that the style had changed in the time it took to move from one door to the next, but that old designs accumulated in builders' stores and these happened to be the designs available from stock at the suppliers. In one house there is a complete mixture of cast-iron fireplaces. Delicate Victorian designs, almost Regency in feeling, one with Egyptian designs direct from the French Empire, another in swirling Art Nouveau. It all depended on the stock which Bond & White's held that day.

Internal doors were often of the simplest type, with panels made of unplaned wooden strips covered with Anaglypta wallpaper, which has a heavily embossed surface to imitate plasterwork, and then painted to give a rich appearance. Add to that stamped fingerplates in thin brass and one had a door which looked expensive, but was not. Many doorways had overdoor panels in fretted wood, or even in metal, while corridors were shortened by fretted screens, again selected from a catalogue.

The builder, with his team of skilled and experienced men, was able to vary houses as he chose, rather as an impressionist painter paints the same scene again and again in different colours and moods, as the light changes.

Typical catalogue items found in Collins Houses

A Victorian fireplace design

An art nouveau design

A fretted wooden over-door decoration

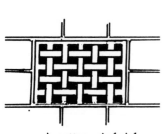

A pottery air-brick
from Cascade Avenue

A stained glass window ▶

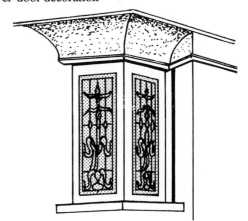

J. Edmondson & Son

Although Edmondson built some of the most impressive houses and parades of shops in Muswell Hill, little is known about him compared to Collins. The head office was in Winchmore Hill and he had other offices in Sydenham, in South London, and at Leigh-on-Sea. The Archive at Southend-on-Sea has drawings of his houses in the neighbourhood.[41]

At the turn of the century he bought The Limes and Fortis House estates to create a block of thirty acres at the top of Muswell Hill. On this he built the royal roads; Queens, Kings, and Princes Avenues. He also bought the Elms estate,North Lodge and Wellfield, in Colney Hatch Lane. On the Elms grounds he built the sweep of shops called the Exchange, on Muswell Hill roundabout and also Duke's Avenue. By combining The Elms estate and Wellfield, he was able to create Methuen Park and Wellfield Avenue. This is an impressive list.

The Limes had been the home of Mudie, the librarian, who ran the highly successful lending library which delivered books to towns and cities all over the British Empire and could make, or break a book. On any day in the year, Mudie's brass-bound book boxes were in vans and trains all over Britain and in the holds of ships on every ocean. Publishers walked in fear of Mudie's: if the library with its huge advance orders for popular novels would not stock a book, sales were doomed.

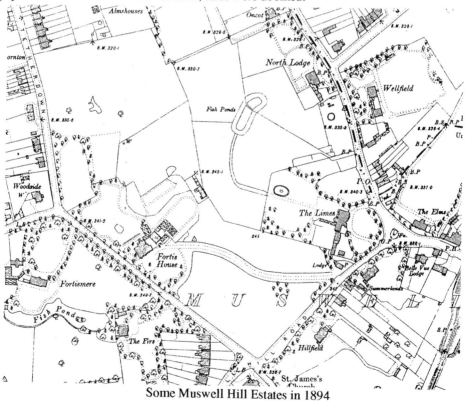

Some Muswell Hill Estates in 1894

From 1842 Mudie had run a very successful book lending business at the cut-throat price of a guinea a year (later increased to two guineas) which was far below the prices charged by rival libraries. At the same time his range was wider - poetry, history, travel, science, biography, adventure, religion and fiction, including all the latest fiction (providing it was respectable) in vast numbers from his premises in Southampton Row. The Library, which had footmen in waiting, was declared to be 'the literary shrine of fashion'.[13]

At this time novels were issued in three volumes at half-a-guinea a volume. A guinea and a half for a novel was more than a working man's weekly wage, so the subscription to Mudie's Library was a bargain. Soon he was dealing in huge quantities - 3100 copies of Silas Marner, 2000 copies of King Solomon's Mines, and 2500 copies of Macaulay's History of England - which amounted to eight tons of paper, so overwhelming the publisher's hand-barrow that Mudie had to collect it in his own horse-drawn vans. Cecil Rhodes ordered 15,000 in one lot for the Kimberly Free Library, in South Africa.

Only when the demand for a book through the lending library had fallen, was it issued by the publishers in a single volume at six shillings and later at two shillings and sixpence. By that time Mudie had already taken his profit, for anyone who wanted to keep up with the latest novels and could not afford to buy them outright, had to borrow from Mudie's. Then, when the demand slackened, he sold his stock of old titles cheaply to a willing public. 'Those once trimphant three-deckers were to be had for almost the price of waste paper'[13], and people like Gladstone flocked to buy.

But they were selected novels. Mudie advertised his library as a 'Select Library', which was a polite way of saying that he censored the type of book which he lent ruthlessly. In doing this, he shaped the nature of the Victorian novel and emasculated it.

In 1883, Mudie banned George Moore's novel 'A Modern Lover' from his list because

Mudie's book distribution office

143

two ladies wrote to him from the country objecting to the scene where a girl sat to an artist as a model for Venus. Only two years later Mudie banned 'The Mummer's Wife' and provoked a violent reaction from Moore, who never forgave him. Moore wrote:-

'At the head, therefore, of English literature sits a tradesman who considers himself qualified to decide the most delicate artistic question that may be raised, and who crushes out of sight any artistic aspiration he may deem pernicious. And yet with this vulture gnawing at their hearts writers gravely discuss the means of producing good work; let them break their bonds first.'

The argument of censorship versus freedom of expression will never end, but in Victorian times Mudie held the purse strings. Editors went through manuscripts line by line, excising any pieces likely to be frowned on by Mudie. If a Hardy heroine could not be carried in the hero's arms, but instead had to be wheeled in a wheelbarrow, it was because of the Mudie factor. If a writer complained that he could describe his characters right up to the bedroom door, but not beyond, it was Mudie who was holding the door shut. It is strange to think that the morality of Victorian England and indeed the British Empire, was controlled, not from Parliament, or Canterbury Cathedral, or Buckingham Palace, but from The Limes, Muswell Hill.

Mudie had expected that, on his death, he would be succeeded by his son, but unfortunately the son died a few months before the father. Thus on Mudie's death the Limes estate was sold for development[13]. Fragments of the brick and terracotta from the building were built into the front garden walls of the Fortismere Estate, instead of the iron railings which had been promised in Collins' original plan. The present Public Library and Barclays Bank were both built on the grounds of The Limes.

A second large house, adjoining The Limes, was Fortis House, which stood on a site which is now the corner of Princes Avenue and Fortis Green. It had once been occupied by James Renton, a member of the Stock Exchange. Part of his old house is now an annexe to the hotel in Princes Avenue. At the time of the 1861 census he was 40, married to Alice aged 24 and they had three children aged four, two and one year old. There were six servants - a cook, a housemaid, three nurses and a coachman, all but one drawn to London from distant counties.

By 1871 the Renton family had grown, There were seven children ranging from Alice, named after her mother, aged 14 to Henry born in 1870. All the servants had changed: there were two nurses, mature women of 37 and 48, a lady's maid, a butler, a cook, housemaid and kitchenmaid, but no coachman. Presumably they had dispensed with the carriage. Instead there was a governess, aged 26, so the children were being educated at home. We get a picture of a settled, well-heeled, Victorian family living in solid comfort.

Presumably the same family, or one very like it, continued to live in the house until Edmondson bought it.

The combined Limes and Fortis House sites gave Edmondson the crown of the hill and on it he built the royal roads. He cut Queens Avenue to join Fortis Green to Muswell Hill Broadway, with the widest and most impressive road in the district and here he built his largest houses. With their forty-foot frontages they are now hotels, or are each divided into several flats. Unusually for the district, most of the houses in Queens Avenue were sold outright, whereas only two houses in Collin's Church Crescent were owner occupied and the rest were rented. More than three quarters of Collins's Fortismere Estate was rented, while the Imperial Property Investment Company rented out the whole of Onslow Gardens. Clearly the managing directors went to Queens Avenue while their clerks, with steady wages but no capital, went to the smaller houses nearby.

The vast majority of Muswell Hill was built for renting, so the estate offices continued to have enormous control over the appearance of the district right up to the 1967 Leasehold Reform Act. Now there is a danger of people putting in incongruous modern windows and doors and destroying the visual unity of the area, so conservation areas are becoming more important all the time.

Round the edge of the Fortis House and Limes site Edmondson built his splendid shops. They, with their arched fronts along Fortis Green Road and square ones along Muswell Hill Road, give Muswell Hill its shape. In 1976 there was an attempt to demolish the Church at the end of Princes Avenue and redevelop. This would have torn a gaping hole in the unity of the Broadway and made further desecration easier. Fortunately this was prevented and the Broadway, despite some discordant shop fronts, is still most attractive. The campaign to save the Church is described later in a separate chapter.

On the opposite side of Colney Hatch Lane, where Duke's Avenue now runs, was Elms,[21] a large family house with extensive grounds, which was sold in 1880. The sales documents contain three plate-sized photographs of a large ivy-covered house standing on a wide terrace, with a sunken croquet lawn below and landscaped gardens with specimen

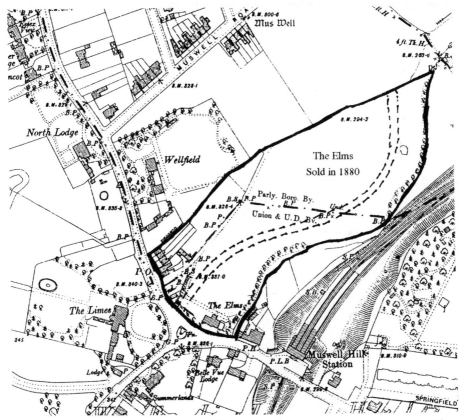

Some Muswell Hill estates as they were in 1894, including Elms estate with the proposed new road offered in the 1880 sale sketched in.

145

trees. There was a broad, gravelled walk through rose arches and, to the north, about two acres of fruit and vegetable garden.

The vendor had bought it in 1857 and was now selling it as either a house and grounds, or, with the cooperation of the Hornsey Local Board, as a building site. This Board had been established in 1867 to control the quality of the houses built in the district. They had established a Museum in Highgate and had, for example, a Catalogue of Sanitary Appliances acceptable to the Board for the guidance of builders.[43] In the Elms sale we can see the Local Board actively supporting the development of Muswell Hill.

The 1880 Sale documents[27] show an estate plan with a proposed road sketched in and say:-

'If intersected by a road which is being offered by the authorities at their own cost would form a most valuable building estate. The enjoyment of the residence with sufficient grounds could be retained without interfering with the development of the estate.'

Potential builders were being offered the inducement of a free road, which is surely most unusual.

In fact the house was to continue as a private residence for nearly another thirty years. In 1907 the Old Tollingtonians Football Club played Alleyns at The Elms.[44] This must have been about the last time the ground was used for football as Edmondson was about to buy The Elms, Wellfield and North Lodge on the opposite side of the road. He combined the first two and built Duke's Avenue, Wellfield Avenue, Elms Avenue and Methuen Park.

The houses are very similar to the larger Collins houses, in a similar red brick, white cavetto mouldings with pargetting below the gutters, and slate roofs. Some have an elaborate brick and plaster vase design built above the front doors as decoration. Panels like this, common in Maida Vale or Chelsea, are rare in Muswell Hill.

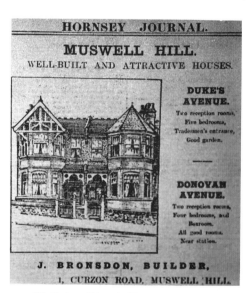

Edmondson did not build all Duke's Avenue

An Edmondson house in Duke's Avenue

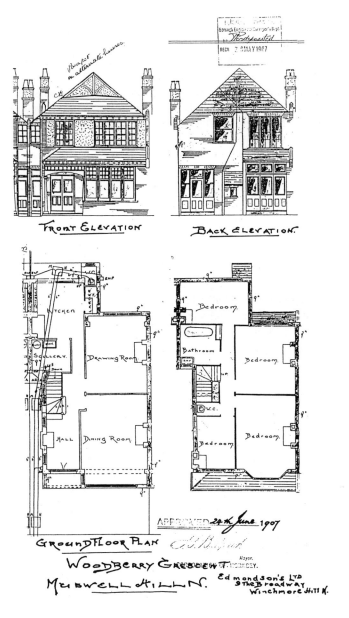

FRONT ELEVATION

BACK ELEVATION.

GROUND FLOOR PLAN

WOODBERRY CRESCENT

MUSWELL HILL N.

APPROVED 24th June 1907

Edmondson's LTD
9 The Broadway
Winchmore Hill N.

Edmondson was building all over the top of Muswell Hill and down the northern slopes on his different estates. Each site had to be developed according to its original shape, so that road patterns and garden fences often conform to old boundaries. Woodberry Crescent is a typical example of a builder cutting his road to suit his field. This simple crescent gave the maximum number of houses on the shortest road length that he could fit into the field. It produced a secluded backwater within a minute of the shops, the sort of layout that some modern town planners seem to think they invented. Collins did exactly the same thing in Church Crescent.

As usual the crescent produced some rectangular plots and some wedge-shaped ones.

The three house layouts which follow show how Edmundson solved the problem of these different shapes. Most houses were given rectangular rooms but the shapes of some of the bedrooms and one kitchen are unusual. In another kitchen the wedge is hidden ingeniously in the scullery.[6]

The houses in different roads differ in size and design but, because so much of Muswell Hill was developed by Collins and Edmondson, who were building rapidly and in a similar style, the district has a unity. This is often mentioned but imagine if they had chosen a different brick. Would Muswell Hill have looked so warm and attractive in cold white bricks or strident purple-reds? Surely a great deal of the unity was due to the pressure from the Hornsey Local Board to use attractive bricks and tiles, build generously rather than skimp, and create wide roads bordered with trees as green foils to the red houses.

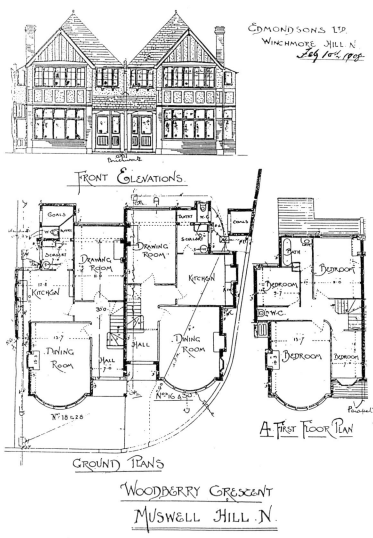

FRONT ELEVATIONS.

GROUND PLANS

A FIRST FLOOR PLAN

WOODBERRY CRESCENT
MUSWELL HILL . N

148

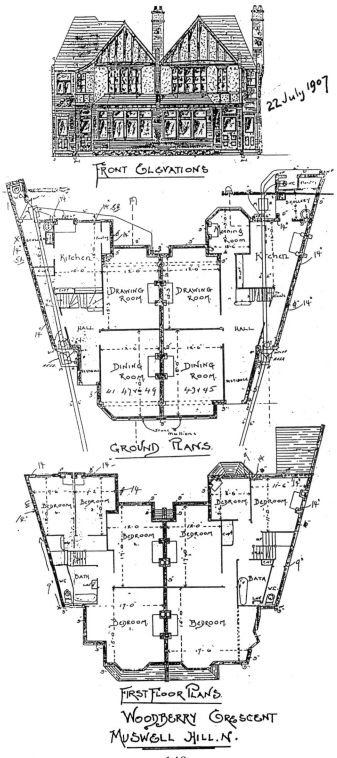

22 July 1907

FRONT ELEVATIONS

GROUND PLANS.

Kitchen

Morning Room

Kitchen

DRAWING ROOM.

DRAWING ROOM.

HALL

HALL

DINING ROOM.

DINING ROOM.

Stone mullions

FIRST FLOOR PLANS.

BEDROOM

BEDROOM

BEDROOM

BEDROOM

BEDROOM

BEDROOM

BATH

BATH

BEDROOM

BEDROOM

WOODBERRY CRESCENT
MUSWELL HILL. N.

149

Midhurst Avenue

Midhurst Avenue was developed slightly later than the Fortismere estate. William Arnold, who had appeared on the 1881 census, was still shown in the 1901 Street Directory as living at Midhurst, but we know nothing about the rest of his family. Street Directories list only the head of house, so we shall have to wait until 2002, when the 1901 census returns are released, before we learn about the others. Certainly the family did not stay in the house much longer, for by 1903 Messrs T.D.Steed and Son had submitted house plans for Nos. 1-27 and 2-36 Midhurst Avenue to Hornsey Urban District Council.

These were approved in October 1903. The designs are not unlike the Collins ones, with the same radiused corner to the dining room, drawn with an old penny. None of these draughtsmen seem to have owned a compass. Instead they used a penny, which on their scale gave about a 15" radius in the corner of a downstairs front room to make space for the stairs.

Steeds & Son, who were substantial builders, appear to have produced their own drawings, but the next houses were drawn by Chesterton & Sons, chartered surveyors, of Cheapside. Chestertons drew up the plans for a Mr W.Oley, who submitted drawings of Nos. 38 & 40 which were approved in July 1907. This was four years after Steeds & Son, so the development was slow. Later Oley built 42-54 to the same design. The fact that he built only two and then a few more suggests that he was in a small way of business.

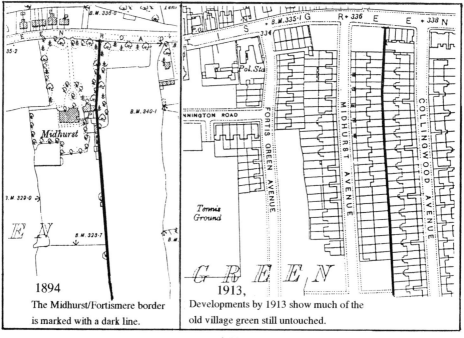

1894	1913,
The Midhurst/Fortismere border is marked with a dark line.	Developments by 1913 show much of the old village green still untouched.

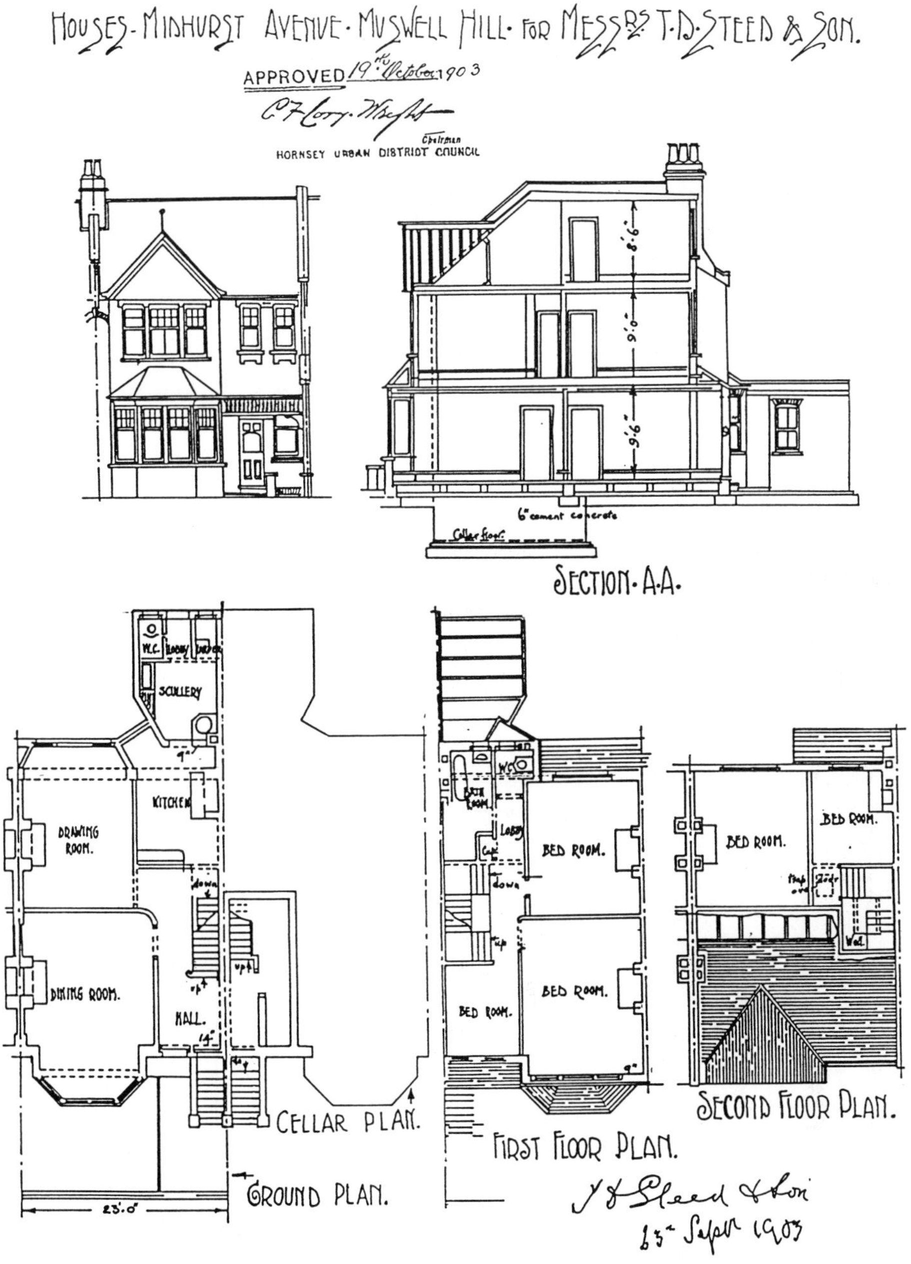
HOUSES-MIDHURST AVENUE-MUSWELL HILL-FOR MESSRS T.D.STEED & SON.
APPROVED 19th October 1903
Chairman
HORNSEY URBAN DISTRICT COUNCIL
SECTION-A.A.
6" cement concrete
Cellar floor
W.C.
SCULLERY
KITCHEN
DRAWING ROOM.
DINING ROOM.
HALL.
CELLAR PLAN.
GROUND PLAN.
23'.0"
BED ROOM.
BED ROOM.
BED ROOM.
FIRST FLOOR PLAN.
BED ROOM.
BED ROOM.
SECOND FLOOR PLAN.
T D Steed & Son
23rd Sept 1903

Two years later Chestertons drew very similar drawings in an identical fashion for Mr F.R.King, builder, of Surbiton. Chestertons is a long established agency which has managed property for years in all parts of London, so they may have been acting for the purchaser of the Midhurst estate and have taken on the drawing as well. Development in this road was a slow, hesitant process, with speculative builders tiptoeing after each other down the road as best they dared. It had none of the all-over planning and self-

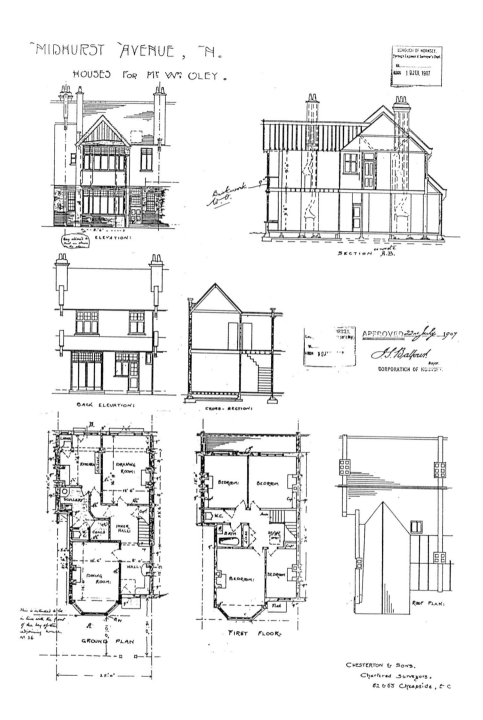

MIDHURST AVENUE, N.

HOUSES FOR MR WILOLEY.

BOROUGH OF HORNSEY.
Borough Engineer & Surveyor's Dept.
18 JUL 1907

ELEVATION.

SECTION A.B.

BACK ELEVATION.

CROSS SECTION.

APPROVED 22nd July 1907
J.S. Balfour
Mayor
CORPORATION OF HORNSEY.

GROUND PLAN

FIRST FLOOR.

ROOF PLAN.

CHESTERTON & SONS.
Chartered Surveyors.
82 & 65 Cheapside, E.C.

confidence of Collins, who had submitted his layout for the complete Fortismere Estate in April 1899 on one huge sheet. This indeed is the difference between Collins and Edmundson, both of whom worked on a large scale, and the other developers who built in small batches.

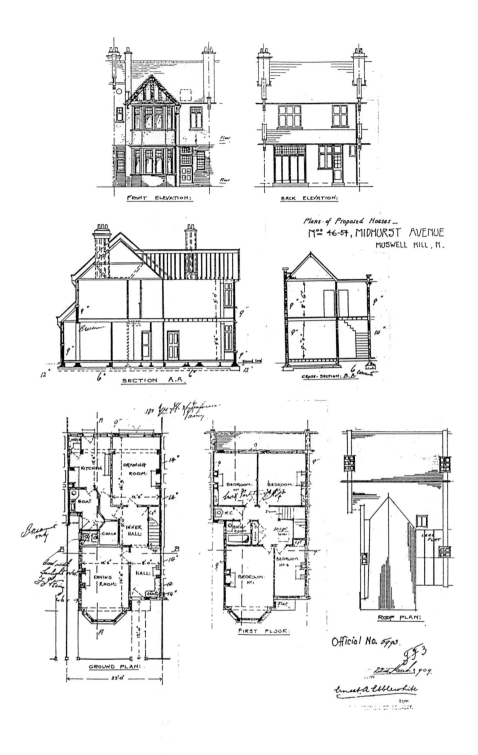

FRONT ELEVATION:

BACK ELEVATION:

Plans of Proposed Houses —
Nᵒˢ 46-57, MIDHURST AVENUE
MUSWELL HILL, N.

SECTION A.A.

CROSS-SECTION: B.B.

GROUND PLAN:

FIRST FLOOR:

ROOF PLAN:

Official No. 5795.

22ⁿᵈ March 1909.

153

A New Midhurst

In 1921 a new 'Midhurst' was built, according to rumour on the piggeries of the old house. The new 'Midhurst' is a delightful Arts and Crafts building, with two gates and a shallow gravel drive curving between them. It is a long rendered building with a round-headed brick doorway and a roof in hand-made tiles. At one end is a coach house or garage, and at the other a wide, recessed entrance to the greenhouse, which must have been a delightful feature but has now been demolished and the entrance walled up. Incidentally this must have made the house much warmer.

The house is laid out in a typical Arts and Crafts manner, with a long hall-passage and staircase on the north side and square rooms facing south over the garden. Rooms have fairly low ceilings and each has french doors opening out to a verandah. The large end sitting room has a ceiling-high fireplace in thin hand-made bricks such as Lutyens loved, with patterns made of creasing tiles. The outside terrace is paved in beautiful limestone slabs, now rich in old lichens, bordered by the same thin bricks. In short, this is a late delightful example of the sort of house that Lutyens and Webb had been building twenty or thirty years earlier.

Many years ago the Midhurst site looked over the Bishop of London's Hunting Park, with deer and boar roaming free. When the present house was built it looked out over the empty Water Board land, but small houses have now been built, fortunately on lower ground, so that from the garden of Midhurst one sees only the tops of their roofs.

The house was built by A.N.Prentice for A.C.Shankland. and the drawings are dated 14 October 1920. By this time Lutyens had moved on to build houses in the Classical tradition, changing, altering and inventing all the while. In the 1920s he was building the flat brick facades like 7 St James's Square, which Billy Collins was to reflect in his Fortis Green flats from about 1925 onwards. Prentice, on the other hand, went back to the 1890s to build this delightful house, long, low and comfortable, taking full advantage of the sun.

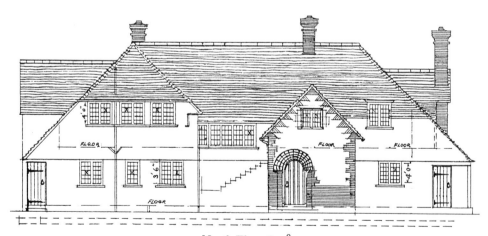

North Elevation[8]

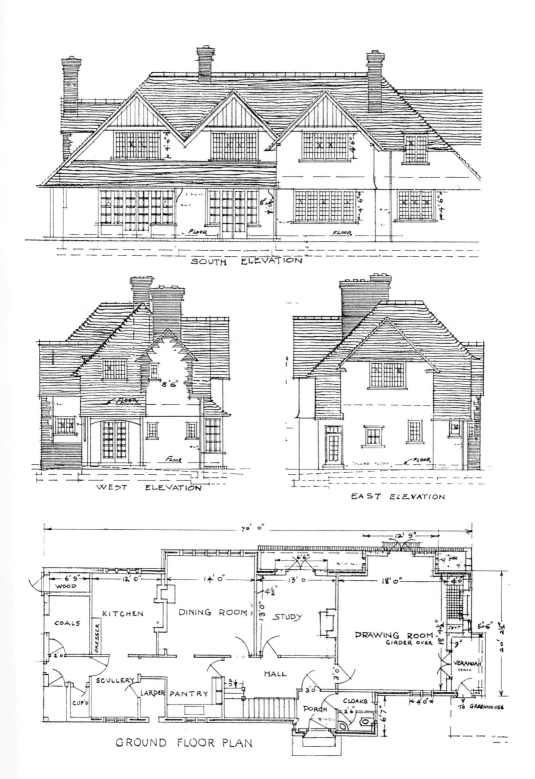

SOUTH ELEVATION

WEST ELEVATION

EAST ELEVATION

GROUND FLOOR PLAN

155

St James's Parish Hall, Fortis Green

G. Grey Wornum, CBE FRIBA, who built St James's Parish Hall, was a most distinguished architect. He was forceful, but had a great social flair and 'nobody in the profession was more liked and respected.' He was born in Hampstead in 1888, son of George Porter Wornum, a doctor of medicine. Grey studied at the Slade in a class of forty girls, for he was first an artist and musician. He could play anything on the violin by the age of twelve and said later that he would have rather been a composer.

He began as an articled pupil to his uncle R. Selden Wornum and studied at the AA where he was awarded a scholarship allowing him to make a 2000 mile bicycle tour of Normandy and the Loire. He gained experience too in various architectural practices and then set up on his own, supporting himself by becoming a reader for Batsford. There he selected thousands of drawings for their popular and authoritative series on the different counties and their building, thus greatly extending his insight.

In the 1914-18 War he served with the Artists' Rifles and The Durham Light Infantry. He was wounded in the leg and suffered the loss of one eye, an even more tragic loss for an architect than for an ordinary man. Later his black rimmed monocle and ribbon were famous, but they were in fact a disguise.

Grey Wornum was president of the AA in 1930-31 and in 1932 he shot to the front rank of British architects when he won the competition for the Royal Institute of British Architects' building in Portland Place, against about 250 other entrants. He had a great sense of design and colour, drawing around him a host of the most prominent young

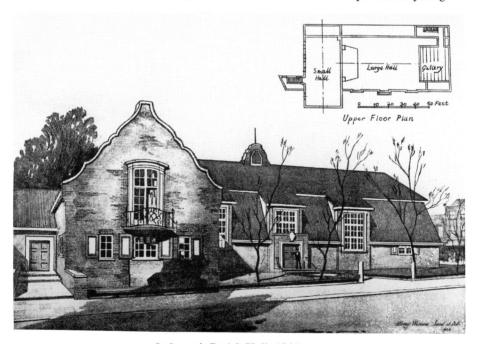

St James's Parish Hall, 1925

156

painters and sculptors. This ability to bring together and enthuse others is shown perhaps most clearly by the success of the decorations for the Queen Mary, for which he was responsible, a ship to be seen by people from all over the world. Their lightness, joie de vivre and originality made them instantly famous.

In 1952 he replanned Parliament Square, while in 1936 he was one of three architects who designed the decorations for the George VI Coronation processional route. He always distinguished between short-term and long-term building. A restaurant, which might be redecorated every eighteen months, or ephemeral bunting on a processional way, could be bright and even garish. A building which was to last, had to use more natural, subtle colours. In the Queen Mary he employed fine wood veneers but, because these would fade and look sad after a number of years, he bleached them almost to white and came back with a different tone. To appeal to him a building had to have a fine scale and employ fine materials. In the RIBA building he used carved Portland Stone, fine marbles and reconstituted stone, brass and terrazo. In the case of St James's Parish Hall there was not that amount of money, but the brick, stone and concrete were carefully chosen for long life and subtle weathering. The building work, by Stevens & Sons, the local builders, was good and carefully supervised, while the profile from both roads was simple and yet surprising.

The Birchwood Avenue elevation is slightly different from the original drawing, with more sophisticated detailing. The limestone doorway has a broken pediment, the top corners of the door entrance are shouldered, and the bases sweep out in beautiful Art Deco curves, while from Fortis Green Road we see a splendid Dutch gable end, with two decorative tie-beam plates shaped to elaborate curlicues.

Wornum always took pleasure in contrasting simple, straight-line designs with sudden, unexpected curves. At the RIBA headquarters, in Portland Place, a building of large and noble rectangular halls, there are two ferro-concrete pillars faced with fluted Ashburton Marble in bold curves. The same contrast can be seen in St James's Parish Hall, where every line is straight except the Dutch gables and the doorway pilasters. A delightful building and an asset to Muswell Hill.

In later life Grey Wornum was severely crippled with arthritis yet, when he was awarded the AA Society Gold Medal in 1952 for distinguished services to architecture, he gave one of the most witty addresses on record, brave, cultured, and charming.[91]

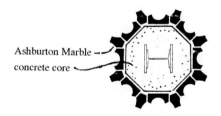

Ashburton Marble

concrete core

A cross-section of a pillar
RIBA, Portland Place [76]

The Nineteen Thirties

From about the age of thirteen or fourteen I took to wandering among the new houses being built in Hampstead Garden Suburb. The centre of the Suburb, with its Lutyens church and houses built in short culs-de-sac, had been started at the turn of the century. By the 1930s, building had reached the Mutton Brook and houses were spilling across Lyttleton Road towards the ridge of East End Road: the whole valley was being engulfed.[2] For years the fields had been used for tennis courts, athletics clubs, and football fields. A few of these still remained, but the majority were being built over. Four or five shops were open in Market Place, set among a sea of building sites and others were waiting to open. This was to be my hunting ground for years.

Half-made gravelled roads led to houses in all stages of building. Some had the foundations laid; others had walls started, or rafters in place, roofs tiled, walls plastered, floors laid, doors and windows glazed, the house painted and decorated - one could follow the progress of building as if in a huge exhibition. Nobody seemed to object to a boy examining everything. In his autobiography, Richard Cobb describes how at my age he walked down the length of a row of new houses with a catapult and, from the shelter of the woods behind, smashed a window in every house. I never saw vandalism like that and do not remember even a night watchman.

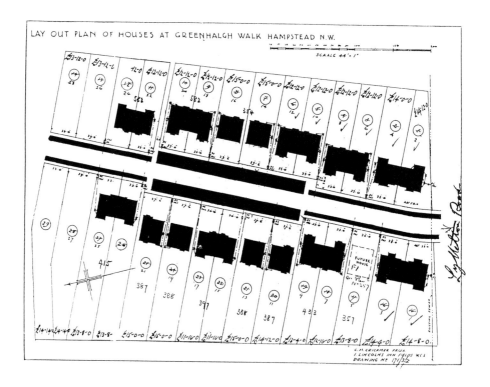

158

When Dame Henrietta Barnett, Robert Hunter, and others first planned Hampstead Garden Suburb, she pressed for a mixture of population, working class, professionals and business people living together in an all-class suburb with shops nearby, in houses of different sizes and rents, but rubbing shoulders as a community. At least one third of the houses were to be for the working class. In the early years a few houses were built with tunnel-backs, small and almost identical with those that the LCC was building at White Hart Lane, Tottenham, at the time. In 1926 she was urging the Hampstead Garden Suburb Trust to build working class flats behind the site which later held the Orpheum

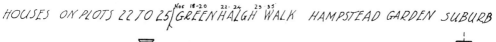

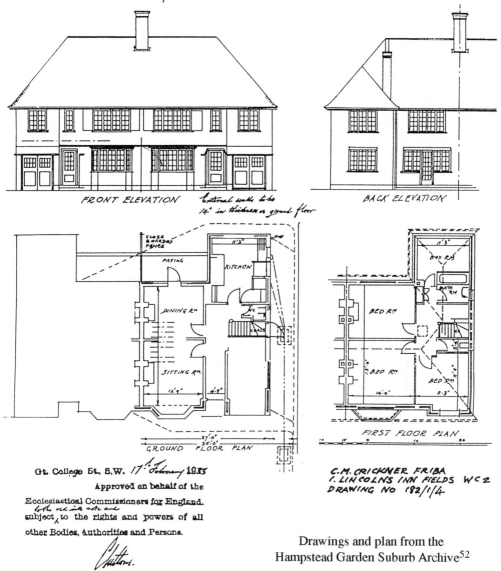

Drawings and plan from the
Hampstead Garden Suburb Archive[52]

Octavia Hill
1838-1912

Courtenay Crickmer, FRIBA
1879-1971

Cinema in Temple Fortune, but was over-ruled. As a result the vast majority of houses were far too expensive for working people and even the few working class houses were soon sold to middle-class people.

The development company called Copartners, owned 300 acres adjacent to the original Hampstead Garden Suburb and acquired other areas as well, so that their holdings stretched from Hampstead Golf Club to Brim Hill. For a time the Trust and Copartners worked together but, especially after 1919, they often disagreed in principle. Copartners traded more and more as a commercial venture, building at whatever price the market would bear. The area was conveniently near to town, yet green and leafy, served by East Finchley and Golders Green Stations, so the houses I used to watch being built in the 1930s were not for the working class. The new owners would be professional people, owners of small factories and others who could afford the prices.

At the week-ends the unfinished streets were full of visitors who had come to look over the houses. For some it was a weekly ritual to view the new buildings in Hampstead, Finchley and Totteridge, or anywhere else along the train routes where houses were being built. The same thing was happening all round London as the building sites moved outwards. An enormous game of leap-frog was taking place. People were moving out from the old centres, leaping from Highgate and Holloway and Clerkenwell, over Victorian houses built in the 1860s and 1880s and the Edwardian developments in Crouch End and Muswell Hill. Some planned to leap a short distance, others leapt further, while some made the extraordinry jump from the East End of London to the edge of the country, a change some of them were never quite to believe could have happened. How could they have made such a transition? What force could have prompted such a leap? People who had never lived far from the juddering rattle of tram wheels, were coming to a narrow, gravelled Lyttleton Road on a No. 58 bus with, in the early days, an open-top. To their amazement these buses would stop at the wave of a hand at any point along the route. This really proved it was the country.

To some house viewers it was a day out to look at a free peep-show, but for many it was a serious quest. In and out of the houses passed a stream of Sunday visitors, in high-heeled shoes and sharp-pressed trousers, hopping over the puddles to examine the new houses. A threepenny bus ride from Highgate Archway took them into the country and perhaps a new life.

These houses were to sell at about £1350 or £1400, well above the price of houses being built further out. £1400 represented a larger plot of more expensive ground, a much larger mortgage, but lower fares than those to Enfield, Potters Bar or Dartford.

The houses in Greenhalgh Walk, for example, were built by Courtney Crickmer, FRIBA (1879-1971). Educated at Highgate School and the AA, he was assistant to Charles H. Mileham, whose daughter he married and whose practice he inherited in 1904. He built houses and churches at Letchworth Garden City and by 1914 he had built seventy houses in Hampstead Garden Suburb. His style varied over the years, so that by the 1930s his Greenhalgh Walk houses had red or purple facing bricks, brown hand-made, sand-faced tiles and metal casements in wooden mullions. Some had half-timbering to the first floor, while other were given more classical detailing.

In Hutchings Walk, Crickmer designed some 'moderne' houses (called Sunshine Houses by other architects). These are the houses using the metal window frames with curved corner windows, long horizontal panes and a chevron vent, which Crittals brought out about 1930. Some architects built these houses with flat roofs, but Crickmer wisely gave them pitched roofs, less attractive in a thumbnail sketch, but far more practical in English weather.[50] [52] [53] Similar houses were built in the same period in Muswell Hill, in Tetherdown.

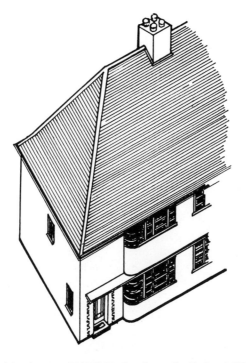

Sunshine houses, 74-78 Tetherdown, built for A.J.Hooper

Crickner also built in Brim Hill and Howards Walk, while many other builders were active around him, so that in a few years the fields were full. Most houses had four or five bedrooms and an integral garage, for each householder aspired to a car. Ground floor rooms had solid concrete floors set with pine or oak parquet in herringbone strips, with curved skirting edges to the floors to make cleaning easy. I was always fascinated by the large baths of pitch and the piles of floor blocks, so regular and exact, each timber with its own particular scent. First the men laid the hollow edge-moulding round the room, set in a bed of pitch. Then the underside of each block was dipped in pitch and placed carefully in position. Two lines of blocks all round the room and the centre patterned. It seemed the ideal floor, watertight and warm.

The smells of the woods were different from today, for the woods are different. When did we last see She Oak, which is really a eucalyptus, or Andaman Padouk which I once handled daily? This was the period of the Empire Marketing Board, set up during the economic slump of the 1930s to promote Empire trade. One of the ways in which Britain hoped to claw her way out of the depression was by Empire Preference, for the British Empire then covered a fifth of the world and much of its trade was protected. The Daily Express, owned by Lord Beaverbrook, who was a Canadian with all the patriotism of a person born on the fringe of a great power, carried a red banner headline each day showing a Crusader battling for the British Empire. Australian beef rather than European, Empire fruit carried in Empire shipping, Empire materials wherever possible. The Northern Line electric trains, which were to bring the householders to East Finchley Station, were being built in the 1930s. The carriages have panels veneered in Indian Silver Greywood, Silky Oak from Australia, and Lacewood cut from Canadian Plane trees. Doors came in their thousands from Canada, as did much of the flooring, but the protection was not complete. Many of the floor blocks found in skips today are in American White Oak and stamped USA.

Gradually the houses were completed and people moved in, commuting from their old factories and offices each evening, splitting their lives into two different and unrelated parts. On a warm spring evening they would open the windows and call excitedly to each

Abbot's Gardens under construction[52]

Martin Hood & Larkin (The Estates Gazette Ltd) Kirby St E.C¹ 13 12 38.

The Elmhurst Sale Map
showing the housing developments up to 1935 [2]

163

other to smell the country air. As the months passed the wonder grew rather than faded, for when the gardens became filled with scented shrubs and the perfumes spread, people arriving from work, their senses dulled by town air, were rejuvenated and walked more lightly. Road after road was built until, by 1939, the back fences of Abbots Gardens and Howard Walk reached the trees of Elmhurst, which Anthony Salvin, the architect who built in Fortis Green, had left in the 1860s. Anne Salvin, Anthony's daughter, wrote that 'the house is closely shut in with trees in all directions', so that today any really large tree still on that boundary may have been planted by Anthony Salvin himself.

After Salvin left Elmhurst it became a private house, a school, and finally the house of Alderman Pulham, Mayor of Finchley. In 1939 it was was sold by auction. By that time Salvin's view across the valley to Bishop's Wood had been blocked by Hampstead Garden Suburb, and later by the buildings of Falloden Way and Brim Hill. As the auctioneer said in his sales notice, Elmhurst was

> 'in a locality which has been in demand for residential purposes for many years and comprises practically the last available site of its size in the district.'

The site was zoned for residential purposes at a density of twelve houses to the acre on the frontage, to a depth of 150 feet and at a density of ten houses to the acre on the remainder. The old house was demolished in 1939, to be replaced by Elmhurst Crescent and Pulham Avenue. Hampstead Garden Suburb had spread from its old centre at The Institute right up to the Bald Faced Stag.[2]

Similar developments were taking place elsewhere in Muswell Hill, where the Church was selling off more land. Coldfall Woods north of Creighton Avenue, which had lost land for Tollington playing field, years before, was being developed. By 1935 Twyford Avenue and Church Vale were complete and two more roads were marked out ready for development.

In 1930 the Ecclesiastical Commissioners had granted a lease to Ernest Nathan Cansick of Royston, Chumley Crescent, Highgate, who was a builder. Two years later he had built Church Vale and was selling the houses. One lease reads:-

> 'the site, the messuage or dwelling house, motor car house and buildings erected thereon' for £1375 and a ground rent of £12 per annum.'

The site was 191 feet deep by 36 feet wide and, like the Greenhalgh Walk ones, it was set in a wide road and well built. These houses, designed for professional people and managers, were among the top of the range for speculative building.

It was only when the lower half of Coldfall Wood was bought as a public open space that the erosion of the Wood stopped. After 1945 the houses marched again: the allotments along Coppetts Road were quickly covered with houses and finally the Coldfall School Playing Field, a wide, open space with splendid views, was sold off and lost.

Then, in 1994 there was a Public Inquiry into the status of the remaining Coldfall School grounds. The DoE inspector told Haringey that these should be designated as metropolitan open land, which would rule out further development. However, in February 1995 it is reported that Haringey may decide to ignore the inspector's report and may sell sell off the land.[76] The jury is out.

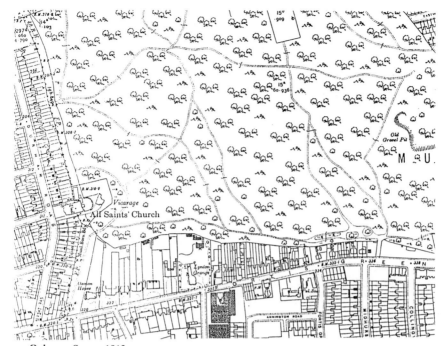

Ordnance Survey 1913

The 1913 map showing Fortis Green and Durham Road, with Coldfall Woods behind.

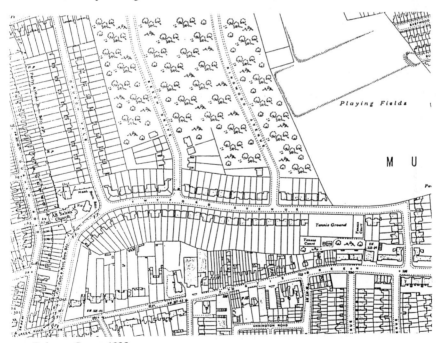

Ordnance Survey 1935

By 1935, Twyford Avwnue and Church Walk are built and other roads marked out.

165

The War Years: 1939-45

A very large number of houses in Hornsey were damaged by bombs during the War. 131 houses were destroyed and a further 611 so badly affected that they had to be demolished. Many more needed repair. By 1945-50, 256 houses had been rebuilt at government expense and blocks of flats were built on other cleared sites. There were 4 rockets, 18 flying bombs, 7 parachute mines, 26 oil bombs, 287 high explosive bombs and several thousand incendiaries.

  I walked into Crouch End School playground one morning in early 1940 to see a boy swinging a bomb round his head. Instinctively I rushed across, only to be greeted with delighted laughter. Teacher had been caught. It was the tail end of an incendiary bomb which had buried itself in soft soil and burnt out safely below ground. When the boy had salvaged it next morning, the fins were complete, attached to a bulb of melted metal and glazed earth. An Air Raid Precautions Officer had declared it safe, so he carried it off in triumph and was now displaying it. Collecting shrapnel, sharp as razors and already starting to rust, was a morning search; everyone had found some, but nobody had ever seen the tail of a bomb before, so he was king for the day.

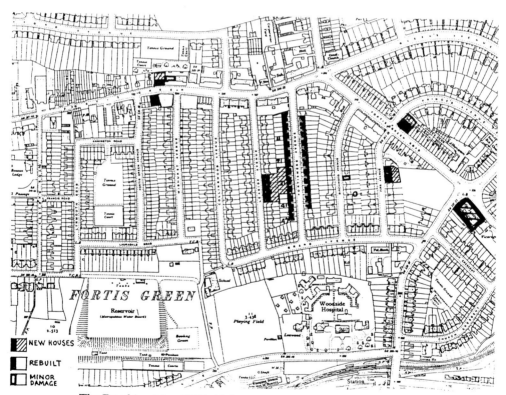

The Bombing Map 1939-45 drawn on the 1935 Ordnance Survey[6]

166

Each borough recorded bombing incidents in its own way. Islington had cards; the LCC had an invaluable set of maps, now at the Greater London History Library, plotting each incident and its gravity. This was drawn as the basis for the Abercrombie Plan for rebuilding of London. Hornsey had an enormous grey book in which every incident is recorded.

Some were bombs; some were our own anti-aircraft shells, exploded or unexploded. In Birchwood Avenue an unexploded bomb was reported but could not be found. In Fordington Road a high-explosive bomb made a crater 14 feet across and 16 feet 6 inches deep. In Duke's Avenue an unexploded bomb caused 80-100 people to be evacuated until it was defused. So the list goes on; ten incendiaries in Barrenger Road and, in April 1941, two incendiaries which gutted St James's Church. At the top of Firs Avenue, opposite the stables, three houses were bombed by a high explosive and some incendiaries, setting fire to the gas and bursting the water main. These houses have now been replaced by modern ones.[6]

A flying bomb which landed at the top of Midhurst Avenue destroyed buildings on both sides of Fortis Green. Nos 3 and 4 Lime Tree Cottages, 1,2,3 and 4 Cheapside, all cottages like those still existing further along the road, were destroyed and the west corner of Long Ridges, Billy Collins's five storey block of flats in Fortis Green was partly demolished. Damage to surrounding property included shops, the electricity sub-station and a first aid post. Thirty persons had to be accommodated at St James's Rest Centre. The photograph below shows the scale of the damage, with furniture exposed, balanced on the edges of broken floors. The 1913 map (page 165) shows six shops with

Destruction by a flying bomb in Fortis Green.[6]

Today a block of post-war flats in an older terrace may well pin-point a bombing incident, while the change of brick colour in a gable wall may reveal that the building was once damaged and repaired.

flats above, at the corner of Fortis Green and Fortis Green Road. On either side of Midhurst Avenue were two small public gardens. The 1935 map on which I imposed the Bombing Map (page 166) was the same, but the photograph shows how three of the shops were destroyed by bombing. After the War the original public garden was extended to cover the lost sites. The photograph must have been taken from the top of Midhurst Avenue looking west.

A landmine destroyed Nos 26 to 36 Leaside Avenue and houses in Fortismere Avenue. It so damaged others that almost all of Fortismere Avenue had to be rebuilt. Some houses were rebuilt approximately as before so they do not look different, but in fact only the two extreme ends of the east side of Fortismere Avenue are untouched. One block, bridging the centre of the damage in Leaside and Fortismere was completely demolished and was replaced by modern houses. These are unmistakable, with their tunnel entrances to rear garages.

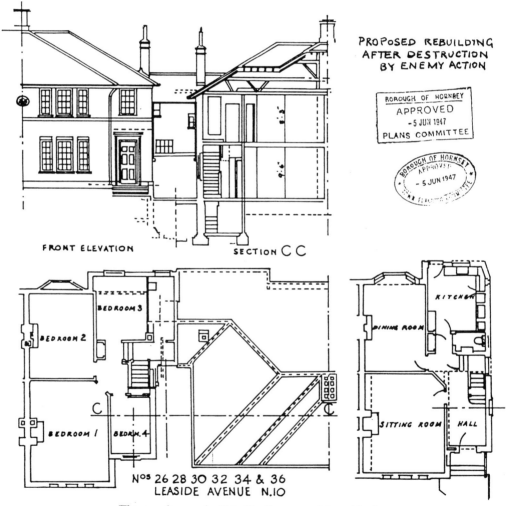

The new houses built in Fortismere and Leaside Avenues
to replace bomb damaged property.[8]

A bomb fell in Fortis Green Road, at the end of Princes Avenue, destroying four shops and sending shock/blast waves in all directions. The buildings were so damaged that they had to be demolished. The site was purchased by Messrs Courage who planned to build a public house there sometime in the future. After the Second World War there was a campaign to make the Borough more beautiful by opening small parks on derelict sites. Messrs Courage consented to this site being included in the scheme and contributed £200 towards the cost. A book called Beauty and the Borough[86] was later published, with photographs, including the one reproduced here. It shows the Princes Avenue site, with the end of the shop terrace rendered to keep out the rain, but before landscaping. In 1959 the John Baird pub was built on the site.

On the opposite corner is a small public open space with a conifer in the centre. One might be tempted to think that the bomb had destroyed a couple of shops on that corner too and a park had been created. However, the flank wall of the shop terrace is completely undamaged and has original windows in it. The wall has not been rendered with sand and cement like the one opposite. The story goes back to 1900.

When Edmondson bought the Fortis House Estate, the entrance to Fortis House stood at the present entrance to Princes Avenue and on this corner was a magnificent Cedar of Lebanon, said to have been one of the most beautiful trees in London. It was so mature and beautiful that Edmondson could not bring himself to fell it. Instead, he presented the tree and the corner site to the public as a garden. When the bomb fell the Cedar must have taken some of the blast, protecting the end of the terrace and perhaps saved lives. It was not destroyed, surviving until the 1950s.[87] Perhaps someday, when the present tree is very old, it may be replaced by a Cedar of Lebanon as a reminder of 1900.

The cleared bomb site at the end of Princes Avenue, on which the John Baird was built.

The Conversion of the Coppetts Road Estate in 1957

For thirty years the lack of a bathroom in these houses had caused resentment. People objected to the lack of privacy and the inconvenience, but the Council was in a dilemma. They had no money for conversion. Central government ruled that houses which had attracted grants when first built could not be given further grants. Sympathy was expressed but it was financially impossible. The Council made more representations with the same effect. After considerable pressure from many parts of the country the government relented, allowing architects to modernize the houses.

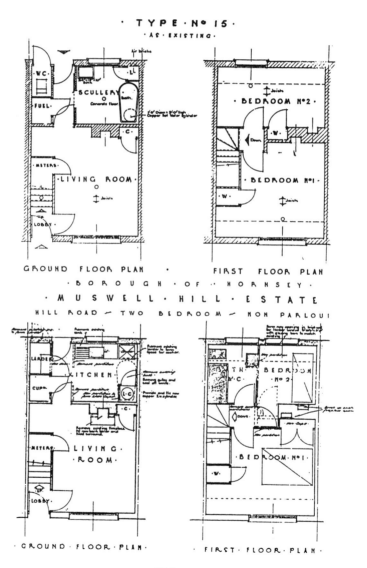

In some cases, such as Type 15, a small bedroom was converted into a bathroom; the scullery was enlarged into a full-width kitchen and the houses were transformed. There was some hesitation about how to convert the larger Type 12 houses as the Council needed to retain the full number of bedrooms for its larger families. It was thought that a complete new bathroom would have to be built on to the back of the houses, an expensive and inconvenient solution. Eventually the large back bedrooms were divided into a bathroom and a narrow bedroom. At last the houses had bathrooms and were as they should have been built originally.

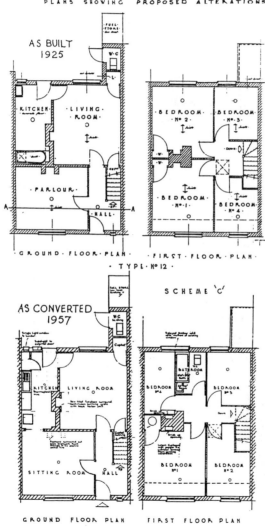

· B O R O U G H · O F · H O R N S E Y ·
· M U S W E L L · H I L L · E S T A T E ·
COPPETTS · ROAD ~ FOUR BEDROOM PARLOUR · TYPE ·
PLANS SHOWING PROPOSED ALTERATIONS

Westside

Westside and its neighbouring large houses in Fortis Green must have been built in the 1860s, in the heavy Victorian Gothic style which is still to be seen nearby in Bernard Johnson House. Westside and the next door house were demolished and redeveloped in the 1960s, but it was in the late 1930s that they first became well known as Fortis Green School. Indeed, at one time, to the outside world Fortis Green was not a road but the name of a school.

When I first went into the house, about 1937, it had been empty for several years. The roof leaked; vandals had damaged windows and doors and the place reeked of damp. Walls were covered in mould, while a huge fungus, like a yellow-purple serving dish, was growing from a picture rail in the front dining room. The back garden, which had once been elegantly laid out with lawns and marble slabs round a large sunken pool, was a shambles. All the marble had gone except for a few broken corners, damaged in the removal. In its place was a gigantic cardboard beer bottle from some off-license window display, draped with lengths of 8mm film of Neville Chamberlain. The scene was a surrealist nigtmare.

BEATRIX TUDOR–HART : 1903 – 1979

photograph by Wolf Suschitzky

172

I was acting as an architect's assistant, being paid ten pence an hour, to hold the tape for a friend called David Pine. He was an architect who had been commissioned to convert the building and the one next door into Fortis Green School. We measured, he sketched, and I learnt to calculate the height of a building by counting the brick courses. For some while we seemed to have lost a brick: the flank wall appeared to be one brick lower than the back elevation, with the whole building balanced uneasily on one leg, but it came right in the end when we discovered the brick course hidden under ivy on the kitchen extension.

Fortis Green School was the creation of a remarkable teacher, Beatrix Tudor-Hart, who had founded first The Heath Nursery School for children aged 2-5, in Hampstead, and was now to open Fortis Green School for children aged 4-11. It was a co-operative non-profit-making co-educational school owned and democratically controlled by a society of parents, teachers and educationalists.

Beatrix had taken a degree in psychology and then done post-graduate studies in Vienna, Germany and USA. She was tall and striking looking, completely unself-concious and without any inhibitions. Beatrix drove a tiny car which flipped about like a shuttlecock, much to the consternation of her passengers.

After her death, one of her friends wrote that Beatrix had 'a kind of divine contempt for bureaucrats' and that summed her up. A child's opinions were important and should be taken seriously; most adults were reasonable and responded to a direct, warm approach; bureaucrats were hidebound, knew nothing and cared less. The best thing was to ignore them and get on with the job.

Fortis Green was a very succesful school - successful in the broadest sense of preparing children to be rounded, mature adults. When one compares the atmosphere and aims of Fortis Green School and the atmosphere promoted by the Ministy of Education today, one despairs. This is not the place to tell the story of the school, except to say that it flourished for some years, but later, as costs rose, this sort of

Drawing by Jennifer Jones of the Westside flats[57]
The final ones were not so tall.

173

education became too expensive for the kind of parents who believed in it. The School became a Nursery School only, as it is today.

Beatrix's architect daughter, Jennifer Tudor-Hart married Colin Jones, another architect, and they rebuilt Westside and School House as two point-blocks of flats, with room for a Nursery School in one block. These flats make a delightful impression, warm welcoming and humane. They are even more interesting than one would imagine from a quick glance, as they are of a completely original design. The flats are four-and-half storeys high, on seven levels. They are built in load-bearing brick cross-walls with reinforced concrete slab floors, and the plans appear normal, but they are not, These are Scissors Flats, very well known in the sixties. The concept of scissors flats was developed by two or three L.C.C. architects, of whom Colin Jones was one. The L.C.C.went on to build a number of blocks, many of them far taller than the ones in Fortis Green.

Typical floor plan of point block. Scale: 1/24-ins. 1: Living Room. 2: Dining. 3: Kitchen. 4: Bedroom. 5: Linen and Heating Unit. 6: Optional balcony.

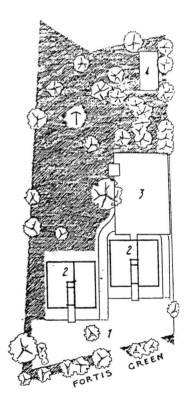

SITE
The second site to be developed by the Housing Partnership is about 1¼ acres in Fortis Green. The site, which previously contained two large Victorian houses, is to be redeveloped with two 7-storey blocks of flats, a caretaker's bungalow and a large semi-sunk car-parking area. Development in depth was not permitted by the planning authority so that the proposed new layout continues the scale and siting of the surrounding large houses.

ACCOMMODATION
Twenty-four dwellings in addition to the caretaker's bungalow. The 3- and 4-room flats have exceptionally large room sizes (certain living rooms, for instance, being over 300 sq. ft.). There is basically no subdivision in the kitchen-living room-balcony area but tenants can have light sub-divisions installed to the architect's detail if they so require. Generosity is again shown in such a detail as the bathroom, which allows space for a washing machine. As at the "Roundacre" scheme the heating is by a recirculating warmed air unit sited at the core of each dwelling. This "Harton" unit also heats the domestic hot water. It is intended that two of the ground floor flats will have minor modifications to permit their use as a Nursery School, which will have direct access to the large paved deck over the semi-sunk parking area. The latter provides for more than 100% car ownership.

ARCHITECTS
Colin Jones and Jennifer Dennis, A/ARIBA.

Plan and site plan[24]

174

Colin and Jennifer Jones were also in private practice and Jennifer developed the concept at Fortis Green. Similar low-level blocks were repeated by the LCC in Malden Road, Camden; in Broadley Street, St Marylebone; and at other sites all over London.

Each flat is built on two levels, with living rooms at one floor and the bedrooms a floor higher. In between the front and back rooms are the kitchen and the bathroom. The kitchen is always on the living room floor, and the bathroom is between floors, at the half stair level. Another flat with living room above and bedrooms below, fits round the first, with its bathroom occcupying the other half of the centre section. Thus the flats fit round each other like the two blades of a pair of scissors.

The idea came from the arrangement of the rooms in Victorian By-law houses, which have a passage and stairway which leads to a back addition at a different level from the front of the house. A return stair then leads to the first floor rooms. The architects imagined two of these houses fitted round each other and evolved this unusual arrangement.

The sectional perspective shows flats at six levels including the penthouse, yet there are only three access corridors. The four floors at Fortis Green need only two, a ground floor access and one corridor above. This is possible because in Scissors Flats one corridor serves two levels of flats. Two front doors, side by side, each lead to a small entrance hall and a half flight of stairs, one to the flat above and the other to the flat below. This reduction of corridors saved a great deal of space so the flats could be made that much bigger. Inside each flat there is another half flight which completes the movement to the rear rooms.

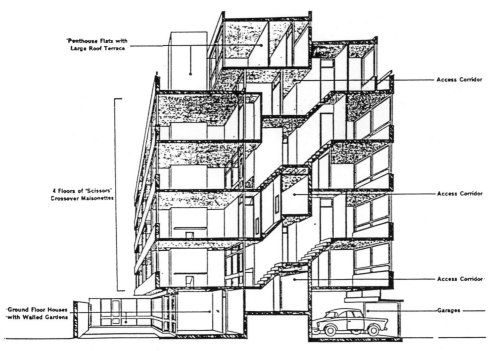

Housing in the 1960s, by A.W.Cleeve Barr[57]   RIBA JOURNAL APRIL 1962

A sectional perspective of a block of Scissors Flats

The design is very flexible since it can be built economically on uneven ground, with the back levels higher or lower than the front. This saves money and time by reducing excavation. The design also gives space for garages on one side. The space saving and the flexible nature of the design made these flats very attractive.

The section on page 175 shows a six storey block with penthouse and garages. It is rather difficult to illustrate the concept, which is more easily understood in a model, but to simplify matters the drawing shows the staircases for only three flats. One must imagine a second set of stairs in the opposite direction serving the other three flats, making each staircase into an X, with people walking up and down past each other, with a party wall between them. If you do find it difficult you are not alone. Even the contractors found the layout a little difficult to understand: they complained that it was difficult to supervise their men, who always claimed to be in another flat, but they are a very satisfying design for living in. They are comfortable, commodious, and have weathered well.

Beatrix Tudor Hart.

photograph by Wolf Suschitzky

176

Road Widening

In 1966 the Ministry of Transport wanted to widen Fortis Green as part of a large road improvement scheme. Road traffic was going to increase, the North Circular Road would become overloaded, so new orbital roads would be needed. The Ministry proposed to improve the A504 road to link Edgware Road at Hendon and Tottenham High Road. The route ran from West Hendon, through Barnet, along East End Road Finchley, Fortis Green, down Muswell Hill, along Priory Road to Turnpike Lane, and through to Tottenham. It would destroy the rural character of Fortis Green, fell the trees and turn it into a three-lane highway.

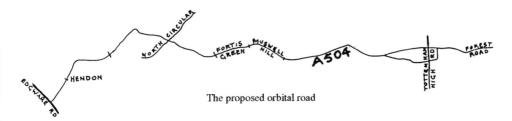

The proposed orbital road

The Minister of Transport offered a grant and, in 1969, Haringey Council served a Compulsory Purchase Order on the householders in Fortis Green. Westside would lose approximately 445 square yards of its front garden; Bernard Johnson House, 175 square yards; 288 from Priory Grange; 103 from Albion Cottage; 90 from Albion Lodge; 232 square yards from Lynton Grange; and so on along the road. Each garden would be truncated and the traffic brought nearer.

Immediately the Muswell Hill and Fortis Green Association protested. They claimed that traffic flowed smoothly and rapidly along Fortis Green, any congestion occurring at the two ends, at the bottlenecks of The Bald Faced Stag and Muswell Hill Broadway. Residents should come before traffic and they accused the Council of having a hidden motive. In recent years eight old houses had been demolished and five blocks of flats erected in their place, increasing the number of housing units from 8 to about 110. The sewers were decayed and overloaded. The Council would have to bear the full cost of replacement but, if the road were widened, the Ministry of Transport would pay three-quarters of the cost. They suspected that the Council was prepared to sacrifice both the residents and the area for the sake of the grant.

Several householders made personal protests. I have kindly been given access to a thick file created by Mr Corfield[81], who was then the owner of Albion Lodge and a driving force behind the protest. He began his objection in this way:-

'Albion Lodge, erected 1815, stands some 90 feet from the road with its other half, Albion Cottage. Both houses are attractive in appearance, with great charm and character. The old, established gardens have two very fine old horse chestnut trees, one to each plot, which are under a Tree Preservation Order.'

177

Others protested in similar vein. A deputation met members of the Planning Development Committee to present a petition signed by over 300 people opposed to the widening scheme. Although the Chairman and Mr Corfield addressed the Committee, no reply or comment was made. The Council was holding its cards very close to its chest.

Haringey Council had asked Ove Arup, the famous civil engineers, to produce a report on the road. By some means the Residents Association obtained a copy of the Report, so that they knew the case for the other side, but had to go to some lengths to conceal their knowledge. Ove Arup had concluded that the road from Tottenham to Hendon and the Edgware Road was an essential link and widening, while regrettable, was inevitable. The real problem was the narrow stretch at Fortis Green. The existing carriageway width varied from 19-21 feet and it was proposed to widen it to 33 feet. There might be a case for widening the road still further at a later date. It might be possible to reduce the footpath width to 8 feet instead of the existing 10-12 feet, but the need for the new road could not be denied.

Instead of agreeing to the widening, the Residents put forward alternative one-way schemes:-

1. While most of Fortis Green was quite wide, the 350 yards from the 'Clissold Arms' was only 19 feet wide. Therefore this should become one-way, with a return flow along Twyford Avenue.

2. The whole of Fortis Green should become one-way, with the contra-flow going along Creighton Avenue.

A third scheme, not mentioned in Mr Corfield's file but bruited at the time, was the threat of a contra-flow system from East Finchley, along Baronsmere Road, Southern Road, a new stretch of road over Water Board land to Grand Avenue, and through to Muswell Hill Road. This plan was particularly unpopular with parents who had children at Tetherdown Primary School, at the corner of Grand Avenue, as the school would have been cut off by a flood of traffic. The idea appears to have dissolved before the Residents made their reply to the Council, but caused alarm at the time.

A Public Inquiry into the Road Widening was held under P. St L. Lloyd, OBE, ACGI, C Eng, MICE, in 1970. He took great care to brief himself on the issues, visiting all the sites and meeting representatives of the opposing sides.

At the Inquiry, Counsel for the Opposition, well briefed by Mr Corfield, claimed that the average speed along Fortis Green was 22 m.p.h. - well above the London norm. The 'improvements' would make the road, which was then virtually accident free, very dangerous. The proposed widening would increase the danger without improving the flow and a unique stretch of road would be spoilt for ever.

The pavement near the shops had been widened voluntarily by the shopkeepers throwing in their frontages to add to the pavement width. If the road was widened at the expense of the pavements in front of the shops, they would become very narrow. Indeed, when the 'Clissold Arms' opened its cellar trap to take a delivery, the pavement would be virtually impassable.

Under the proposed plan the trees on the south side would have to be removed and those on the north considerably mutilated by removing the lower branches to allow double-decker buses to pass within eighteen inches. This would be unsightly, to say the least.

At the Inquiry, Roy Dunn, Deputy Borough Engineer and Surveyor, said that Fortis

Green was an essential route for traffic and traffic flow was high. The average carriageway was about 30 feet wide at the eastern end but at the 'Clissold Arms' it narrowed suddenly to 19 feet. It was this narrow section which it was sought to improve.

The Muswell Hill and Fortis Green Association had protested in 1968. As a result the plan was reconsidered, but no alternative route parallel to the North Circular Road had been found. It was now proposed that the scheme should go ahead, but be limited to the narrow stretch beyond the 'Clissold Arms' public house.

The trees on the north side would be preserved by routing the footpath behind them. Objectors considered that the real congestion problem was at each end of Fortis Green and that bus bays would solve the problem. The Council claimed that the road was so narrow that one parked car stopped the traffic flow in one direction.

Local householders objected to the footpath being put behind the trees. It was claimed that this would preserve the trees, but in doing so it would trap the householders and prevent them from getting their cars out on to the road. The trees were old and large, with some trunks up to a yard in diameter, so they would completely block the view of the road from any emerging car. At present cars leaving a house to join the traffic flow, moved slowly across the pavement width until the driver was able to see the traffic, before turning into the road. If the carriageway came right up to the trees, a driver would have to push his car blindly into the oncoming traffic. Accidents would be inevitable.

The objectors continued that the suggested road 'improvement' would suck traffic into the area. Indeed the reason why the Council was asking for a 14 foot verge was so that the proposed three-lane road could be turned into a four-lane one in the future.

Fortis Green was one of the few remaining tree-lined North London roads and the trees should be preserved. Trees should not be sacrificed for cars. The objectors then finished with a ringing call to make Fortis Green the turning point in the fight against 'the ever-increasing four-wheel invaders.'

In July 1971 the Minister decided not to confirm the Order to requisition the land for road widening and this strip of Fortis Green, with its over-arching trees, was saved - for the present.

Highgate Woods

The woodlands of Hornsey are very old indeed, likely to have existed without a break from prehistoric times.[63] The parish of Hornsey today contains four oak/hornbeam woods, Highgate Wood, Cherry Tree Wood, Queen's Wood, and Coldfall Wood, with a total area of 97.5 hectares. There is documentary evidence that Bishop's Wood, now built over, had been managed as far back as the 13th century. No doubt the same applies to all the other woods.

A pollen analysis of an area in Hampstead Heath about three km to the south-west of Highgate Wood (Girling & Greig 1977) showed that before 3,000 BC the area was covered with a mixed deciduous forest predominantly of small-leaved lime, *Tilia cordata* and also contained oak, elm, birch, Scots pine, alder and hazel.

In the second phase, around 3,000 BC there was a decline in elm and lime and the first appearance of cereals and the weeds of cultivation. Heathland vegetation, which often accompanies the signs of human activity, also appeared. Charcoal found in the third phase of the Hampstead sample, on the light Bagshot Sands, suggests that this area was cleared for cultivation, probably by burning. Without more evidence however it appears unlikely that there was any extensive clearance in Highgate Wood before Saxon times, as it is on the much heavier London Clay. Small clearances would not have had any permanent effect on the wood as a whole as it would have quickly regenerated.

The Roman Pottery

About AD 60, in Roman times, the timber and clay supported a pottery, which helped to supply the needs of London. In 1974, A.E.Brown and H.L.Sheldon reported on the excavation of a number of kilns in Highgate Wood. The fragmentary remains of one kiln was found, with its fire-bars lying in a mass of burnt clay and pottery debris. Lower down was a puddling pit containing clean green clay. Nearby were other kilns, so that the picture emerged of a pottery which was developed and redeveloped over a period of time, in a series of production phases between AD 50-60 and AD 140-160. It was not a permanent settlement, but the clay ridge 'appears to have been visited for the purpose of pottery manufacture for a period of perhaps some 100 years.' The number of kilns and the amount of debris suggests that total production must have been small and no permanent buildings were found. The archaeologists considered that the potters were itinerant, visiting the site occasionally and working for a few weeks to supply local needs before moving on.[64]

A large number of pottery sherds were recovered, enabling no less than 95 different vase and bowl shapes to be recognised. These were classified into different phases and dates which showed that early ware was produced by local potters to supply pre-Boudiccan London, while later pottery was of a finer quality for a more selective market. For some reason production stopped about AD 160, perhaps because it became cheaper to transport pottery from further afield, or it may reflect the fall in population known to have occurred at about this period and with it, the lack of demand.

As was mentioned earlier. Highgate Wood became part of the Bishop of London's Hunting Park. Hornbeam, which was not mentioned in the Hampstead Heath tree survey, is very common in Highgate, Queen's and Coldfall Woods. It was traditionally coppiced by cutting areas down to ground level and allowing the roots, or stools, to regenerate as slender poles. In Epping Forest, another area rich in hornbeam, the trees were coppiced at shoulder height so that horses would not stumble on the low stools. The same shoulder-height coppicing was used on the western edge of Queen's Wood so as to put the attractive new leaf growth above the reach of any cattle in the adjoining field. If coppiced at ground level the browsing animals would have prevented the trees from growing again.

This coppicing was carried out systematically, cutting different woods or sections of woods in turn, to provide a constant supply of fuel to London. In the 17th century local woodland was far more extensive than it is today. The map below shows the wooded areas in middle of the seventeenth century. The Hunting Park was divided into two parts, the Great Park to the west of the Great North Road and the Little Park (Highgate Wood) to the east. All the woodland in the Great Park, apart from Turner's Wood, has now disappeared.

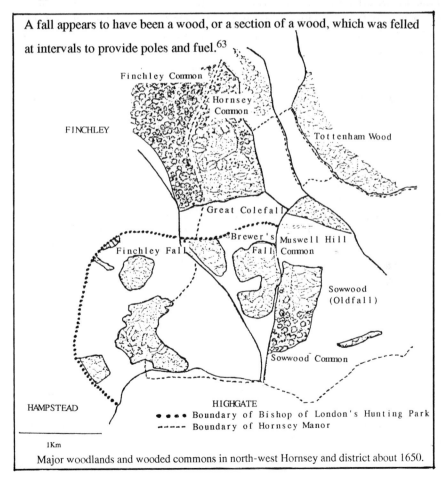

A fall appears to have been a wood, or a section of a wood, which was felled at intervals to provide poles and fuel.[63]

● ● ● ● Boundary of Bishop of London's Hunting Park
－－－－－ Boundary of Hornsey Manor

1Km

Major woodlands and wooded commons in north-west Hornsey and district about 1650.

181

About the time when the Archway Road was built, Brewhouse Wood became known as Gravel Pit Wood. 'The area from which the gravel was extracted is at the north-west corner of the present Highgate Wood, and can be readily distinguished by the unevenness of the ground and by the wavy hair grass *Deschampsia flexuosa* growing on the acid soil of the site.'[63]

Lord Mansfield leased the wood in 1842 and 'there is some evidence to show that the Gravel Pit Wood at least was not coppiced after about 1840. The effect of this neglect over the following forty years was to allow a dense undergrowth to develop, which probably resembled parts of Queen's Woods today.'[63] However, changes to the nature of the wood were soon to come.

The Acts of Parliament

The 1855 Metropolitan Management Act gave the Corporation of London powers to levy a tax on all the grain entering the City of London for sale, for the preservation of open spaces in the neighbourhood of London. This was an old way of raising money; the rebuilding of London after the Fire in 1666 had been paid for by a tax on coal. Gradually the City became responsible for various open spaces, churchyards and parks.

The 1878 (Open Spaces) Act extended this power, giving the Corporation the right to acquire and manage certain open spaces within twenty-five miles of the centre of London and keep them open for the use of the public. The Corporation could dig gravel sand loam and turf therein for the management of the properties, but could not sell them, thus excluding the mining companies from the public lands. They had the right to build lodges and other suitable buildings for the use of their employees and the public and to create cricket pitches etc. for the use of people of local parishes. The 1878 Epping Forest Act gave the Corporation similar powers over that area as well.

In the 1880s the Church Commissioners planned to develop Gravel Pit Wood (now called Highgate Wood) by building rows of houses as they had done in other parts of the Borough. It was their property and they had the legal right to do so, but the public outcry was so great that the Commissioners decided to build a road instead through Bishop's Wood (Bishop's Avenue) and to give Highgate Wood to the public. They asked the City of London to accept and maintain the Wood as an open space.[67]

The 1886 Highgate and Kilburn Open Spaces Act was passed enabling the Church Commissioners to transfer some of their lands to the Corporation as permanent open spaces for the use of the public. The wording shows that, while generous, the Commissioners were not entirely altruistic in giving the land to the public. They recognised that permanent open spaces near to their own existing housing estates, or ones to be built in the future, would make the houses more attractive and more valuable. Just as Victorian builders knew that a good church near their new estate would help to sell the houses, the Church Commissioners saw the advantage of local open spaces.

'And wheras the conversion of such lands into public parks or open spaces will be of advantage to the Commissioners as owners of adjoining and neighbouring lands will be of great public benefit and it is expedient that the provision of this Act contained should be made with reference thereto:'

The Corporation of London's powers over their new property were quite closely defined:-

'As regards the said lands at Highgate the Corporation shall at all times as far as

182

possible preserve the natural aspect thereof and as regards all the said lands shall take all necessary steps for the protecting of timber and other trees pollards shrubs and underwood heather gorse turf and herbage now or at any time hereafter growing thereon and for preventing the felling cutting lopping or injuring thereof or the digging of the gravel and clay loam and sand therein except as may be necessary for the purpose of this Act.'

W.H.Hudson, the great naturalist, described the wood only three years after the City of London took over the unmanaged Wood:-

'A very large proportion of Highgate Wood is veritably a wood, very thick and copse-like, so that to turn aside from the path is to plunge into a dense thicket of trees and saplings, where a lover of solitude might spend a long summer's day without seeing a human face'

Apparently the City of London began to cut undergrowth and saplings soon after it took control of the Wood and an unpublished photograph of Highgate Wood mentioned by Silvertown, shows bundles of wood stacked by newly cut coppice stools.[63] The effect was to open more parts of the wood to the public, with the consequent trampling of the ground and destruction of wild flowers. In March 1894 A.E.Houseman, who lived opposite Highgate School and walked regularly in Highgate Wood wrote a letter to the Standard.

Highgate Wood

Sir, in August, 1886, Highgate Wood became the property of the Mayor and Commonalty and Citizens of the City of London. It was then in a very sad state. So thickly was it overgrown with brushwood, that if you stood in the centre you could not see the linen of the inhabitants of Archway Road hanging to dry in their gardens. Nor could you see the advertisements for Juggins' stout and porter which surmount the front of the public house at the south corner of the wood. Therefore the Mayor and Commonalty and Citizens cut down the intervening brushwood, and now when we stand in the centre, we can divide our attention between Juggins' porter and our neighbours' washing. Scarlet flannel petticoats are much worn in Archway Road, and if anyone wishes to feast his eyes on these very bright and picturesque objects, so seldom seen in the streets, let him repair to the centre of Highgate Wood. Still we were not happy. The wood is bounded on the north by the railway to Muswell Hill, and it was a common subject of complaint that we could not see the railway from the wood without going quite to the edge. At length however the Mayor and Commonalty and Citizens have begun to fell the trees on the north, so that people in the centre of the wood will be able to look at the railway when they are tired of the porter and the petticoats---[68]

The letter appears to have had little effect because in 1916, in an article on the botany of the district, Nicholson wrote:-

'Highgate Woods, which thirty years ago were a blaze of colour in spring, are now so intersected by cinder and asphalt paths that their beauty has almost been destroyed. Bluebells are practically non-existent, and the thousands of wood anemones are now represented by a few miserable clumps of leaves here and there. The better drainage of the woods has destroyed numerous plants, and several fine clumps of such as *Carex pendula* and *Carex vesicaria* have been lost.'[69]

These three descriptions by Hudson, Houseman and Nicholson are reported time after time in different articles and reports on Highgate Wood. Perhaps one more time will not matter, especially as they highlight the ever recurring problems of managing an urban wood to the satisfaction of everyone in the neighbourhood.

The 1976 Various Powers Act

The 1976, the City of London [Various Powers] Act was passed in response to all sorts of new duties which had been imposed on the Corporation by new British and European laws. The Local Government Act of 1972; International Health Regulations governing the quality of water; The Medicines Act of 1968, which affected in particular the Port of London; the safety of traffic and prevention of accidents to the public in connection with the Blackfriars Underpass; and a multitude of other recent enactments had affected the City of London, its Port and Open Spaces. Therefore the Various Powers act was passed.

The Act dealt with, among many other things, the Rights of Common in Epping Forest etc. In the early drafts the Act included Highgate Wood. The Act dealt at length with the grazing of animals (which is not applicable to Highgate Wood) but it also included some very broad references to closing off certain parts of the Forest and building access roads, which might be acceptable in such a large and varied area as Epping Forest but were far too broad and draconian for Highgate Wood. This is so small and heavily used that it needs very delicate and sensitive treatment. A very few people, notably Sally Vernon and David Jones, made it clear to the City that if these wide powers were extended from Epping Forest to Highgate Wood, the City would be faced with a very strong public protest campaign and their whole Act could be delayed, or even endangered. In the end Highgate Wood was excluded from the 1976 Act and the Corporation's powers there are limited to their original 1886 ones.

The City of London and Highgate Wood

Highgate Wood consists of London Clay, ideal for the growth of oak, hornbeam and wild cherry.[71] In the south-east section the clay is covered with Claygate Beds. This geology had a profound effect on the nature of the Wood and should be borne in mind when reading various biological reports which are mentioned later.

The City of London cut undergrowth every winter until at least 1906 despite complaints from the Chairman of the Hornsey Board. The annual cutting allowed visitors to enter more parts of the wood and trample the soil which made it difficult for plants to take root in the hardened soil. The effect was to change the wood into a wooded park with a high tree canopy and little undergrowth.

A number of fenced enclosures have been made in Highgate Woods at different times in the century in the hope of regeneration. One became a bird sanctuary but when the fences were removed there was little evidence that new trees had become established, probably because the dense tree canopy and the compacted soil combined to prevent it. However, some areas which were fenced between 1947 and 1955 now contain a number of self-sown trees, including oak, hornbeam and birch, but there is very little ground flora. These areas are now unfenced and the thickets which have grown up in them appear to have thinned out due to the competition and damage by visitors'[63]

The cutting back of undergrowth and the burning of leaves ceased after about 1967 and dead wood, or fallen trees were no longer removed except in the vicinity of paths, so that they provided habitats for many insect and fungus species. Limited plantings of native flowers, such as meadowsweet, wood violet, wild campion, comfrey, herb robert, ground ivy, wild garlic, pendulous sedge and male fern were made. It was a deliberate policy not to plant alien or exotic flowers. In the same way it was decided to remove areas of rhododendron, not a native English woodland species and to replace with native shrubs such as hawthorn, holly and elder and, in damper sites, willow and guelder rose. It was resolved that tarmac paths were to be replaced with gravel 'hoggin' paths. The grey squirrels were subject to control, with about 100-150 culled each autumn.

About 1969, under increasing pressure from local residents, attempts were made to increase the diversity of species and to help natural regeneration. Coniferous trees including Douglas fir, Western hemlock, Norway spruce, Corsican pine, Red oak, Turkey oak, Norway maple, and Swedish whitebeam were planted. Areas were fenced and underplanted with beech; other areas were replanted with oak, hornbeam, hazel, cherry and fenced to allow the trees to establish themselves. Apparently the object was to change the nature of parts of the wood from the ancient hornbeam/oak wood into an arboretum containing a great variety of trees, a contradiction of the earlier policy.

In 1977, The Muswell Hill and Fortis Green Association commissioned Mr P.F.Garthwaite, a consultant on Forestry, to report on the Wood.[71]

He questioned the policy of planting a wide variety of species not found naturally in the ancient wood. Beech preferred a lighter soil with better drainage and mature beech trees shade out all other growth. There is no undergrowth in a beech wood. The planting of conifers was also doubtful. Scots pine and Western hemlock gave little bird shelter and suffered from atmospheric pollution in towns, while Scots pine did not grow well on clay.

The policy of fencing off areas of two or three acres for tree regeneration put a great strain on the rest of the wood. The public was confined to the unfenced areas causing the soil to be heavily trampled, compacting the soil and perhaps shortening the lives of the trees. Instead, much smaller areas should be fenced, irregularly spaced where the tree cover was broken, or a dead tree had been felled.

The report suggested the planting of container-grown oak trees, each three or four feet high at about 10 metre intervals, with intermediate planting of holly, hornbeam, wild cherry and rowan, on small parcels of land. Each block would form its own little thicket and there would be plenty of room for the public to wander in.

The public did not want to walk at the edges of the wood bordering the Archway Road and built up areas: the denser these were the better. Groups of holly and hawthorn should be planted here, as these were more effective in creating a screen than conifers. On the roadside horsechestnuts could be added. Where it was safe, dead trees should be left to improve the habitat for wild life, and where it was not safe, the trees should be left on the ground to rot.[71]

At the Joint Consultative Committee meeting in October 1977 Mr Garthwaite's report was considered and was dismissed, in the words of David Jones who represented the

Muswell Hill and Fortis Green Association, 'as though it was the gibberings of a half-wit.' Instead the City was set on its own policy. When asked about further plans the Committee was told there were no plans, yet in February, four months later, the City felled more than fifty trees in the Wood, clearing an area almost as large as a football pitch. They would be replaced with very small oak and hornbeam trees.

Immediately the Residents Association wrote an angry letter to Hugh Rossi, the local Member of Parliament, saying that the Association did not say that the policy [of regeneration] would not work, but that it was brutal and heavy-handed, wholly inappropriate in a highly used urban woodland of which there were so few.

The Residents Association protested to the City of London and asked that the matter should be put on the agenda for the next meeting. They also attempted to have the control of the Wood moved from The City of London to Haringey Council.

The Chairman of the City of London Open Spaces Committee wrote to the Hampstead and Highgate Express stoutly defending the felling, saying that young oaks needed light if they were to grow and suffered badly by trampling, so an area to be reforested needed clearing and fencing. Without this the young trees would die. The Superintendentt of Highgate Wood was selecting the weakest parts of the wood for replanting. The size of the replacement areas and the care with which they were chosen was reflected by the fact that the National Trust estimated that it would take 300 years to replant the whole wood at the present rate of progress.[72]

This never ending conflict about the management of the Wood is in fact a sign of the importance of Highgate Wood to the local community and is a most healthy sign.

In 1983 a report on the biology and management of Highgate and Queen's Woods [70], said that Highgate Woods were notable for mature and old hornbeams, uncommon wild service trees *Sorbus tormanalis*, rowans and midland hawthorns.[70] As the trees were no longer coppiced the hornbeams in particular had now developed into large trees in their own rights, a thing that would never have happened when the woods were 'managed' and wood was cut at regular intervals for fencing and fuel.

'The flora of Highgate Woods is very limited because of past management and public pressure. The heavy tramping of sections of Queen's Woods too may have given rise to the predominance of grasses. The flora of the stream valley in this wood however is still rich.'

'The woods are an oasis for other wild life. Foxes have bred, green, greater and lesser spotted woodpeckers and nuthatches are present the last three species breeding regularly here, regular summer visitors include chiffchaff, willow warbler and blackcap and the butterflies include speckled wood, holly blue, comma, painted lady and red admirals. Occasional rarities are observed: a golden oriole was recorded in June 1983.'[70]

The report then gives maps of both King's Wood and Queen's Wood, divides them into sections and describes each in detail, with lists of trees and plants in each.

In Queen's Wood it was decided to cease all further deepening of the stream bed and the dumping of the spoil on the forest floor, as this would lower the water table. Queen's Wood is the only site for a damp woodland-valley flora and this would be destroyed if the water table was lowered. Indeed it would be be best to raise the water table level, increasing the dampness and encouraging the growth of water-loving plants. A dam creating a small pond, or damp site, could be an attractive feature as well as diversifying the habitats and encouraging particular plants.

186

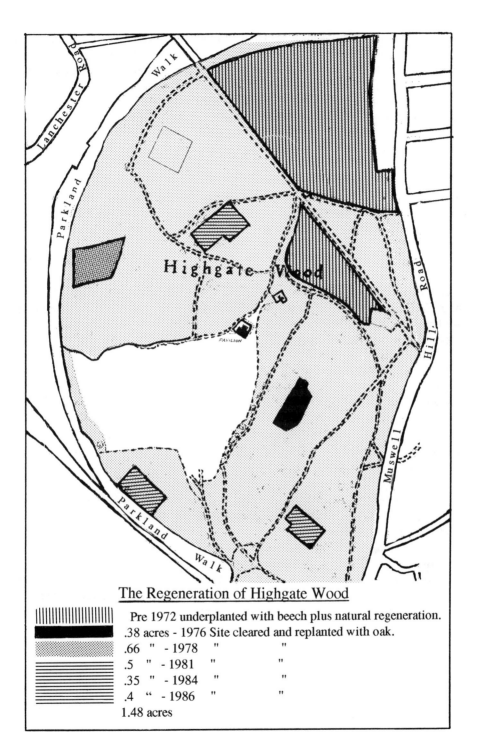

The Regeneration of Highgate Wood

Pre 1972 underplanted with beech plus natural regeneration.
.38 acres - 1976 Site cleared and replanted with oak.
.66 " - 1978 " "
.5 " - 1981 " "
.35 " - 1984 " "
.4 " - 1986 " "
1.48 acres

As I write, the problems of maintaining the Wood as a rural retreat in the middle of the urban throng has been highlighted once again. In January 1995 London Transport destroyed a copse of trees near Highgate Station which used to screen Highgate Wood from the Archway Road. The copse included a dozen mature trees which it will take years to replace. London Transport said that they needed the land for more track and, because they were on London Transport land and not part of Highgate Wood, no outside permission was required. The land was needed to lay more track and the public would benefit in the end. In the meantime the view from the Wood has been blighted for years.[77]

There was immediate cross-party complaint. People in Highgate no longer wear red petticoats and Juggin's Stout is no longer brewed, but the seclusion of the Wood has been breached yet again. From its centre we can now see hurtling cars and poster boards and hear the roar of traffic. The protection of Highgate Wood is a never-ending care.

HIGHGATE WOOD, c.1906

189

The Broadway Church

St James's Church had stood on the same site at the end of Muswell Hill Road for many years but, when Muswell Hill expanded suddenly about 1900, there were no churches for the Nonconformists. Edmondson, who was a Nonconformist himself, gave sites for the Presbyterian Church at the end of Princes Avenue and the Baptist Church at the top of Duke's Avenue. Both are placed with an architect's eye, so that today the Broadway has a church at each end and one in the centre, facing Hillfield Park. Muswell Hill Broadway had been given a commanding form for ever. In 1976 an attempt was made to demolish the Presbyterian church and redevelop the site for commercial purposes. This is the story of an attempt to destroy Edmondson's vision of a unified Broadway and its defeat.

The Broadway Church, Muswell Hill

The Presbyterian Church at the end of Princes Avenue, now known as The Broadway Church, was built in two stages. The first church was built in 1898 in Princes Avenue by Arthur Breeds F.S.I. who also later built the Baptist Church. It was opened as a church in its own right but later became the Church Hall. Only four years later, in 1902, the Presbyterian Church was built on the corner of The Broadway by George and Reginald Palmer Baines. The two churches merged both physically and organizationally to form one.

George Baines probably began his career in Accrington but was established in London by 1874. By 1900 he had designed at least 30 churches, mostly for the Baptists, some in the Italian 'rundbogen style' and others in Gothic. When he was joined by his son, Reginald Palmer Baines, in 1899 there was a sudden explosion of creativity. The son's vitality fused with the experience of the father led to a great expansion of church commissions. They were to build at least 86 in the fifteen years between 1899 and 1914.

Nonconformist churches are arranged so that everyone can witness what is happening at the communion table and The Broadway Church was a good example of this. The interior was a wide space with a central pulpit and curved benches arranged concentrically, hardly interrupted by columns. It was designed, in fact, like a modern theatre.

Muswell Hill Broadway showing St James's Church and the Broadway Church which both give dignity to the shopping parade.
Andrew Golland, 1976.

191

The outside is very striking in a highly inventive free Gothic-Art Nouveau manner, in white flints with red Costessy Ware (terra-cotta) dressings from Norwich, clearly designed to catch the eye but also selected to withstand the grime of the urban situation.

As church congregations have fallen over the years, various denominations have combined to create the United Reform Church. Here various denominations worship together, so creating a surplus of buildings for which there is no further use as churches. The buildings can either be converted to new uses, redeveloped, or left to rot. The Broadway Church was last used as a church in 1973 and the Hall behind last used in 1976. The congregation had been told that the building, and especially the roof, needed expensive repair. There was some doubt about this, but on this basis the congregation was persuaded to leave the building, which was much loved, and move to the church at the top of Tetherdown. Immediately plans were announced to demolish the Broadway Church and redevelop the site.

This was greeted with alarm by a wide range of people who saw it as an attack on the Edwardian facades of Muswell Hill. Indeed The Broadway Church was the jewel in the crown. Remove what was undoubtedly the finest building in the facade and the rest would crumble. We had already seen the effect of what can only be called the 'Sainsbury disaster', where the Athenaeum, which had been designed as the end-stop to a splendid array of shops, had been replaced by a characterless block. Another faceless slab would destroy the Broadway.

BROACH

Broadway Church Action

The BROACH logo.

Immediately protesters formed BROACH,[36] Broadway Church Action Group, to campaign for the retention of the Church building, to raise funds and place the building in Trust. The Trust would maintain the building and establish appropriate community uses for the premises. A concert hall, rehearsal studios, or a recording studio seemed possible.

Support came in from all sides - amenity groups; the Chamber of Commerce, who said that shops and offices were empty in the Broadway and they did not want more; eminent art historians and musicians; and ordinary people who had been brought up with the church and could not contemplate the destruction of an old friend.

Broach asked everyone to protest against the demolition and letters came flooding in. Sir John Summerson, the great art historian wrote:-

'It is an interesting and eloquent piece of architecture -- characteristic of a period when the Nonconformist Churches were trying to 'modernize' the Gothic Revival while retaining its most romantic features.'

'It is full of daring strokes carried out in rather unusual combinations of materials and with Craftsmanship of a kind now exceedingly rare and enormously expensive. To destroy this kind of work is horribly wasteful.'

'And in suburban London we desperately need to keep the inherited landmarks. These give character and quality to an area which no modern building can. It is very much part of Muswell Hill and I sincerely hope that local feeling and effort will succeed in saving it.'

192

Sir Hugh Casson, architect and later President of the Royal Academy, said that the church was:-

'a building of architectural merit, conspicuously placed amd making a highly individual visual contribution to the street scene. The building style is becoming increasingly admired for its originality and richness. It is good economic sense to use sound buildings for many years of valuable, if changed, use.'

Hundreds of individuals and organizations, from Yehudi Menuin to the Greater London Council's Historic Building Division, wrote to the Haringey Planning Department and the Department of the Environment to make their views clear. Broach collected over 9000 signatures against demolition and held a protest celebration outside the Church, with a street organ playing all day to attact the passers by.

Sir Nicholas Pevsner, who had included the Broadway Church in his Buildings of England series, said,

'Baines was the very best architect of Nonconformist churches and he is still easily recognisable. This building should in no circumstances be pulled down.'

The end of Princes Avenue. Andrew Golland, 1976.

Sir John Betjeman wrote:-

'The church is to Muswell Hill Broadway rather what St Martin's-in-the-Fields is to Trafalgar Square , or St Paul's to the City. By its outline and distinctive style it gives an identity to the district.

'Muswell Hill without the Broadway Church would not be Muswell Hill, but some soulless suburb,'

Julian Barnard, the art historian,[37] wrote:-

'The style is reminiscent of the work of the Glasgow designer Charles Rennie Macintosh and has the same sparkling 'jewel-like' quality as his work. The main structural lines of the church are in red terra-cotta while the infil panels are faced with cut flint, an unusual and particularly attractive combination of materials that does so much to brighten and enhance the street.'

The Ancient Monuments Society wrote:-

'The Muswell Hill Church is in the Nonconformist tradition epitomised in the Octagon chapels of Norwich and Wisbech and the Union Chapel in Compton Terrace, Islington. We would like to reassert our view that it is a building of character, quality and of individuality and we cannot believe that the Minister will allow its destruction.'

As a result of all this protest, the Department of the Environment responded to the public mood by listing the Church Grade II as 'being of special architectural and historic merit.' This listing was for the outside of the building. Unfortunately for the later story of the building, nobody noticed at the time that the inside, which was outstanding, was not separately listed. This was a fatal mistake which was to have very serious effects later and lost to Muswell Hill, among other things, an organ worth £50,000 at 1976 prices. Haringey Planning Department rejected the application to demolish and redevelop. The exterior of the Church was safe and with it the integrity of the Broadway shopping facade. BROACH had won the first battle, but victory was not yet secure.

In February 1977 the Church appealed against the rejection, despite the fact that the building was now listed. BROACH opposed as strongly as before and circulated all previous supporters, asking them to protest once again. The Planning Committee, strengthened by the listing, rejected the application once again. The building appeared to be saved so BROACH concentrated on the future.

Alternative Uses of the Building

Nonconformist churches were often designed for singing and music and The Broadway Church was famous for its sound. Felix Aprahamium, the music critic for the Sunday Times, had lived in Muswell Hill all his life and knew the church well. He wrote:-

'It seems to me utterly incredible that so well preserved a gem as the United Reform Church in Muswell Hill should be subject to commercial whims. I have heard music-making there and I know the acoustics are ideal for this purpose as well as the spoken word. I will help in any way I can to keep the building intact for cultural purposes. I believe that posterity will judge very harshly those who today oppose or hinder its retention.'

The Presbyterian Church organ, which was known for its high quality, was still in place.

1 Contrast of shops and church showing the two schools of architecture at work -
   Classical and Gothic side by side
2 View along the street showing the high degree of flamboyant detailing of the shops
   and the church.

   Andrew Golland, 1976

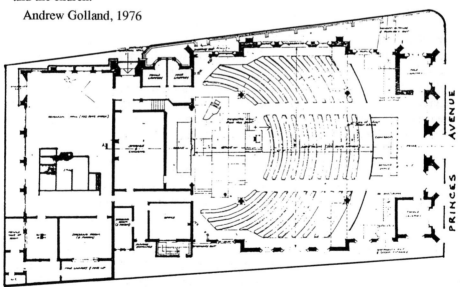

Plan of the church showing the curved pews
wrapped round the altar.

Some small pipes had been been stolen by vandals but these were covered by insurance and BROACH was promised that if the hall was used for concerts the organ would be properly restored. On a Sunday in March 1977 musicians and public gathered in the church to hear the organ and other instruments played, in what everyone thought would be the first of many concerts.

The acoustics were perfect. Felix Aprahamium, writing on behalf of the Alexandra Palace Arts Society, stated:-

'We know the sound of music in this building and assure you unhesitatingly that its acoustic ambience is ideal for concerts, --- The windows will need sound-proofing against noise from outside.'

Mr Keith Rose, ARIBA examined the building and reported :-

'A relatively long reverberation time is always desirable for classical music and the results obtained in this survey confirm the statements by musicians who have tested the church that it is ideal for classical concerts.' He considered that all windows should be triple glazed and the balcony used as a meeting or assembly area, with a glazed screen to the auditorium to reduce noise from the street.

Clearly the Church was an ideal size for chamber concerts, jazz concerts, piano and organ recitals, with an audience of 500 on the main floor. Hall design is a very sensitive art and this one was particularly successful as it created an intimate atmosphere in comfortable surroundings for quite a large audience. There were plenty of exits which needed only minor alterations to conform to the Fire Regulations.

The building could also be used as a recording studio, with the equipment and controls

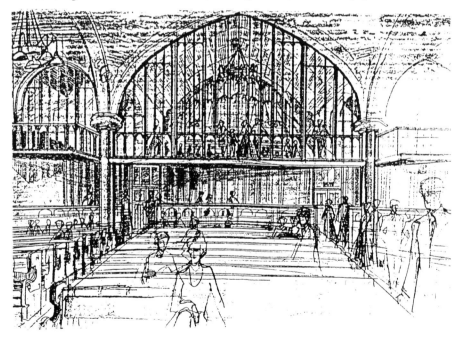

Sketch of the proposed conversion of the church with the balcony glazed in as a separate circulation space.

Andrew Golland, ARIBA, 1976.

196

housed in the Church Hall behind. Various record companies, including EMI were interested.

It would provide excellent rehearsal facilities for small and medium-sized orchestras. Plans were made to put the curved pews on runners so that they could be slid back to provide more space.

There were inquiries from The National Theatre Student Company, a film society, craftsmen wanting a venue for a monthly market, and more. The possibilities seemed enormous. BROACH produced an impressive Feasability Study which was well received.

In the midst of this creative planning the church authorities appealed over the head of Haringey Council to the Department of The Environment for permission to demolish and redevelop the site. The DOE arranged for a Public Inquiry on 15th and 16th November 1977 at Hornsey Town Hall, which was later postponed to 2nd and 3rd May 1978. BROACH had to postpone planning and fight for the church for the third time.

The Inquiry

BROACH assembled an impressive array of experts including Sir John Summerson, then Curator of the Soane Museum; David Adler, consulting engineer; Christopher Wakeling, who was completing a thesis on Nonconformist churches and had visited dozens of Baines churches; Felix Aprahamium and other musicians who confirmed that the church had an outstanding acoustic; Dr Joan Schwitzer of the Hornsey Historical Society, and many others.

David Adler's evidence was critical because the church authorities were trying to say that the roof was unsafe and the building should be demolished for safety reasons. As luck would have it, Alistair Service, the writer on Edwardian Architecture,[31] had just sent a letter to BROACH saying:-

'The roof structure is one of the most ambitious and successful designs of its sort in London. It is an early example of roof trussing by a light steel frame developed by Messrs Dawnay & Sons and was illustrated as an example to be followed by other church architects (Vol 4 of Modern Buildings: Their Planning, Construction and Equipment, by G.A.T.Middleton, 1907).'

This letter arrived by final post on the first day of the Inquiry, with David Adler due to give evidence next morning. At 10 o'clock the next day I was at the the doors of the Royal Institute of British Architects Library as they opened, and twenty minutes later I was in a taxi on my way to the Inquiry with a photocopy of the roof truss. As David Adler was talking we were able to put the truss design in front of him. He said that the truss was not well designed and one member had probably collapsed when the roof was first built, but this was not of any importance. Muswell Hill had lived with the roof as it was for eighty years and could live with it for another eighty.

The Inspector rejected the application to demolish and advised conversion to a use which required an enclosed space of a high standard. He suggested a Concert Hall or Library. It was this suggestion which was to founder because the inside had not been listed.

Haringey Council renewed its offer to buy, but the Church prevaricated. They were slow at answering letters and set up obstacles. When Broach produced a carefully

197

costed plan for a Concert Hall, with a restaurant and bar in the then Church Hall, the Church authorities countered by limiting the times and nature of the bar, knowing full well that the scheme was not viable in those conditions. Haringey wanted to buy the building freehold but the Church offered only a lease, and that with conditions: the building could not be used in any way for business or commercial purposes other than as a concert hall. This would have precluded use as a bank, shopping mall, etc, precisely the uses which the church had in mind if they ever succeeded in demolishing the site. Obstruction went on for months.

Late in 1977 Haringey resolved to make a cash offer, but it appeared that the church authorities had lined up potential purchasers and were determined to obtain the highest conceivable price for the site. The advising surveyors had the effrontery to claim that the building was not worth saving, despite the views of the highest architectural historians and the protest of 9000 local people. Broach issued a press release in February 1978 calling on the church authorities to negotiate fairly and asking the old congregation of the church 'not to accept this profit-motivated vandalism', but the negotiations still dragged on.

In January 1979 Andrew Golland, Dip Arch RIBA applied on behalf of Broach for Listed Building Consent to convert the church into a Concert Hall with restaurant and bar. Permission was granted by Haringey Planning Development Committee under the 1971 Town and Country Planning Act. [32]

Haringey reserved the money to buy the building but, with increasing pressure on its budget, was not able to retain it for the following year and was therefore no longer in a position to buy the building outright. By 1980 the financial climate was forbidding, which made it difficult for BROACH to raise funds for the conversion. Recording companies were worse hit than most and major orchestras were being affected by public expenditure cuts. The BBC was pruning orchestras which would reduce demand for rehearsal space.

BROACH now suggested that the building should become a Library, while still retaining facilities for small-scale recitals. There was a suggestion that Bond & White's should move in, but that would have altered the front elevation in an unacceptable way. In any case, there was no room for builders' lorries to park and load on this busy corner of the Broadway. A developer wanted to turn it into a shopping mall, but failed to complete. There was a proposal for nine flats and later another scheme for ten flats.

In the end another developer converted the Church Hall in Princes Avenue into flats, which are still in occupation and appear to be perfectly satisfactory, but the story of the Church is a complete disaster. Because the interior was not listed, the developer was free to put in a floor at balcony level, the pews and organ went to the four winds and the church became offices.

For some time Haringey Borough Council rented the offices for the Housing Department, but there were complaints about the ventilation. The staff did not like the conversion and, as the economic climate became more hostile, the Housing Department moved out, no other tenant was found, and the building remained empty.

The integrity of the shopping parade has been saved. Edmondson's vision of a unified architecture for the Broadway remains, but even if a tenant is found for the building the noble space of the church had been destroyed and Muswell Hill deprived of a fine concert hall for ever.

The logo of Broadway Church Action

The logo I drew based on the church window, when we hoped that the interior space and organ would be saved and the church become a concert hall. Unfortunately this nightingale never sang.

At Christmas 1994, Taylor Walker applied to Haringey Planning Committee for permission to convert the Church into a public house and brewery. The plan had the advantage of preserving the building and finding a viable use for it. They proposed to remove the new floors put in by the previous developer, opening up the internal space.

Taylor Walker's design for converting the church into a public house.
Presentation drawing by Paul Dickinson and Associates.

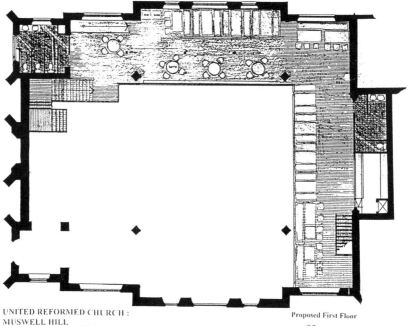

UNITED REFORMED CHURCH :
MUSWELL HILL

Proposed First Floor

The proposed mezzanine floor on two sides[80]

so that one could see the original ceiling once again. They would build a small brewery on one side of the ground floor and increase the floor space by building a mezzanine floor on two sides. The plan is self-descriptive.

The application to open a pub was greeted with alarm by people in neighbouring streets, who were very concerned with the effect of a pub drawing in young people from a long distance, especially on Friday and Saturday nights. Taylor Walker had already attempted to open a pub further along the Broadway and, in face of local opposition, had decided instead to open Café Toto, a thirty five seat restaurant, near Boot's. Now they were trying again.

Local residents, concerned about increased noise and car parking, held a protest meeting in The Crocodile antiques shop opposite the Church. These protests continued at the Council Planning meeting. Suggestions of an extra restaurant or a community centre were made, but not backed by any realistic money. On the other hand everyone agreed that a viable use for the building had to be found or it would decay.

The meeting was adjourned to give everyone a chance to produce alternative schemes, but when it was reconvened, on 30 May 1995, no such scheme emerged. The Council then gave Taylor Walker planning permission to convert the building providing it was adequately insulated against sound.

Some people still object. There is talk of a public inquiry which would be extremely expensive to the Council and time consuming, but may well happen. Readers will have to complete this chapter for themselves as the story continues.

An artist's impression of the new interior, with a bar and mezzanine floor above.
The roof should be a four-sided dome, not a continuous vault, but the general
impression is not unlike what might be built if the work went ahead.

Paul Dickinson & Associates

The original vault[6]

Muswell Hill Odeon

Muswell Hill has had four cinemas; The Athenaeum, built as a dance hall on what is now the Sainsbury site; The Summerland at the bottom of Summerland Avenue, now a car park; the Ritz, built in 1936 opposite The Green Man, demolished and now offices and flats; and the Odeon, opened four months before the Ritz. Only the last has survived.

To understand the importance of the Odeon to Muswell Hill we have to go back a number of years. The Athenaeum had been a dance hall and when it became a cinema it was always clear that we were sitting in a converted building with high ceilings and irrelevant decoration. The Summerland was like a theatre at the end of a seaside pier. The Ritz was purpose-built, but was of only minimal interest as a building, but the Odeon was the result of one man's passion for the Cinema. Oscar Deutsch was the centre of a hectic cinema building boom which began in the early nineteen thirties and stopped only with the opening of the Second World War.

Born in 1893 in Birmingham, his parents were Jewish immigrants from Central Europe and his father had been successful as a partner in a scrap metal firm. Oscar Deutsch

The Odeon, Muswell Hill

202

started in the family firm but was soon attracted to the cinema, so in 1920 he went into partnership with Michael Balcon and Victor Saville to form Victory Motion Pictures Ltd. The other two later created Marlborouh Films and became film makers, while Deutsch was more attracted to film distribution. He bought his first cinema at the age of twenty-five and soon bought a number of other small cinemas in side streets. He then decided to become a national distributor and commissioned a number of Midlands architects to build cinemas for him between 1930 and 1934 in a variety of styles.

When he invited Harry Weedon, yet another Midlands architect, to co-operate in the interior decor of the Odeon, Warley, which opened on 22 December 1934, a new design flair and speed of building became evident. Larger cinemas were completed in a year or less and smaller ones in seven or eight months, while a new ODEON house style also appeared.

Clavering, a young architect on Harry Weedon's staff, who had qualified only in 1933, had became interested in the ideas of Courbousier and the Germans. Erich Mendelsohn's Universum Cinema in Berlin, built 1928, was particularly influential. Many early cinemas were converted theatres, with their high fly-towers and several levels of galleries, so the ceilings were high. This height was not necessary in cinemas as there was only one balcony and a low screen, so ceilings could be lowered, reducing the building costs, giving a warmer, more intimate atmosphere and moving the projection box down so that films could be projected with less distortion.

Most cinemas at this period borrowed from Classical styles, Chinese, the Moors and especially from the Egyptians. Any romantic style would do and the more that cinemas looked like bizarre film sets, instead of buildings, the better. Instead of this, Odeon Cinemas developed a plain, modern style, simple and bold. They were characterized by a large fascia to the street in faience, or terracotta and the name ODEON lit by a halo of red neon light. This, with floodlighting from above the entrance canopy, made a dramatic impact at night. As a result, the cinemas had a characteristic style which could be recognised from one end of the country to the other.

The expansion and building were organized on almost military lines, with a precise brief for each building, the latest cinema equipment, bulk buying of carpets, settees and even ash trays. Frequent and close inspection of each stage of building, with rigid attention to fire-regulations and local bye-laws, was standard so that nothing should interfere with the buildings being accepted for showing films by the designated opening day.

The people involved were almost cut off from the outside world by their obsession for opening cinemas. Sixteen hours a day were normal. R.A.Bullivant, one of the architects involved in the building of the chain of Odeons, said in 1979:-

'I was reminded how myopic a view I had [of the Nineteen Thirties], yet I was constantly travelling the country when motoring was still a delight and I was conscious of my good fortune at a time when many architects had little or no work to do. At first I was only vaguely conscious of what was going on outside.

'Later it was impossible not to be aware that war would come again, but war was not discussed and sites were acquired and openings planned into 1940 and 1941. We became anaesthetized against the inevitable.'[60]

As an example of the pace at which they worked, Muswell Hill Odeon was one of thirty-two Odeons opened in 1936 alone.

In 1935 George Coles, who was an experienced cinema architect, was commissioned by Oscar Deutsch to build the Muswell Hill Odeon, together with a complex of nine shops and ten flats, with a private car park behind for the cinema goers. Although Deutsch had no interest in shops or flats he was often forced to build mixed complexes if his cinema plans were to be accepted by local planners, who wanted something extra besides the cinema as a planning gain. Thus at Muswell Hill and no doubt elsewhere, he built shops and flats but immediately sold them off when his cinema was opened.

The site was at the corner of Muswell Hill Road and Fortis Green Road, opposite St James's Church. All but a couple of the 1860s terrace of houses, once occupied by surgeons, doctors and other professional people, were demolished to give Coles a commanding corner site on which to make his statement, with the height of the original terrace dictating the building height. Coles placed the cinema entrance boldly in the corner as a flaring display, the main feature of the complex, not unlike the Astoria at Finsbury Park. The St James's Church congregation was immediately roused to anger by this flamboyance. The sedate and respectable church would be faced by enormous posters of naked film stars and violent gangsters, floodlit and topped with a dramatic neon sign flaming red against the night sky. This, in of all places Muswell Hill, was completely unacceptable. Muswell Hill would not tolerate such desecration.

George Coles quickly rethought his design. He built flats and shops all along the Muswell Hill Road frontage and curved them sharply round the corner, so that the

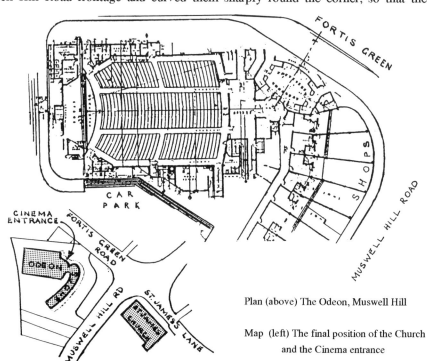

Plan (above) The Odeon, Muswell Hill

Map (left) The final position of the Church and the Cinema entrance

Church was faced by a quiet, simple frontage in a warm brown brick, midway between the traditional Muswell Hill red brick and the grey Ancaster and Bath Stone of the Church. The Cinema remained where it was, but the entrance was moved along to the end of the site and into Fortis Green Road. Movement from the foyer into the cinema was skewed. A slip road was built in front of the shops, distancing them from the Church, while the sharp curve of the shops and a group of trees formed a screen, discreetly hiding the Cinema from religious gaze. A most sophisticated solution.

The top of the flats is horizontal and the long Crittal windows, typical of the period, stress the horizontal form of the design and make the building appear lower than it is. The architect has cleverly disguised the fact that the site is sloping. To achieve the level top to the flats and so give peace to the design, the shop ceilings have to vary in height. The ground slopes downwards towards the car park entrance, so the heights of the shop ceilings gradually increase as one moves from the corner of the building towards the car park entrance. Thus all the shop ceilings are at the same level and the flats can have a horizontal roof. When Bond & White's took over a row of four adjacent shops and knocked them together, the changes of floor level became apparent. Today the floor rises and sinks in Bond and White's, as we move, vaguely bewildered, from one level to the next. This change would not have been noticed when the shops were separate.

Since the whole cinema complex had to conform to the rigid Fire Regulations governing cinemas, all the materials had to be fireproof. Thus the buildings are in steel framed construction, concrete and brick, with aesbestos roof tiles for the cinema and asphalt for the floors and roof of the flats. The speed of construction was astonishing. The Cinema and flats each took eight months to complete, but the flats were not started until the cinema walls were almost complete and were not finished until four months after the cinema had opened.

The Odeon was a modern, purpose-built cinema, not a converted theatre and the shape reflects this. Coles designed a splendid Art Deco interior, with the ceiling sweeping down from the balcony to the screen in great curves. The concealed lighting in the long central ceiling light and the sweeping curves which carry the ceiling down to the screen create the appearance of a giant cash register, with the seat backs as keys. Fortunately, despite the conversion of the cinema into three smaller units, the view from the balcony is unimpaired and can still be enjoyed as an excellent example of Art Deco design.

Oscar Deutsch had boundless energy, was able to work until two in the morning, and is said to have needed only three hours sleep at night. He built some 140 cinemas, acquired about the same number of existing ones and spent more than £10 million in capital outlay.[61] The expansion had been so rapid and everyone was so fully committed that, as was mentioned earlier, they were all oblivious of what was going on in the world outside. This lack of perspective allowed Harry Weedon to take Bullivant and two others into partnership in April 1939 and in September they were operating from four offices with a total staff of 160. War was declared on 3rd September 1939 and all the work they were engaged on came to a full stop the next day.

The War caused a complete crisis in the cinema industry. Anticipating immediate mass raids, cinemas and theatres were closed by order. No cash was coming in and cinema shares could not be sold for fear of a price collapse. After several weeks the Government decided to allow places of entertainment to reopen and audiences soon reached all-time records. Thus the cash flow and bank credits were eased, but building

The interior fron the balcony

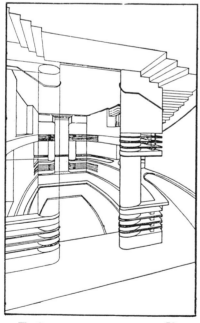

The foyer and the balcony staircase[79]

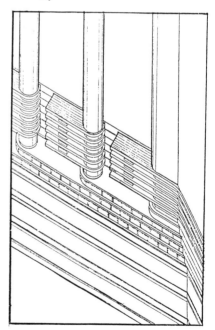

The art deco flank wall[79]

virtually ceased. For years there was a half-built Odeon in Junction Road, Highgate, one of the first casualties of the War.

Oscar Deutsch had been in hospital several times and recovered, but in 1941 his illness recurred and he died of cancer at the early age of forty-eight. This came as a great shock to all his associates who had no inkling that he was so ill. Even if he had survived, it is most unlikely that the cinema building boom would have been resumed. Quite apart from the War, that particular phase was gone.

In the nineteen forties and fifties the cinema flourished, with huge audiences and films appealing to all ages. By 1960 other forms of entertainment, including television, drew people away from the cinema so that profits fell and by the seventies some were trading at a loss. As audiences continued to fall, land values and property prices began to soar as the property boom began. Land was more valuable than cinema seats.

The Summerland was demolished and then the Athenaeum was rebuilt as a Sainsbury store. The Ritz ABC cinema at the top of Muswell Hill was demolished and rebuilt to provide 25.000 sq. ft. of office space on the ground, first and second floors, with the basement and sub-basement providing car space and, on the third floor, flats with extensive views over London. The original design was a stark brutalist block of the worst sort, but protests and some professional advice led the Council to insist on the present Mansard roof, which is a considerable improvement.

This left the Muswell Hill Odeon as the sole cinema. In 1974 it was converted to three screens and in 1976 the Council took over the car park for public us. However, it was not until 1981 that Muswell Hill became fully aware of the threat to its last remaining cinema when Rank Entertainment Ltd attempted to demolish the Odeon and redevelop, perhaps as another and larger Sainsbury store.

The Muswell Hill Odeon appeared to be reasonably successful and had just fitted a bar in the cinema, but The Hornsey Journal reported that of the three local Odeons, both Wood Green and Holloway were trading at a loss while Muswell Hill was 'in the black' and Bar sales had also improved profitability. However, both Sainsbury's and Tesco were interested in the site which was large, central and with an integral car park. Rank's saw the opportunity to make an immediate cash profit - to asset-strip the site - and to this end they claimed that the cinema as an entertainment form was dying. Rank's were being forced by the public to move out of cinemas.

Shortly before this Muswell Hill and Fortis Green Association had joined in a bid to have the 1930s art deco Odeon building listed and the decision was pending. Nearly 4000 signatures were collected protesting at the closure. Mr Rossi, then MP for Hornsey, wrote to the Rank Organization but met with a blank refusal to reconsider.

David Atwell, who was the Information Officer for the GLC's Architects' Department and one of the most influential experts on 1930s architecture, had written a book on art deco cinemas which featured the Muswell Hill Odeon. He was "appalled at the idea of demolition" especially as he had only just before recommended the Muswell Hill Odeon for listing, together with three other cinemas. All were approved except the Odeon which then became the only 1930s cinema in London not listed. He said,

"Without doubt Muswell Hill Odeon is the best surviving interior in the country." ---"I can't understand why they did not agree".[65]

Finally the mass protest by the public had its effect. In September 1981 the Rank Organization announced a reprieve for the Muswell Hill Odeon, one of thirteen London cinemas which had been destined to close, because its profits had apparently improved.[66] In 1984 the Cinema was listed Grade II* and is now far safer than it was. Long may it last.[74]

CHURCHYARD BOTTOM WOOD, HIGHGATE.

Between 1860 and 1880 the centre was torn out of the City of London to build sewers, railways and new roads.[38] Houses were demolished without regard for the tenants who had to find whatever accommodation they could. Managers went to live in Kensington and St John's Wood, while the poorest crowded into the rookeries like Seven Dials and Lisson Grove. For those between, the clerks and skilled workmen, the speculative builder put up row after row of terraced villas and Mr Pooter moved into Holloway. The people of Muswell Hill watched houses creep across the fields of Finsbury Park, up Crouch Hill and down the other side, so that by 1880, Crouch End was being developed and there seemed no way to stem the flow. Ten years later the large estates of Muswell Hill were being sold. Upton Farm was sold and the Ecclesiastical Commissioners wanted to develop Churchyard Bottom Wood, now called Queen's Wood. The story would have made an Ibsen play. Two groups of honest, highly motivated people fighting for what they each thought was right. The Ecclesiastical Commissioners on the one hand and the Committee of the Hornsey Charities on the other, both believed they were doing their best for other people, and the public rose up against them both in indignation.

At that time Muswell Hill Road was a country road, with Southwood Hall at one end and Upton Farm at the other. By 1894, Onslow Gardens was built, Connaught Gardens marked out, and builders were poised to develop the Woodlands estate. Cut out of Churchyard Bottom Wood was a group of tumble-down cottages, on a triangular site. An undated map, held by the Ecclesiastical Commissioners[3,] shows six Wasteland Cottages with an opening between them - not a road, not metalled, but a way through to the strawberry beds behind. Further along was another gap which led to footpaths through the wood. These two openings were to be the basis of the plan. The same two gaps and the cleared ground, which was the strawberry field, can be seen in the 1894 map below. They are shown as 'Muswell Hill Cottages' and, quite in passing, Peter Sellers was to live on the same site much later on. To develop the wood as a housing estate, the Commissioners needed to drive two roads through from Muswell Hill Road and build houses along them. The Muswell Hill Road frontage alone would not have provided room for enough houses to make the venture worthwhile.

The land and cottages had been given much earlier as almshouses to house old people and were held on their behalf by the Trustees of the Hornsey Charity Commissioners. By the 1890s the cottages were tumble-down, in need of major repair. Public-spirited, wishing to do the best for their old tenants, the Trustees could not improve them since they had no money. Some years before the Ecclesiastical Commissioners had planned to develop Gravel Pit Wood (now Highgate Wood) as a housing estate, but this had met such opposition that they backed down. Instead, in 1886, they gave all 69 acres woodland to the public. At the same time they offered to sell Churchyard Bottom Wood to Hornsey Urban District Council for £25,000, but this was too much for Hornsey to raise on its own. The Council said that people living outside Hornsey also enjoyed the

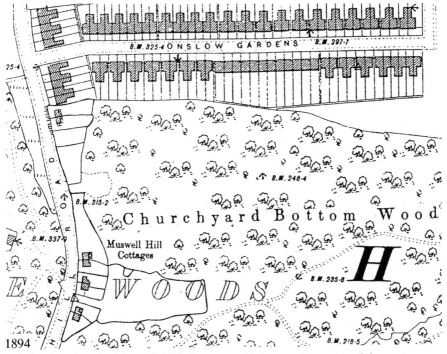

Map showing the Muswell Hill Cottages which were the centre of the controversy.

209

wood and other authorities should help, but no help was given. In the end the offer fell into abeyance.

The Ecclesiastical Commissioners wanted to raise money for its church work here and abroad. They considered that they had been given the land to be used for the propogation of religion and if this meant selling off land or woods, it was a lesser evil than restricting the work of the church. They had given Gravel Pit Wood to the public: in its place they would develop Churchyard Bottom Wood.

The Trustees of the Hornsey Charities wanted to produce an income to help their poor people, so they made an offer to the Commissioners. Their triangular piece of land was too awkwardly shaped to be developed economically, but if the Commissioners would grant them some more land to make it into a square site, they would build twenty-five neat villas. These would bring in ground rents of £225 per annum, which could be used to relieve the poverty of Hornsey people. In return they would permit the Commissioners to cut two roads through their land so that the Commissioners could develop the woods.

When this offer became known people immediately reacted with alarm. On the 16th December 1893 Mr Carvell Williams MP asked in the House of Commons, if the Ecclesiastical Commissioners had consented to sell a strip of land to the Hornsey Charities Trustees on condition that an existing road be widened to 40 feet, whether this was a preliminary to a building scheme and if the House of Parliament would have an opportunity to express an opinion.

Mr Leveson Gower, a Church Estates Commissioner replied',"Yes" to the first part.

Mr Carvell Williams, "Do I understand it is the intention to destroy that portion of Highgate Woods by building on it?"

Mr Leveson Gower, "No Sir. My Hon Friend must not understand anything of the kind."

Two days later The Star published an article worthy of any modern tabloid.

'Parliament must keep a keen watch on those old vandals and confederates of the jerry-builder the Ecclesiastical Commissioners. They are always alienating some piece of land or are favouring the builders as opposed to the general public. The Commissioners would not sell the Churchyard Bottom wood to the ratepayers but now propose 'to open it up' by cutting two wide roads through it in connection with one of their numerous building schemes. Will not someone ask a question in Parliament and check the brick and mortar policy of the Commissioners?'

By the time this was printed, the question had been asked and the answer was either untrue, or devious. Other papers took up the story. The Times, in a long report, said that the Commissioners were not prepared to give an undertaking that Parliament, or any other public body, should have an opportunity of considering any scheme for building on the site of the wood.

The situation simmered for eighteen months until the Ecclesiastical Commissioners were forced to open an enquiry, which began at Highgate on 31 May 1895, chaired by an Assistant Ecclesiastical Commissioner. The Inquiry produced a flurry of newspaper letters of which this was the most important.

The Daily Chronicle, 5 June 1895
VANDALISM AT HIGHGATE

Sir - One of the most lovely bits of woodland in suburban London is threatened. Will you help us to ward off what would be a calamity, not only to the immediate district, but to the whole of densely-populated North London? In no part of the metropolis has the builder been more active than in Crouch End and Hornsey. The beautiful meadows of a year or two ago are now houses and shops. Ballast heaps have taken the place of stately elms and chestnuts, and once pleasant villages are sharing the fate of Stroud Green, Harringay, Finsbury Park, Highbury and Islington. ---

---- The object is the construction of two forty-foot roads through the woods. We in this district know the meaning of forty-foot roads through woods. It means that the woods are doomed. Ten years ago agitation saved the sister-wood of sixty-five acres - The Gravel Pit Woods - and no one who saw the Bank Holiday crowds flocking up the Archway Road from the dreary streets of Holloway, Islington and Clerkenwell, and watched the keen enjoyment of the children and family parties picnicking on the grass and among the trees, could fail to realise the immense boon that the grant by the Ecclesiastical Commissioners of this wood has been to the whole of North London, but the Lower Wood of sixty acres has always been regarded as a natural complement of the other. ----

--- The Ecclesiastical Commissioners own nearly one-third of the large parish of Hornsey. By the liberal expenditure of the ratepayers' money in the opening up of roads and the general development of the district, the value of their property has been enormously increased, and from this unearned increment they each year draw large revenues. Surely the ratepayers whose money has thus aided in creating the immense estate may expect liberal treatment in return. ---

Yours obediently,

Signed by The Vicar of St James', Muswell Hill, the Minister of Park Chapel, Crouch End, a barrister living in Onslow Gardens and three members of the District Council.

It was a shot right across the bows of the Ecclesiastical Commissioners. Religious leaders and the District Council all up in arms saying in effect that the church was too rich and should be charitable, not greedy. The inclusion of the two clergymen was a shrewd move.

The Evening News, 7 June 1895 said:-

"If the Ecclesiastical Commissioners are not tackled at once, the building octopus will get a grip of the wood which will be very difficult to loosen later on, ---. Therefore it behoves Londoners to be up and doing if they would save one of their most delightful bits of rustic scenery. The public inquiry stands adjourned to Thursday next, and before then something must be done to convince the Commissioners that the citizens of London will not tolerate the confiscation of one of their favourite playgrounds.'

A letter in the Daily Chronicle the next day said:-

' ----It was with great relief that that the residents, some ten years ago, heard that the purchase of the Upper Wood had been effected; and how delightful a boon this has proved, anyone who visited them can testify, but all who exerted themselves to save these upper woods, which lie on the west side of Muswell Hill road, felt that their victory was incomplete so long as the sixty acres on the east side remained in danger. It is, as it were, an accident that the woods are divided by a broad high road. Can anyone doubt what the effect would be if the Churchyard Bottom Wood were replaced by rows of small villas, each sending out its contribution of smoke and soot? Can anyone doubt, too, the serious difference it would make to the picturesque setting of the purchased woods if a line of staring new houses were to be run up right over against their leafy frontage?'

This expressed the opinions of many people. In fact, the Gravel Pit Wood, which the writer calls the 'Upper Wood', had not been purchased, but given to the district by the Ecclesiastical Commission, a point they were to reiterate time and again over the years, but most people ignored it. The Commission was not going to give away a second wood whatever anyone said, and held this position to the end.

H.S.Chamberlain, of 5 Cranley Gardens, in a letter to the Times dated June 8, 1895, urged purchase.

I know that it is common to speak harshly of the Ecclesiastical Commissioners, but as the trustees of a fund they are bound to administer it to the greatest advantage, and therefore, if anything is to be done to save the demolition of the wood, it appears to me that it can only be effected by the purchase of the property from the Commissioners, who I know, are fully alive to the protection of free and open spaces for the people, and who, I feel sure, would be disposed to treat the matter of a purchase in a free and liberal spirit, as they have already done in the matter of the Shepherd's Cot-field, by granting a lease to the Crouch End Playing-fields Company - a small company in which I own a few shares, a small company which was formed exclusively for the purpose of securing the fields for cricket, tennis etc.--

As Chairman of the Muswell Hill Conservative Association, I am constantly in touch with the inhabitants, and I can safely affirm that every person resident in the neighbourhood would do anything in reason to preserve this beautiful wood from the destroyer.

Might I suggest that the parish of Hornsey should raise a loan for the sole purpose of purchasing the wood, and make it an open space, free and for ever, for the use of the public? ---

The Inquiry

An Inquiry was opened but adjourned because the Ratepayers' Association wished to obtain a full expression of public opinion. In the meantime a letter appeared from H.R.Williams, a Charity Trustee of Hornsey. His Trust was responsible for providing charity to the Poor of Hornsey and he argued the case for building the 25 villas. He had been active in the campaign about the wood for years and had nothing to gain personally: all he wanted was Charity income to support his poor people. He demanded his acre of land - not a great deal surely - he believed the Commissioners' assurance that the wood was not in danger. 'Muswell Hill Road was one of the best in Hornsey and would remain equally beautiful, houses or no houses', and then came the great rhetorical flourish. 'Are the poor to suffer because of the sentimental objections and the hysterical cry of 'wolf' just raised by your correspondents? Something must be done and that soon. An acre of back-land added to the charity estate would make no appreciable difference to the land remaining, while the profit derived from it would succour many poor old and deserving persons in their declining years and enable us to hand over to our successors an estate which in the distant future would be of great value in the rendering of charitable aid to the deserving poor of the parish of Hornsey.'

Reading his letter one senses hysteria very near the surface. Why did he think the Commissioners wanted to build a road? Why should they spend all that money if not to build houses? He never seemed to realise that for an acre of land the the whole wood would be lost. But he had been with the problem for a long time. He was the person to whom the Commissioners had made the offer of sale for £25,000 years before and it is his name which is honoured in a plaque on Crouch End Clock Tower for saving the wood, but his trust in the Ecclesiastical Commissioners seems naive. It is sad that at the Inquiry he was to be cast as the devil.

The adjourned Inquiry opened in Highgate on 15 June 1895. Expecting a large gathering, the Council Chamber had been changed completely. The usual tables had been removed and the room filled with chairs. By half past seven the room was crowded, with people jostling for seats.

Mr Murray, the Commissioner, said the Inquiry was really a simple one. Hornsey Parochial Charities wished to purchase a piece of land adjoining their charity property at the back. The question was whether the Charity Commission, which controlled all charities, had enough power to stop them. The Church Commissioners were prepared to sell the land at very favourable terms and the income of the Charity would be very considerable increased.

Against this there were three classes of objection. The original Trust was for the purpose of providing cottages for the Poor, but the trustees were proposing to build villas which would be too expensive for the Poor. However, it was within the power of the Trustees to vary the terms of the Trust, so they could build villas if they thought that the Poor would benefit in the end. The poor people themselves might object, but liberal provisions had already been promised for them. The third objection related to the aesthetic and public side of the question. He took it from what he had read that the Charity Commission ought to interfere to prevent the Ecclesiastical Commissioners from exercising their own discretion in dealing with their own property.

The Inquiry discussed fine points, but the speakers kept coming back to the major problem of preventing any destruction of the wood. The Vestry Clerk of Islington, representing 300,000 people, made a formal protest about any part of the wood, so valuable for the people of Islington and Hornsey being used for private purposes.

Mr Wilfred White said that if the Commissioners would give them time they would be able to raise the money to compensate the Trustees. Mr Beaumont said they did not want villas, they wanted cottages for poor people who were being driven out of the district. Others said that there was no money to build cottages to replace the present delapidated ones but villas would be an economic proposition. Others retorted that there were score of villas to let in Highgate. The Wood was sacred. Stick to the question of the Wood.

Dr Fletcher said the cry among the working people was that there was nowhere to go. Working people came to him with the cry, "We are driven out of Highgate and are obliged to go to Highgate New Town."

If the Muswell Hill Road frontage was sold there was no question but that roads might be cut right through the woods in the direction of Hornsey, but if the Commissioners could not get the land from the Charity Commission they could not cut the road.

He was very sure the cottages could be put into a fit state of repair. He was asked by the poor people, by the police and by a number of the working classes to represent these two points, that cottage accommodation was very sorely needed in Highgate and that if they once allowed the land to be sold, there was no telling where the hand of the builder would be stayed.

(Loud and prolonged cheers).

Numerous other people spoke and the Commissioner summed up by saying that he took it that the prevailing opinion was in favour of retaining the cottages but the meeting should draw no conclusions from what he had said (Groans).

Others said that the Trustees of the Charity had failed in their duties by letting the the cottages fall into disrepair.

Mr H.R.Williams, the Trustee who had written to the paper earlier, said that he had it on the best authority that the Church Commissioners would make no roads whatever and they would not be benefitted one iota by the actions of the Charity Commissioners. Others were far less trusting and the meeting closed after nearly three hours.

Drawn from Hornsey & Finsbury Park Journal & North Islington Standard report, 15 June 1895).

Another article from an unknown and undated paper[3] says:-

'We are faced with the fact that in Highgate and Muswell Hill there are a number of persons who want the Churchyard Bottom Wood and will not be happy until they have got it - while nobody appears willing to spend a farthing to pay for it. Everyone says it would be a fine thing to have the wood as open space, but everybody thinks it is the duty of someone else to make it one. The Islington Vestry has 'resolved' on the subject, but the Islington Vestry does not offer a penny piece towards the purchase. - -- There is no more difficult problem for the community or the individual to solve than how to gain possession of other people's property without paying for it.'

Paying for it was indeed the problem as Churchyard Bottom Wood became the subject of intense local and national debate. A joint committee was formed to raise money to save the wood. On 20 November 1896, C.F.Cory-Wright, Hon Treasurer, wrote to The Standard, a daily paper at that time, appealing for help. He reminded everyone of the danger of losing the wood and said it could only be saved by buying it. The Church Commissioners would sell for £25,000 and an extra £5,000 would be required for fencing and drainage, making a total of £30,000. This was too much for Hornsey Council to raise but they had already voted £10,000 towards the total. The woods were of inestimable value to all of North London so he appealed to public bodies and private people to raise the remaining £20,000. He warned that the present offer from the Church Commissioners was open only to the end of 1898. After that the builders would move in.

The appeal was warmly welcomed by the press. A Private Bill was rushed through Parliament and the Highgate Woods Preservation Act, 1897, became law. The Committee now had the right to advertise for contributions towards buying the Wood and preserving it.

In a fairly short time almost all the money was raised, but the last few thousand proved very difficult to raise and the Commissioners' deadline was a matter of weeks away. Mr Cory-Wright wrote pleading for more time but was granted a mere three months and then only if interest at 4 per cent was paid for the extra period on the full sum. In the end the London County Council, which had originally offered £2,500, made this up to £5,000 and the total was reached, but it was a close-run thing.

The Council decided to re-name the Wood as the 'Queen's Wood in honour of Queen Victoria's Diamond Jubilee and Hornsey put on a fine display of bunting when the Duchess of Albany formally declared the Wood open 'for the free use of the public for ever'.

MUSWELL HILL ROAD IN 1880.
W. WEST.

Muswell Hill Road about 1880 [94]

It seems probable that these three pairs of cottages
were the ones at the centre of the dispute.

How the Money was Raised

While the campaign to save Churchyard Bottom Wood was run and directed by local people who felt passionately about this particular piece of woodland, they called on the help and experience of a vast network of people, some of whom had worked together on similar campaigns for over thirty years. The Committee issued an appeal, printed on very good quality paper and bearing some famous names.

The questions of open space and public health were major subjects of the Victorian vision. Octavia Hill, the great housing reformer, who had begun with three old houses in Marylebone, bought for her by John Ruskin, had quickly become an expert on housing poor people in the healthiest conditions possible. Her way was to buy leases and then knock down some of the crowded houses in order to bring light and air to the rest, believing that fresh air and sunlight were the the only way poor people could be

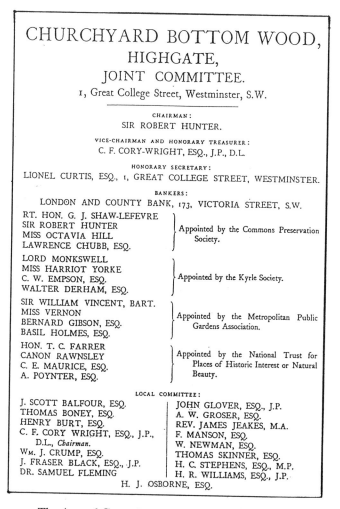

The Appeal Committee set up to save the Wood

saved from 'putrid fever'. She had learnt this as a child from her grandfather, Southwood Smith, who developed his theories at the Fever Hospital at King's Cross. He had built the first Industrial Dwellings for poor people and had proved statistically that good air and decent drainage saved lives.[51]

Open spaces and the opportunity to breathe clean air, were essential for people living in one or two crowded rooms. Octavia Hill took her charges from the Lisson Grove slums, up Fitzjohn's Avenue to Hampstead Heath. She so loved the Fitzjohn's Avenue fields that she tried to buy them as a public park. They were to cost £10,000 and within three August weeks £8,500 had been raised. It needed only the end of the summer holidays and the return from holiday of sympathetic friends and the further £1,500 would have been raised, but the owners suddenly withdrew their offer. Despite all pleading, the fields were covered with large houses. From this developed the campaign to save Parliament Hill, the next open space, buying up fields in the path of the builders to make a permanent cordon sanitaire against the advancing bricks. The Parliament Hill Fields campaign was so successful that the Heath Bill was passed and there was money over from the appeal. From this money and the impetus towards open spaces, was to develop the National Trust. Octavia Hill had been interested in protecting areas like Church Bottom Wood for years, so she and the National Trust were natural allies in the fight to save the wood.

The Commons Preservation Society also, was familiar with this kind of agitation and money collection. They had torn down fencing when lords of the manor had enclosed pieces of common land, leading both legal and illegal battles against the arrogant privatization of land traditionally free. Robert Hunter, their Honorary Solicitor from 1868, was always concerned with securing open spaces, large or small, for the public. He, now Sir Robert Hunter, became the Chairman of the Church Bottom Appeal. The Chairman of the Commons Preservation Society was Mr Shaw-Lefevre MP (later Lord Eversley) who played a big part in this and other campaigns in the House of Commons. Octavia Hill had been involved in their work from about 1875.

At the same time Octavia Hill was campaigning for a Burials Bill. City churchyards had become so full and so serious a hazard to health by contaminating wells from which people drew their drinking water, that City burials were no longer permitted. Instead, cemetries were created on the outskirts of town. There was then a movement to remove the headstones to the edges of the old town cemetries, re-inter the bodies elsewhere and turn the cemetries into gardens and open spaces, instead of building on them. This land in the centre was very valuable and speculators were avid to obtain it: even the Quakers had built over one of their cemetries and threatened to do so again by building over Bunhill Fields. Octavia Hill had a network of allies, so her help to save the wood was invaluable.

The Metropolitan Gardens Society, set up in 1882, had laid out about two hundred small gardens in city centres by 1890, which they later handed over to the Local Authorities, so their support for the Churchyard Bottom Wood Appeal was assured from the start.

The Kyrle Society is forgotten now, but in its day had great influence on town planning and open space legislation. The Society had been set up about 1875 for 'the Diffusion of Beauty', to bring colour and interest into the lives of people living in dull, drab surroundings. Bright colour to walls and decoration, good singing, open spaces, Nature, Literature and Art. All these fell within the Society's remit. There was a

Decorative Branch, for whom William Morris lectured; a Musical Branch to promote choirs and Happy Evenings for people in local school buildings; and a Literature Branch. This appealed regularly by letters in The Times, to 'the richer classes' for books and periodicals to be distributed to boys' and girls' clubs, almshouses and elsewhere. However the Open Spaces Committee was the most active. The very name 'Kyrle' came from Pope's The Man of Ross, the philanthropist who gave his birthplace to the people as a public park.[25] [48]

Sir Robert Hunter
1844-1913

The bas relief of Mr R.H.Williams
on the Crouch End Clock Tower

In 1982, Liza Chivers, who had been born in 1908, wrote a delightful account of her childhood as the daughter of John Sparrow, 1869-1947, the Keeper of Queen's Wood.[17]

It paints a picture of a wood far more heavily used than today, with people living more closely within their own neighbourhoods, shopping and walking locally, instead of driving past. The Lodge, combining the Keeper's house and a tea room with its open verandah, had cost £1,223 to build and the tea room was then a busy place. In daytime the wood was full of people, while at nightfall, with the wood fenced off all round, the sub-keepers dispersed, locking the different gates behind them as they went home. Then the Keepers' seven children had the wood to themselves for another night.

The Keeper and his family lived in the Lodge and the tea rooms were let out to contract. A picture shows her father armed with a rook rifle standing beside three assistant keepers, for there were four men on duty in the woods in those days. Mature, responsible men, the assistants in waistcoats with watch-chains across their chests while the Keeper is in his official uniform of a stiff peaked cap and a raincoat. Another photograph shows the Keeper holding a dead rabbit and pointing upwards with a stick, while his assistant shoots at a squirrel. Grey squirrels had so increased that they were a nuisance, damaging the trees and taking bird's eggs. The Keeper's children lived in a splendid wood, their lives poor but idyllic.

The Keeper's Lodge and Tea Room in Queen's Wood

219

Queen's Wood in the Nineteen Nineties

A century after Churchyard Bottom Wood was saved, the situation has altered drastically. Just as beautiful and even wilder, for fallen branches are no longer collected and burnt on the Keeper's fire, there is no money to maintain four keepers: the Lodge is empty and the tea room has long closed, yet the local council, short of money, is still responsible for the wood and Lodge.

On 9 December 1993 Haringey Council announced their intention to 'dispose' of the Lodge. They would sell the Lodge and its garden with sufficient land to make a drive to the Lodge through the wood.

Immediately a group called 'Friends of Queen's Wood' was formed to fight against this sale. The Council had no right to sell any part of the wood, which had been bought by subscription and gifts to be kept 'in trust for the free enjoyment and benefit of the people for ever.' The Lodge was part of the wood, having been built with some of the £30.000 originally collected. It could not be separated from the wood. Building an

---

HARINGEY PLAN TO SELL OFF
QUEEN'S WOOD LODGE

THE LONDON BOROUGH OF HARINGEY
LOCAL GOVERNMENT ACT 1972 -
SECTION 123 (2A)
QUEEN'S WOOD LODGE,
42 MUSWELL HILL ROAD, LONDON, N10

1. Notice is hereby given pursuant to Section 123 (2A) of the Local Government Act 1972, (as amended) that the Council of the London Borough of Haringey intends to dispose of the vacant premises and land described as follows:
A 3 bedroom single storey, former park keepers lodge together with surrounding land situated within the boundary of Queen's Wood and being approximately 0.43 of an acre in total.
2. A plan numbered BVES(A4)114B showing the above-mentioned land and, premises is available for inspection at the Offices of the Borough Solicitor, Alexandra House, 10 Station Road, Wood Green, London, N22 4TR, between 8.45am to 4.45pm on Mondays to Fridays until 6th January 1994.
3. Any objections to the above proposal should be made in writing to the Borough Solicitor at the above address quoting reference LEG/AS by 6th January 1994. Any such objections will be considered by the Council before the disposal.

Dated this 9th day of December 1993.

JULIA C. LOMAS,
Borough Solicitor,
London Borough of Haringey,
Alexandra House,
10 Station Road,
Wood Green,
London N22 4TR

Sale Notice

THE FRIENDS OF QUEEN'S WOOD OBJECT TO THIS PLAN

We have support from:

* The City Parochial Foundation
Friends of the Earth
The Highgate Society
London Wildlife Trust
The Museum of Garden History
* The National Trust
* Open Spaces Society
SAVE Britain's Heritage
* The Selborne Society
The Victorian Society

(* Supporters in the 1880s/90s, and now)

Those in Opposition

220

access road would involve cutting down trees and the loss of part of the wood. The same arguments which had applied a hundred years ago against taking the acre of wood and adding it to the Charity Land so as to build the 25 houses, applied today. The sale of woodland to make a drive to reach the Lodge was not acceptable and moreover, it was now illegal as there was now an Act of Parliament to forbid it.

No less than four societies which had supported the original fight to obtain the wood, again protested against this attack on the wood and they were joined by a number of others. It seems ironical, but somehow fitting, to celebrate the centenary of the opening of Queen's Wood by a campaign to save it for the next millenium, using the same arguments of public need over hundreds of years against doubtful short-term gain. The problem has not been solved. The Lodge is empty and no proper use has been found for it, but the whole of the Wood and the Lodge are still in the public domain. Despite all attempts they have not been sold off. It would be interesting to know what someone else will be writing a hundred years from now when we have run out of petrol and may spend more time in our own neighbourhoods. There might then be need for the Tea Room again.

The four keepers in Queen's Wood: Mr Martin, Mr Smith, Mr Sparrow (father of Liza Chivers who wrote the pamphlet) and Mr Duke[17.]

Appendix 1

Housing

In the nineteen-twenties Housing was the responsibility of the Ministry of Health, so the reports of the Local Medical Officer of Health are revealing. In 1921, after the First World War he wrote:-

'On the whole the property of the Borough is of very good quality --- There are no houses in the Borough that are so dangerous or injurious to health as to be unfit for human habitation and there are no insanitary areas.

'In parts of Highgate, Crouch End, and Hornsey there are collections of houses occupied in many instances by more than one family and some houses exist which the tenants seem to make no efforts to keep reasonably clean. Sanitary defects in these and other houses have been brought to our notice from time to time throughout the year and it may be said generally that the activities of the Health Department have resulted in the amelioration of many conditions adverse to health.

Overcrowding

'It cannot be said that there is any acute shortage of working class houses in the Borough, chiefly because it is not a working class district. But that there is a certain amount of overcrowding is undeniable. I do not consider that the provision of, say, a hundred more houses for the working class would diminish the overcrowding to any appreciable extent, for the reason that it is largely financial in origin. For example, a family occupies a house and, because they are in need of money, they sub-let three rooms and crowd themselves into the remaining two. The sub-tenants themselves begin to take in lodgers and these lodgers may in their turn take in other lodgers. The final result is an over-crowded house. To offer each family in such a house a separate workman's dwelling would not remedy the overcrowding, for none of the families could afford to accept the offer.

'The whole problem of overcrowding has given the Health Department much trouble during the year, [because] it is so difficult to find the correct remedy. To take people to the police-court and prosecute them for overcrowding is no remedy, for the infliction of a fine would merely add to the distress. Efforts have been made from time to time to find accommodation in other and more satisfactory places and by this means the conditions in some of the over-crowded houses has improved.'

In 1922 the MOH reported that many of the houses neglected during the War, because of labour shortage and high costs, were now being repaired, but he had to return to overcrowding.

If two, three, or four families share a sink or a water-closet, it is nobody's business to keep it clean. It is the business of nobody to look after the common passage and the common back-yard.

--- many of the families have no proper cooking place: there is only one cooking range or gas-cooker in the house and only one family has access to it. The others have to get on as best they can by cooking on a bedroom fire, or a gas-ring. Hot water and baths are unknown luxuries in many of these houses and it is not to be wondered at that sometimes vermin are found in the houses.

These reports were duplicated in every borough and town in the country and were ventilated day in and day out in Parliament and the press. In Hornsey the 1923 Report lays out the situation of some tenants baldly, but there is some hint that the reports are beginning to have some effect.

--- There are a few houses which, under pre-war standards, would be closed for not being 'in all respects reasonably fit for human habitation'. Having regard, however, to the post-war shortage of alternative accommodation these houses are occupied, in some cases by a bad type of tenant. Many of the occupiers take in one or more lodgers, or sub-let one or more rooms for the purpose of augmenting their incomes.

'The Hornsey Town Council is preparing to build some houses for the working classes: and it is undeniable that these houses will be very readily taken by decent people, many of whom are newly married persons who for many years have been looking for houses. But, very properly, the Town Council demands that its tenants shall be fairly respectable and decent people: and the shiftless and bad tenant will not, and should not, find his way to a new Corporatin house. He would make a pig-sty in a month, would take lodgers in every room and be evicted before he had paid any rent. So it must not be thought that the provision of Corporation houses will render more practicable the closing and demolition of, say Ward's Cottages, a block of six back-to-back houses in North Hill; for the tenants there are not the sort that would be received into a Corporation house.

'The sub-letting of houses and the taking in of lodgers, to which I have referred, is especially in evidence in the Campsbourne area, although it exists in other parts of the town. Practically every house in certain streets is sub-let, and in some instances the original tenant makes a good living out of letting his rooms. Overcrowding can be considered from two aspects: there is a legal overcrowding where each person has less than 300 cubic feet of space (I believe there is none of that in Hornsey): and there is the moral overcrowding where more than one family share a cooking range, a sink, a water-closet and a copper - and of that there is a very great deal. It is economic in origin. One family cannot afford to live in a five-roomed house: but five families can afford to live there. Overcrowding of this nature will obviously not be remedied by the new Corporation houses; although these are emphatically needed by a large number of persons able and willing to pay the rents and behave like decent citizens.'

As result of reports like this Hornsey Borough Council, like other councils, resolved to build houses for those who could not find clean, affordable housing elsewhere and so helped to produce a generation of healthy citizens.[6]

Appendix II

How Tuberculosis affected the Design of Schools
in Central London

St James's Elementary School was in the clean air of Muswell Hill but many London schools were in polluted air so that the children were particularly likely to contract TB. Here is the story of how one London school building, not so very far away, was adapted in the fight for good health.

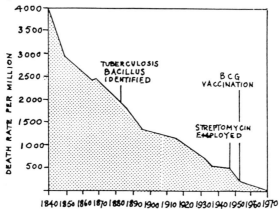

The Graph of Deaths from Tuberculosis

As described in the chapter on St James's School, Muswell Hill, there were 4000 deaths per million from tuberculosis in 1840. Slowly better living conditions, better food, and the cult of open-air exercise, reduced this but, by the time the tuberculosis bacteria was identified in the 1880s, there were still 2000 deaths per million. There was then no prospect of an early cure. The only hope was to feed people better and to give them fresh air, in the hope that their bodies would be made strong enough to resist the disease. This is why fresh air and exercise played such a large part in the conscious planning of child health.

The London County Council developed open-air school sites in Muswell Hill and other sites on the outskirts of London. Classes from the centre of London visited them for one day a week, to work in open-air classrooms, botanise, and play games, away from the befouled town. In town, schools had lessons and exercise on the roof. This emphasis on physical exercise which would ensure deep breathing, was the other side of the coin. Exercise yards can still be seen on the tops of some London Schools.

An example is Queen's Head Street School, in Islington, now part of Islington Green School. It was built in 1884, on a long narrow site where there was hardly space to move.

224

Queen's Head Street School, Islington[78]

In the 1880s the London School Board had the duty to build schools but often had extreme difficulty in finding sites they could afford, or even finding sites at all. Islington had once been open country, a place for gardens, duck shoots and ponds. Sadler's Wells had been a Hampstead Heath of London. In 1559, Anne Packington (the wife of Sir John Packington, chirographer (a writer of legal documents in the Court of Common Pleas) bequeathed to the Clothworkers' Company an estate of 60 acres and 31 perches. This produced rents of £16.16.9d per annum, which were to be for charitable purposes.

The Clothworkers built almshouses, collected the rents for houses and farms and no doubt their members shot duck. By the end of the eighteenth century the situation was changing: Islington had become the fashionable place to live, in the fresh country air, within walking distance of the City of London. Each evening the managers of London firms heaved themselves up the hill to the high gravel ridge near The Angel, to tend their gardens and live a suburban life.

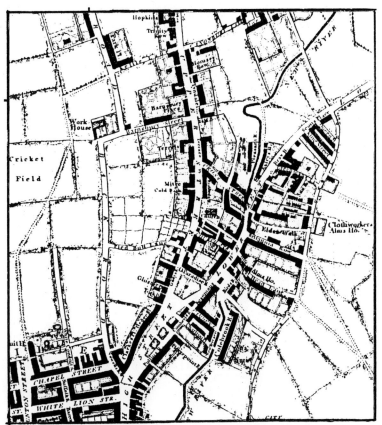

A map showing Islington when it was still open countryside, on the borders of London.   Baker

225

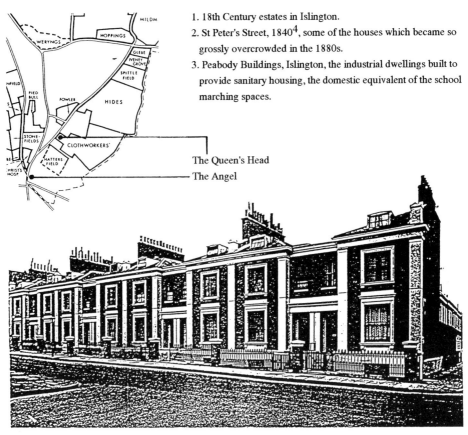

1. 18th Century estates in Islington.
2. St Peter's Street, 1840[4], some of the houses which became so grossly overcrowded in the 1880s.
3. Peabody Buildings, Islington, the industrial dwellings built to provide sanitary housing, the domestic equivalent of the school marching spaces.

The Queen's Head

The Angel

226

By the 1880s industry and a flood of population had changed the situation completely. Muswell Hill was still far out in the country, but London was expanding and Islington had become overcrowded. The area had become delapidated when houses were split into floors and rooms, while Industry established itself in outbuildings and basements. Some areas became slums. In Booth's 1889 Map of Wealth and Poverty, he printed the streets of London in seven colours according to the incomes of the occupants. Yellow showed great wealth and black extreme poverty, with dark blue and light blue only slightly better off. Upper Street, Islington, is marked with large areas of poverty. The site of the present Peabody Buildings, those monuments to Victorian philanthropic drive, is marked in black or dark blue. This is where the London School Board was searching for a site. Finally the Clothworkers' Guild offered a row of decrepit houses at the end of their leases, many used for small industry, which had caused the Clothworkers trouble over the years and which they were glad to sell.

'The Masters, Wardens and Commonalty of Freemen of the Art or Mystery of Clothworkers of the City of London' sold the property which consisted of workshops, machine rooms, engine and boiler house, sheds, covered yards, yards, roadways and outbuildings in Rheidol Terrace and St James's Street. Two school buildings with high-pitched roofs were erected in 1884, one of which is illustrated on page 228.

When the school was enlarged in 1892, the original Nursery School building was extended to cover much of the playground, making the free space even more restricted. In 1910 the London County Council (which had taken over from the London School Board) installed hot water radiators and built a boiler house below. Before this there had been no need for a boiler as each room had an open fire with its own chimney. Each day every fire had to be cleared out, ashes removed, the fire relaid and lit before the classes arrived. The smoke from all those chimneys produced pea-souper fogs.

It is rather sad that some modern children, brought up in centrally heated houses, have no idea what a chimney does. They draw houses in the traditional way - a square box with a door and windows, and a pitched roof with a chimney belching smoke. But in the children's minds there is nothing under the chimney. It does not connect to anything. The chimney is a sort of appendix to the house, a folk memory of an earlier functioning chimney as the human appendix is a relic of an earlier digestive system.

By reducing the number of fires in the school, pollution was slightly reduced, but not enough to counter TB. At the same time, in the hope of warding off illness, the LCC put on a flat roof surrounded by high walls and large wrought iron grilles, to form an open air Marching Space, so that exercise could be taken in all but rain. Cups and shields were awarded for competitive marching, but the real purpose was health.

The Chairman of the School Board for London said in 1884:-

'At the instance of the Chairman of the Works Committee, whose connection with measures for arresting disease in London is well known, special attention has been paid to the sanitary condition of our schools, and it may be safely said that this is now as well considered and as complete as in a first rate hospital. At a time when dangerous epidemics threaten the metropolis, I feel this will be a satisfaction to the public mind. In some of our schools considerations of expense and contracted sites have compelled us to provide playgrounds on the roof. It is worthy of note that the winning school in the drill competition this year was confined to an airy but confined space of this kind.'

227

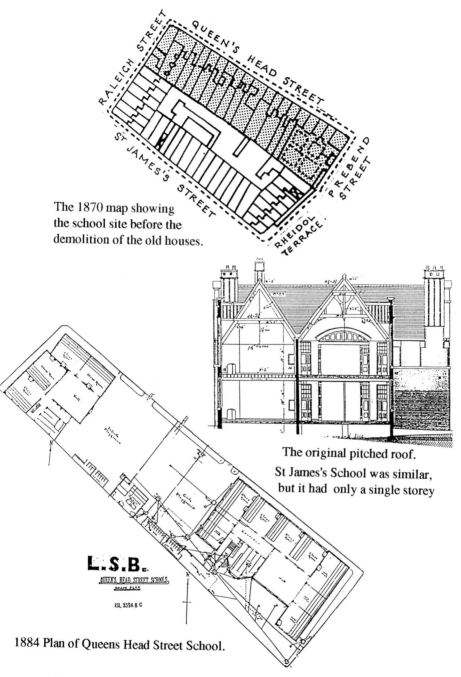

The 1870 map showing the school site before the demolition of the old houses.

The original pitched roof.

St James's School was similar, but it had only a single storey

L.S.B.

QUEEN'S HEAD STREET SCHOOLS,

DRAIN PLAN

ISL 359A B C

1884 Plan of Queens Head Street School.

Queen's Head Street School, Islington[78]

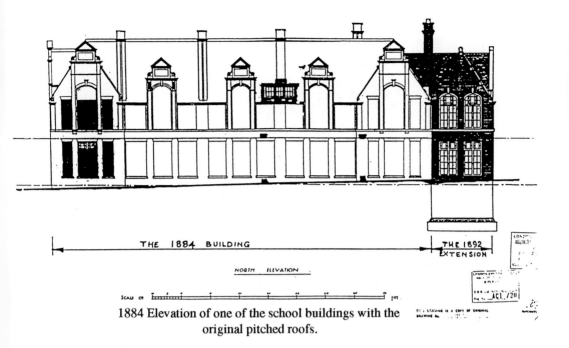

1884 Elevation of one of the school buildings with the original pitched roofs.

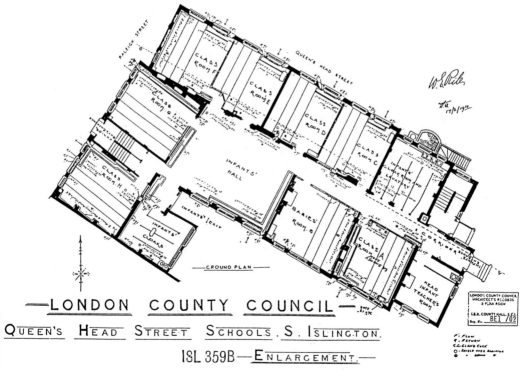

ENLARGING THE NURSERY SCHOOL BUILDING IN 1892

LONDON COUNTY COUNCIL

QUEEN'S HEAD STREET SCHOOLS. S. ISLINGTON.

ISL 359B — ENLARGEMENT.

229

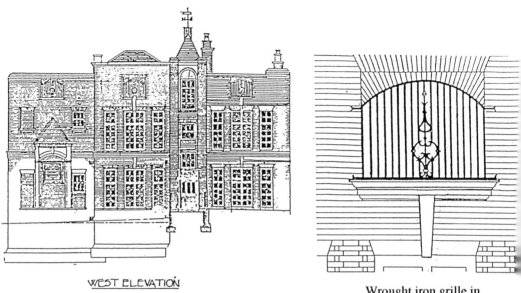

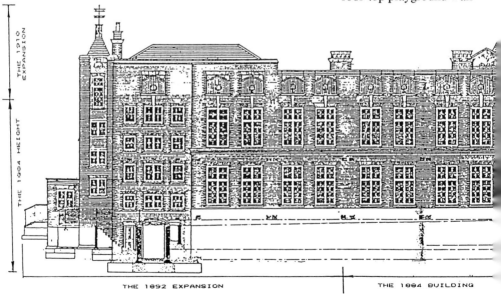

Wrought iron grille in
roof-top playground wall

Elevation of the enlarged school building with the flat roof.[78]

The change in the treatment of tuberculosis since the 1950s is illustrated by the case of the writer Katherine Mansfield. Today she would have been cured, but she lived too early. After the First World War she searched everywhere for a cure. Away from home, in sanatoriums in France or Switzerland, any rumour of a cure was followed up. Separated by TB from Myddleton Murray, who had to earn a living as a jobbing writer back in London, Katherine Mansfield, in foreign pensions among strangers, lived out her last short years obessionally trying to write against the background of perpetual illness. In doing so she spoke for all those thousands of inarticulate sufferers from tuberculosois, describing their sense of the shortness of life and the unceasing search for a cure. In the end she died while trying out yet another promised nostrum.

When, in the end, streptomycin was discovered, the bacteria was defeated. Large isolation hospitals were closed; open-air balconies in London hospitals and the open stairways in blocks of industrial dwellings, which had been built in Victorian times as the last word in health protection, could be glassed in and the buildings made warm at last. An architectural concept had been changed.

This then was the reason for the high roof with no ceilings in St James's School, its large windows and the love of bright sunlight. These were the only measures likely to keep children healthy in a world without modern drugs. Each child was guaranteed a fixed cubic capacity of air to breathe and a high roof was required to provide it. Only when modern drugs were available could classroom ceiling heights be lowered.

The Muswell Hill Solution

St James's School playground in 1925, showing the open-air hut
and desks under the oak trees

The hut and trees disappeared when Charles Clore House was built on the old school site. Then, in 1994, Haringey Council built sheltered housing on the municipal yard beyond Clore House. Perhaps some of the boys and girls who sat in the hut in 1925, have come to live on the site in later life.

Sources and Bibliography

1 BL British Library

2 BRO Barnet Record Office

3 CER Church of England Record Office

4 GLRO Greater London Record Office

5 GL London Guildhall Library

6 HA Haringey Archives, Bruce Castle.

7 HHB Hornsey Historical Bulletin

8 HBC Haringey Building Control

9 The Diary of a London Schoolboy 1826-1830, by John
  Thomas Pocock, Camden History Society, 1980.

10 Anthony Salvin: Pioneer of Gothic Revival Architecture, by Jill
  Allibone, Lutterworth Press, Cambs, 1987.

11 Salvin, The Sunday Times 28 Aug 1988 p.17.

12 Nevil Smart, Barnet Press and Finchley News 14 Dec 1935.

13 Mudie's Circulating Library and the Victorian Novel, by G. Griest.

14 Herbert Collins: Architect and Worker for Peace, by Robert Williams,
  pub. by Paul Cave, Publications Dept Ltd, The City of Southampton.

15 Homes Fit For Heroes, by Mark Swenarton, Heinemann, 1981.

16 Ancestors and Friends, by John Lehmann
  Autobiography I, II & III, by John Lehmann, Eyre & Spottiswoode

17 Memories of Highgate from a Keeper's Lodge, by Liza Chivers, 1982, pub Hornsey Historical Society.

18 Hornsey Urban District Council Review of the Years 1896- 1900, by
  the Chairman of the Council

19 HHB No 28, Rookfield Garden Estate: a study of the influence of the
  Garden City, by Kate Trevett.

20 HHB,A Tour Round Muswell Hill and Fortis Green, by R.W.A.Smith

21 The Story of St James's School, by I.T.Plant, 1950

22 The Glacial Drifts of Muswell Hill and Finchley, by Henry Walker,
  republished with a postscript by Eric Robinson, 1994, by Jack Whitehead

23 HHB No 23, How the Archway Road was built, by Arnold Lynch

24 Keystone, Fortis Green, Spring 1961 pp. 2-5

25 Octavia Hill, by William T. Hill, 1956, and many other biographies

26 BL The Muswell Hill Record and Tradesmen's Advertiser, 1907

27 British Library Maps Dept, Sale documents of The Elms, 1880

28 Greater London, by E. Walford, 1881

29 GLRO, 1815 Enclosure Map of Hornsey

30 HHB No 25, Highgate Hunting Ground, by Malcolm Stokes

31 CER, Hornsey and Finsbury Park Journal, 15 June 1895

32 Haringey Green Paper 'Urban Design & Environment', Planning Dept. 1960s?

33 Paddington Children's Hospital records.

34 Islington Borough Council Architects' Dept.

35 The Builder, 25 Nov 1932

36 The BROACH file, Haringey Archives, Bruce Castle, N17

37 The Decorative Tradition, by Julian Barnard, 1973

38 The London Building World of the 1860s, by Sir John Summmerson, 1973

39 Edwardian Architecture, by Alistair Service

40 Haringey Planning Committee 8 Mar 1979, Item 5

41 Essex Record Office, Southend-on-Sea, ref. D/BC/1/4/12/2055

42 Hornsey Journal 1905

43 The Growth of Stoke Newington, by Jack Whitehead

44 Growing, Autobiography of Leonard Woolf, 1972

45 Huntingdon Library, California

46 Highgate Tunnel: or The Secret Arch, 1812, by Joan Schwitzer, Hornsey
   Historical Society Bulletin No 32

47 RIBA Drawings Collection

48 Octavia Hill, by Gillian Darley

49 Information from Mrs Niblett

50 Hampstead Garden Suburb 1907-1977: A History, by Brigid Grafton Green,
   1977

51 Results of Sanitary Improvements, illustrated by the Metropolitan
   Society for Improving the Dwellings of the Industrious Working Classes,
   etc, by Southwood Smith MD, 1854.

52 Hampstead Garden Suburb Archive, Big Wood House, Big Wood Rd, NW11,
   Coparts Ref: 582

53 Hampstead Garden City, by Melvyn Miller & A. Stuart Gray

54 The Edwardian House, by Helen Long

55 The Gardener's Magazine, Feb 1840

56 Information from Robert Andrewes

57 Housing in the 1960s, by A.W.Cleeve Barr, RIBA Journal April 1962

58 Library London, by Beckles Willson, in Living London, ed. G. Sims

59 Beatrix Tudor Hart Remembered: memorial publication, by Jennifer Jones

60 Talk by R.A.Bullivant ARIBA, at the Victoria and Albert Museum, 1979

61 Finchley Press 24.6.1977

62 David Jones interview with 'Billy' Collins

63 The History of Woodlands in Hornsey, by Jonathan Silvertown, The London
   Naturalist, No 57, 1978

64 Highgate Wood: the Pottery and its Production, by A.E.Brown and
   H.L.Sheldon, The London Archaeologist, 1974

65 Ham and High 27.11.1981

66 Ham and High 27.7.1981

67 The Ecclesiastical Commissioners Estate Committee, 22.1.1885

68 Literary Associations of Hornsey, by F.W.M.Draper

69 The Botany of the District, Transactions London Naturat History Society,
   1915: 40-43, by Nicholson C.S.

70 Highgate and Queen's Wood Biological Survey (undated but
   recent)

71 Report of Highgate Wood Management Policy, by
   P.F.Garthwaite, May 1977

72 Ham and High 14.3.1978

73 Obituary, Finchley Press, 24.6.1977

74 Mrs S.Heathcote, Thesis on the Odeon Cinema, Muswell
   Hill, deposited at RIBA

75 Rails to the People's Palace and the Parkland Walk, by Reg. Davies,
   Hornsey Historical Society, and The Parkland Walk, by David Bevan.

76 Journal of RIBA, 6.11.1934.

77 Ham and High, 24.2.1995.

78 Architects' Dept, Islington Borough Council

79 Source unknown

80 Paul Dickinson & Associates

81 File lent to me by Mrs McKnight

82 Hornsey Journal 1905

83 Ham and High

84 The Little School, by Joan Schwitzer, Hornsey Historical Society

85 House Decorating Whitewashing, painting, paperhanging etc. Ed. Paul N. Hasluck, Cassell, undated, but
   Victorian/Edwardian.

86 Beauty and the Borough, by Councillor F.E.Cleary, 1949, pub Hornsey Council.

87 A Walk Around Muswell Hill, by Ken Gay, 1987

88 The Archive of The Clothworkers Guild, Mincing Lane.

89 Elsie Higgins

90 Looking at Muswell Hill, by David E.D.Freeman, 1984

91 Architectural Association Journal, July/Aug 1957 p.59

92 From Highgate to Hornsey: A Portrait in Old Picture Postcards, by Ken Gay and Dick Whetstone

93 Private collection

94 Hornsey Historical Society photograph collection.

Map Sources

Many of the maps used in the book are old Ordnance Survey maps, available at Haringey Local History
Archive, Bruce Castle. The Godfrey reduced size copies of some Ordnance Survey maps are readily available,
cheap and very convenient.

The 1815 Enclosure Map for Hornsey is held at the Greater London History Library.

The Milne 1800 Land Utilization Map is reprinted by the London Topographical Society, as is the
John Rocque 1762 map. These and other London Topographical maps may be purchased at Bishopsgate
Library, London EC2.

Index

242